MW00571679

BEHIND THE LINES

365 Daily Challenges for Military Personnel

ADAM DAVIS AND CHAD ROBICHAUX

BroadStreet Publishing® Group, LLC
Savage, Minnesota, USA
BroadStreetPublishing.com

Behind the Lines: 365 Daily Challenges for Military Personnel

978-1-4245-6178-0 (faux leather)
978-1-4245-6179-7 (e-book)

Stock or custom editions of BroadStreet Publishing titles may be purchased in bulk for educational, business, ministry, fundraising, or sales promotional use. For information, please email orders@broadstreetpublishing.com.

Typesetting by Kjell Garborg and design by Chris Garborg | garborgdesign.com

Printed in China

21 22 23 24 25 5 4 3 2 1

Dedication

For those who serve.

Contents

Foreword

You hold in your hands one of the most powerful, important books you will ever read. After reading God's Holy Word in the Bible, spending time with a book like this is one of the most important things you can do in your life. Seeking God's Word and wisdom every day is essential if you are to survive and triumph as you battle evil in this world.

As you serve our nation, you will stare into the face of evil. In distant lands and (all too often) at home, you will witness the works of evil. If you personally have not already seen evil at work, you most assuredly will in your future.

Evil. What else can you call it when helpless bound victims have their heads cut off, when people are burned to death in cages, and when airliners full of men, women, and children slam into buildings to murder thousands of other terrified civilians? *This* is the face of evil, and you must understand that you are a living shield of flesh and blood standing between evil and precious, innocent lives.

If you believe in a force of evil, and who can deny it, then you are doomed in your battle if you do not also believe in a superior force for good and apply that force for good in your daily life. There is a mighty, awesome force for good in this universe. He loves you, wants you to thrive, and will give you all that you need to triumph in this battle. Indeed, the presence of evil is solid proof of God and his holy forces of good. Consider what happens when the moon eclipses the sun. We cannot bear to look directly at the sun, but the darkness of the eclipse proves the presence of light. So, too, does the darkness of evil prove the presence of good.

The opposite of love is not hate; it is evil. Evil is the absence of love, just as darkness is the absence of light. And God *is* love. God is love, and all love emanates from God. His love for us is infinite and beyond any earthly love that we can comprehend.

As you put on our nation's uniform and place your mortal body in peril, you must understand that no one does this job for the money. Love is what motivates us. Love for your nation, love for your way of life, love for your family, and love for your comrades. And love is what motivates God.

"To live is Christ and to die is gain" (Philippians 1:21). Think about that. The world says, "Life is hard, then you die." But God says "to live" is to be "in Christ," which is an amazing life of love, joy, and peace. And "to die" is even better. Study those two options and decide now which one you would choose.

Again, the opposite of love is evil, and hate is not necessarily bad. God tells us that there are things in this world that we should hate. Amos 5:15 affirms this in six of the most powerful words in the Bible: "Hate evil, love good; maintain justice." Merriam-Webster defines *hate* as: "intense hostility and aversion usually deriving from fear, anger, or sense of injury." We do not fear evil, for we are strengthened by God's love, and we are told that "love drives out fear" (1 John 4:18). But we should have "intense hostility and aversion" toward evil. We should also have a sense of anger toward evil, and we do indeed have a "sense of injury," for we fully comprehend the great grievous injury that evil would inflict upon all that we love.

In our book *On Spiritual Combat,* Adam Davis and I describe this mighty, epic, global battle against evil:

> You can think of this like the United States during World War II. The entire nation was focused on winning that war. The farmer in the field and the clerk in the store were striving, working in their jobs with victory in mind. They bought war bonds. The students in school wrote letters to our troops, collected scrap metal, and bought "war saving stamps." Every other citizen, everyone in between, accepted war rationing, and they all worked together for victory, leading ultimately to the troops in the front lines.

All of them were part of a concerted effort to defend our nation and defeat our enemy.

In the same way, every believer in Christ is part of a similar, vast endeavor, striving toward a single goal. In World War II we won, in large part, by killing the enemy. *In this war, we win by saving lives!*

Our goal is to save lives, and you can think of "saving lives" spiritually and eternally like this: in the physical realm, one "ultimate evil" can undo a lifetime of good. No matter how many good deeds and wonderful works you have done, if you unlawfully, willingly, directly take the life of a single innocent person, then you will spend the rest of your life in prison or possibly face execution. This one "ultimate bad" of murder will undo all the good in your life. And, in the world's eyes, society often holds those who hunt down murderers in highest esteem. That is just the way the universe works.

In the spiritual realm, one "perfect good" can undo a lifetime of bad. The "ultimate good" of Jesus' sacrifice upon the cross to pay the price for our salvation saves us spiritually—eternally. That one perfect good undoes a lifetime of bad. Think about that: every bad act in our lives—past, present, and future—is forgiven if we accept the price that Jesus paid upon the cross. And in God's eyes, those who save lives by bringing the gospel, the "good news" of salvation through Jesus, are held in highest esteem. That is the way the universe works.

As you begin to work your way through this book, renew yourself daily with the amazing insight, deep wisdom, and powerful Scripture provided by my dear brothers, Adam and Chad.

In my book *On Combat,* I introduced (and received a US Government trademark for) the concept of "sheepdog as a protector." In *On Spiritual Combat,* Adam Davis and I took this model a step further, introducing the concept of "sheepdogs under the authority of the Great Shepherd." We are the hounds of heaven—God's faithful, loving, obedient sheepdogs. I love my master, the Great Shepherd. My love is all I have to give to him, and it is all he asks of me.

Will Rogers said, "If you get to thinking you're a person of some influence, try ordering somebody else's dog around." Thus, when the evil one comes for you and yours, look him in the eye and tell him he has no power over you. Just tell him, "Hey dude, I'm not your dog." Read and rejoice daily in this book, my brothers and sisters in Christ—my fellow sheepdogs under the authority of the Great Shepherd!

Dave Grossman
Lt. Col. (ret.)
Author of *On Killing, On Combat,*
Assassination Generation, and *On Spiritual Combat*

A Prayer for Those Who Serve in the US Armed Forces

Heavenly Father,
thank you for the opportunity to serve my nation. Grant me wisdom in the most difficult circumstances. Empower me with a supernatural power to discern right from wrong in the darkest of moments. I ask for your divine intervention, protection, and guidance. May my steps be ordered by you, and may your presence go before me. Thank you for this day and what it means to serve in the United States Armed Forces. Amen.

January 1

Be a People Builder

When you speak uplifting, positive reinforcement to another person, especially your spouse or children, you are giving him or her seeds of life. If you are a parent, your words will linger with your children well into their adulthood and have the potential to shape their perspective about God, their own self-esteem, and life in general. More important than the words, at times, is the tone in which you speak them. Be mindful today that your family is on your side. They are your haven, your place of refuge from a world in turmoil. Take time to think about the words you speak and be mindful of the way you speak them.

It is often difficult to shift from Sergeant or Major to husband or Daddy, and your family deserves time with the real you, not the on-duty version of you. Don't expend all you have and leave those who love you most neglected. Instead, speak love and life, and the fruits will pay great dividends. Focus on investing in the relationships of your spouse, children, parents, family, and friends. You will be glad you did.

> *Heavenly Father, help me be conscious of my words and the way I speak to my family. Amen.*

Encourage each other and build each other up,
just as you are already doing.
1 THESSALONIANS 5:11 NLT

January 2

A Two-Way Street

In regard to the love and respect discussion found in Ephesians, many people often take it out of context and manipulate it for control and power in relationships. However, let's focus on one area of marriage and relationships for today. Loving a wife as Christ loved the church means sacrificial, selfless love. That is precisely the type of love you show the people in your unit every time you put on that uniform.

Your passion to serve is to be commended, and while your spouse is certainly proud of you, your love for him or her will set the tone for your life. Selfish attitudes, poor communication, unforgiveness, and bitterness are all things we must let go if we want the best marriage God has for us. Love is a two-way street. We must love first without demanding the other person to love us in return but allow for love if he or she gives it. This is the way Jesus loves each one of us—perfectly and sacrificially. Today, find a specific way to express love to your spouse, beginning with words of encouragement, appreciation, and love.

> *Heavenly Father, help me to be as intentional and focused on being a godly spouse as I am at being a warrior. Help me to remember the human side of my spouse and that he or she is not my enemy. Amen.*

For husbands, this means love your wives,
just as Christ loved the church. He gave up his life for her.

EPHESIANS 5:25 NLT

January 3

Poisoned Marriage

A terrible relationship with your spouse can make for a miserable life. Being selfish can ruin all your relationships and leave you desolate. Life spent alone is not how God intended it to be, whether you are married or not. God wants you to have friends and family. But no relationship is sustainable if one or both parties are selfish. One of the greatest attributes of a healthy marriage is when each spouse tries to "out-serve" the other, intent on meeting the desires of the other spouse. When we remove the focus from our own lives and shift it to the lives of others, being selfless and kind, being humble and thinking of others, our relationships will take root and grow.

Ask your spouse today if you come across as selfish. Avoid becoming defensive or arguing your way around it but instead listen intently to your spouse's response. Another way to take personal inventory and determine whether you are selfish is to ask a trusted friend who will tell you the truth. Being intentional about putting others first and thinking of others before yourself will position you to be a tremendous friend and an even better spouse.

Heavenly Father, remove from me any selfish attitude toward my spouse and reveal to me any arrogant or prideful ways. I surrender them to you. Amen.

Don't be selfish; don't try to impress others.
Be humble, thinking of others as better than yourselves.
PHILIPPIANS 2:3 NLT

January 4

Captured and Cherished

For the married warriors reading this, your marriage is more important than your career in the military. Our spouses, regardless of whether you are a husband or wife, have many hours, heartaches, and sacrifices invested in our lives, and we owe them our absolute best as it pertains to our relationships. I've often wondered why there wasn't a clear Scripture stating how much of a blessing spouses are to each other, but if you've found a good partner for life, you have found favor from God.

When we cherish our spouses as Jesus cherishes the church, treat them with love and respect, and love them selflessly, we align ourselves scripturally for receiving God's divine blessings and favor, not to mention having a great marriage. Statistics say that if you are married and in the military, your marriage doesn't stand a chance. But the stats don't stand a chance. You are stronger than a number. Be intentional, love your spouse, be quick to forgive, and lean on God through difficult seasons.

> *Heavenly Father, give me the wisdom to lead my family, to love my spouse the way he or she needs to be loved, and to honor you in my marriage. Help me be the best spouse I can be and to meet the needs I was created to meet in my spouse's life. Amen.*

He who finds a wife finds what is good and receives favor from the LORD.

PROVERBS 18:22

January 5

Careful of the Company You Keep

The people you spend time with affect your character. At the end of the day, you will become more like those you allow to invest in your life. This could be detrimental to your marriage. Think about the commitment you share with those you serve with while on duty. If you associate with individuals who are battling substance abuse issues, you are exposing yourself to opportunity for error. Not only that but you are also allowing an opportunity for insecure thoughts to enter the mind of your spouse.

Keeping bad company can lead to a domino effect of negative circumstances. Just like when driving a vehicle, keeping your eyes down the road for any threats and distractions in marriage means you can avoid heartbreak, unnecessary stress, and costly mistakes. Communicate with your spouse your need for friendships outside of work and commit to having friendships that align with the plans and goals you have as a married couple. Ask God to match you and your spouse to a like-minded couple, for this will lead you into more peaceful paths in your marriage.

Heavenly Father, give me wisdom to see and know when the company I keep is not healthy for my marriage and give me the wherewithal to remove myself from those situations. Send my spouse and me godly couples to associate with, who will glorify your name. Amen.

Do not be misled: "Bad company corrupts good character."

1 CORINTHIANS 15:33

January 6

Back to Basics

Life gets messy, complicated, and busy. Getting back to the basics in marriage means we refuse to neglect one of the most important relationships in our lives. We all need to be intentional about communicating with our spouses, loving them the way they need to be loved, and respecting them, not treating them like suspects. Focusing on the basics in your marriage means you are intentional about putting your spouse first (for example, even if you can't make dinner on time, you call home to let your spouse know). As a married believer, God calls you to love your spouse before yourself.

How we love our spouses will reflect on our relationship with Christ. We cannot parade around as heroes in uniforms and abuse our spouses, belittle them with our words, or neglect them and still expect to receive God's blessings. Focus on making things right with your spouse. If that seems impossible, remember that God thrives on the impossible. Ask him for the wisdom and guidance needed to navigate a damaged relationship with your spouse and, above all, communicate with your spouse and pray together.

> *Heavenly Father, I cannot do this on my own. I need your guidance. Help me get back to the basics of being a great spouse; show me how my spouse needs to be loved and bring reconciliation where division has existed. Amen.*

Dear friends, let us love one another, for love comes from God. Everyone who loves has been born of God and knows God.

1 JOHN 4:7

January 7

It Takes Two

There is always a lot of talk about the need for a wife to submit to the husband, but this is only in the context and understanding that the husband is first submitted to Christ. If both the husband and wife do not submit to one another, the seeds of selfishness eventually take root. One main cause of failed marriages is selfishness—the "I deserve" mentality. We should strive to follow Christ and the instructions in the Word of God as it relates to marriage.

We should never treat our spouse like our enemy. If one party in the marriage refuses to work toward reconciliation or is abusive, the situation may require counseling or additional intervention. Be the first in your marriage to submit to your spouse. This drives a dagger through the heart of pride and aligns you with the Word of God. Communicating with your spouse from a place of humility instead of a place of defensiveness means you are giving room for the intervention of the Holy Spirit in your relationship. The day that both of you are fighting over who gets to serve whom is the day you have grasped the true vision of submitting to each other out of reverence for Christ.

Heavenly Father, give me a vision of my marriage where both my spouse and I are submitted to each other and you, for your glory. Amen.

Submit to one another out of reverence for Christ.

EPHESIANS 5:21

January 8

Is It Worth It?

The temptation to stray from your marriage may come. Maybe you are bored at home. Maybe you and your spouse have grown apart, or you feel your spouse doesn't understand you, or you want the attention of someone else. At the end of the day, is it worth it? Your marriage may be going through a rough patch, and your spouse may not "get" you or your stress, but to wander for any reason is an awfully selfish decision to make.

If you have driven down Infidelity Drive and survived, you know the pain that others will suffer for your actions. Anyone with a conscience experiences internal conflict with his or her decision of sexual immorality. It is best to remain committed to your spouse, through the good times and the bad, and find ways to focus on the best in each other. Fight for love instead of finding reasons to just fight. Keep it real and keep it in the marriage.

Heavenly Father, thank you for the marvelous gift of intimacy. Please show me the beauty of this gift from your eyes and how I can fan the flames of passion between my spouse and me and protect our relationship from infidelity. Amen.

*Since sexual immorality is occurring,
each man should have sexual relations with his own wife,
and each woman with her own husband.*

1 CORINTHIANS 7:2

January 9

Fleeing for Freedom

She comes along looking better than sin itself. He comes along flexing, talking smooth, and making promises your man only wishes he could fulfill. How do you respond to the seductive power of a temptress or tempter? You run for your life. At least that is what the writer of 1 Corinthians 6:18 advised. As a member of the US military, you are likely someone who runs away from few situations. But temptation is one you should be willing and proud to flee from.

The price of engaging in sexual immorality goes beyond the initial contact. It brings pain to someone you love and someone who loves you deeply; it brings pain to your children, your family, your friends, and the people who look up to you. Please, heed the warnings. Do not be seduced by the temptations of those who would lure you into their destructive traps. Infidelity will claim your family, your career, and your joy and leave you empty and destitute. Yes, you can rebound in time, but some things take a lifetime to come back from, and this decision is one of them!

Heavenly Father, give me the eyes to see the seductive power of the temptress or tempter and give me the guts to run from it. Amen.

Flee from sexual immorality.
All other sins a person commits are outside the body,
but whoever sins sexually, sins against their own body.

1 CORINTHIANS 6:18

January 10

Passionate Partners

Let's focus on two things today: self-control and passion. If you are physically attracted to someone and in a relationship with them, it is going to be difficult to control your emotions, and at some point, you are going to need to set boundaries of physical contact. Someone in 1 Corinthians 7:9 thought this was important enough to include it in the Bible, so I figured, with some of the issues we have seen in our culture, it should probably be mentioned here.

For some reason, we let the passion fizzle out over time after we say our vows. But before we are married, it takes all the power and self-control we have to remain chaste with our significant other. In marriage, we should focus on nurturing our spouses like we did before we married. We should never base our love on fear or on the reciprocity of love, and we should never stop letting our spouses know just how physically attractive they are to us. Never stop being passionate partners!

Heavenly Father, thank you for my spouse. Thank you for protecting my marriage and giving me the wisdom to nurture my spouse in love and compassion. Amen.

If they cannot control themselves, they should marry, for it is better to marry than to burn with passion.

1 CORINTHIANS 7:9

January 11

Family Time

As parents, training our children is often interpreted as discipline, teaching, or some other external lesson. The life of a service member is a busy one that requires many sacrifices. But one of the greatest things we can do for our children is to make time to be with them, to attend their events, and to spend time with them. Building a healthy relationship with your child begins when he or she is an infant, and that relationship can be lost or destroyed in a short matter of time.

If you aren't a parent, then do what you can to support those who are. I am not suggesting you cancel your plans for theirs, but consider helping make the lives of their children a little bit easier along the way. The sacrifices you make are difficult, and in the long run, they will probably help your career. But don't forget to take time to invest in your children. Starting them off on a solid path and raising them correctly goes beyond discipline. Spending quality time with your child is more powerful than any material possession.

> *Heavenly Father, help me to reflect your nature to my children as a parent, and when life is busy and I get distracted, remind me of my first mission: my children. Amen.*

Start children off on the way they should go,
and even when they are old they will not turn from it.

PROVERBS 22:6

January 12

Time and Love

You see the impact evil has on the lives of others. You see the impact that fatherless homes have on communities, and you see the impact that abandoned children have in schools. From shoplifting to drug possession, juveniles are committing more (and increasingly violent) crimes. It may seem easier to parent like a disciplinarian or authoritarian, but the secret to the heart of our children is quality time and love.

If we are always barking orders, our children's ears will eventually begin to tune us out. Then our voices will become harsher, and eventually, our children will become completely discouraged and disconnected from us. They will quit trying. Holding a standard of perfection means you give no mercy or grace, and while that may work on the streets, there's hardly any place for it in the home. Walk with love and handle the hearts of your children with white gloves. Before you head home from duty, take time to set at the feet of Jesus all the things you dealt with at work. He is strong enough to handle your burdens and carry your load.

Heavenly Father, when my patience runs thin or my temper is short, remind me that my children need me to love them and discipline them but, most of all, to be here for them. Help me, Lord, to be a godly parent and to not exhaust my child. Amen.

Fathers, do not embitter your children,
or they will become discouraged.

COLOSSIANS 3:21

January 13

Give Them Wisdom

As a parent of two boys and a beautiful girl, I can tell you that boys know nothing about balance. And by balance I mean they can eat more than a horse, play for twenty-four hours a day, and never stop asking questions. There is no fear when it comes to danger and no common sense when it comes to risk. While we should strive for balance in discipline, we should not deprive our children of healthy reprimand when they need it. This is the impartation of wisdom we are responsible for giving our children.

The wisdom of God comes to us through reading his Word and gaining knowledge and life experience, and then, with all that, we pass it down to our children through correcting misaligned behavior. If you are like me, you don't like to discipline your children because it doesn't bring you pleasure. But what it does is give you peace in knowing you are passing down valuable lessons that will save them time, pain, and heartache, even if it takes them enduring a moment of suffering at the time.

> *Heavenly Father, as you have loved me, you have disciplined me. Help me to not become overbearing to my children because of the things I see on duty but to love my children and impart wisdom. Amen.*

A rod and a reprimand impart wisdom,
but a child left undisciplined disgraces its mother.

PROVERBS 29:15

January 14

Habits of a Good Leader

It is out of a spirit of immaturity that we attempt to lord over our families with authority or discipline. This type of behavior will only last for so long before those entrusted to us begin to rebel and buck the tyranny of our rule. Instead, those of us who have families should lead by example. If we are overweight and out of shape, it is unwise to think we can expect those entrusted to us to behave any differently than we do.

Our habits become the habits of our children, and our spouses deal with the carnage. There are a few things we can do to change the destiny of our children, but it all begins with our personal habits. We cannot expect our unhealthy behaviors to have no consequences because in due season, we will reap what we sow. Commit to being intentional with your decisions, changing your negative habits, creating new healthy habits, and unifying your family. Set the example, and in time, your family will follow.

Heavenly Father, may I never abuse those entrusted to me by you. Help me in my weakness and set before me the example of your Son as a leader to my family. Amen.

Not lording it over those entrusted to you, but being examples to the flock.

1 PETER 5:3

January 15

Party Killers

When it comes to parenting and discipline, there are as many schools of thought and opinions as there are brands of shoes. But I will say this: we cannot ignore the unhealthy behavior of our children. If you notice, not long ago, the focus was on the other extreme—overbearing, disciplinarian parenting. The key is balance in whatever approach you have in parenting.

If you ignore your children's behavior, it only leads to death. If you are overbearing, it can lead to death too. It is time to kill the party. The relationship between you and your children is a special bond, one that no one can ever replace, but it is not the same as any friendship. Giving your children hope begins with being willing to lovingly confront them when they are wrong but also admitting when you are wrong. Demonstrating godly character as a parent will embed in the minds of your young protégés the necessary images to mimic as adults.

Heavenly Father, teach me the balance of healthy discipline as a parent. Help me to hang up my uniform and gear when I come home and to love my family like they deserve and need to be loved. Amen.

Discipline your children, for in that there is hope;
do not be a willing party to their death.
PROVERBS 19:18

January 16

Don't Raise a Fool

I have seen good parents do all they knew how to do with their children only to see their children end up in prison or even dead. They were good parents, so what went wrong? Your job as a parent is not to raise your children to be good children; it is to prepare your children to be successful adults. Children are not born knowing right and wrong, but they quickly learn the difference. Therefore, we must teach them the correct way of living. If every person in your community caught on to this, imagine how much the schools would change and what future generations would look like.

At the end of the day, your children are entrusted to you. Your duty as a service member is to serve others, to defend our nation, and to protect those who cannot defend themselves. This position often comes with great authority, but your position and authority in the military has no value to your wayward children. They need the effective, present, and involved love of a parent. Today, commit to changing a generation starting with one.

Heavenly Father, help me to be a godly parent and to impart godly wisdom into the hearts and minds of my children. Amen.

Folly is bound up in the heart of a child,
but the rod of discipline will drive it far away.

PROVERBS 22:15

January 17

The Compassionate Warrior

Dealing with the enemy on the battlefield can make you mentally tough, which can either be a good thing or a negative thing. If it costs you compassion toward your children, I'd say it is negative. This is no excuse to raise up weak kids, but it is a reminder that we should leave our military mindset at the door when we arrive home. Loving our families with compassion is one of the ways Jesus would love them. In fact, compassion preceded every miracle Jesus performed.

People pray daily for miracles but often fail to see the power they possess to be the miracle to their own families or to their own children. Showing them compassion, love, and quality time are all ways to demonstrate the nature of God to our families. And as warriors, it is a good reminder that compassion for those whom we serve can go a long way.

Heavenly Father, give me a heart of compassion toward my spouse and children. Help me to love my family like you love me. Amen.

As a father has compassion on his children,
so the LORD has compassion on those who fear him.

PSALM 103:13

January 18

Obedience Creates Breakthrough

If your parents are still living, when was the last time you called them? The older I get, the more I realize the frailty and brevity of life. We are never promised another moment. To think of some of the downright silly things we have allowed to destroy the relationships we have had with our parents, spouses, and children is mind-boggling. Today, begin with forgiveness.

Mending a relationship may not mean you begin with forgiveness if you were wronged, but you begin with forgiveness out of obedience so you can begin the narrative of relationship again with your loved one. As a service member, it is easy to forget someone else gave us life. Call your mom, your dad, or your family and tell them you love them. Go spend time with them. Honor them. Take the risk of mending relationships because, after all, you are a peacemaker. You will be glad you did.

Heavenly Father, give me wisdom and a course to approach damaged relationships; help me to seek forgiveness in areas where I have wronged others and in areas I have been wronged. Amen.

Children, obey your parents in the Lord,
for this is right.
EPHESIANS 6:1

January 19

Lead Them to Life

When my youngest son doesn't get his way, he wants to have a trial on the spot. He wants the facts laid out, and he wants to have a perfectly clear understanding of why the results are the way they are. It is in those moments I have to make it clear through a patient, loving explanation that I do not have to provide him with an attorney, at eight years old, over his inability to get chicken nuggets.

Many of us are the same way when it comes to getting answers from God. We want to know the reasons why things are the way they are or why he said no. God will not lead us to death, but through his Son, Jesus, he leads us to eternal life. We should focus our efforts on leading our children in love. Even when our patience with them grows thin, remember God's love is long-suffering, and he could have brought judgment on us long ago, but instead he gives us new mercies every morning. Lead your children to life daily.

> *Heavenly Father, help me in my moments of impatience with my children. Help me to speak words softly and with love because I know they will remember it forever. Amen.*

If anyone causes one of these little ones—those who believe in me—to stumble, it would be better for them if a large millstone were hung around their neck and they were thrown into the sea.

MARK 9:42

January 20
Lifetime Warranty

New vehicles often come with extensive warranties, providing service for the vehicle according to the manufacturer's guidelines. Proverbs tells us that if we train our children, they will give us peace. Much like automobile manufacturers tell us that if we maintain our vehicles, they will honor a warranty, so we are to properly train our children and expect peace from them as they mature. To discipline your children means to train your children to obey rules or follow certain expected behavior, using punishment to correct disobedience.

Punishment can come in a variety of methods. For some, making their child write a five-hundred-word essay on the topic of obedience is plenty of punishment, while others need more traditional punishment or manual labor. It is your job as the parent to help your child discover the purpose, vision, and mission God has for his or her life. There is nothing more in this life that I can think of that will give parents more peace or delight than to see their children living out their God-given destiny. Training your children from a young age will help them realize this.

> *Heavenly Father, help me to cultivate in the heart of my children the vision you have for their lives. Help me to nurture the purpose you have for them, through properly training them as a parent. Amen.*

Discipline your children, and they will give you peace;
they will bring you the delights you desire.
PROVERBS 29:17

January 21

Take Care of Your Family

Under the uniform of every warrior is the heart of a man or woman who is willing to do whatever it takes to get the job done, to serve their nation, to defend the helpless, and to meet the needs of their own family. There are seasons in life when it is necessary to work more than usual, and communicating with your spouse and children will help you to navigate those seasons in a healthy manner. You should be commended for your service, the risks you take, and the dangers you face for the sake of others.

Most people do not leave for work wondering what dangers they may face that day or whether they'll come home at the end of their training or lengthy deployment. Your faith in God, your strength, your perseverance, and your consistency in service will provide for you and your family for many years to come. Do not become complacent in your duties but learn contentment at home.

Heavenly Father, thank you for the opportunity to serve my nation. Give me favor in your eyes as I seek your ways and help me to provide for my family to meet all their needs. Amen.

Anyone who does not provide for their relatives,
and especially for their own household,
has denied the faith and is worse than an unbeliever.

1 TIMOTHY 5:8

January 22

Sentenced to Life

As you progress in your career, you will obtain promotions in rank, receive pay increases, face cost-of-living increases, and contend with other raises. These times may be tempting to acquire new debt. While a new house or new car may be enticing, consider saving money and paying a large down payment or purchasing a used home or a nice used car. The burden caused by overloading yourself with debt is substantial, and you become a slave to the lender. You have no choice but to work and to work as much as necessary to meet those obligations. This means more time away from your family. Some debt, like a thirty-year mortgage, can seem like a lifetime sentence to debt.

God's ways are always higher than our own plans. It may seem foolish or even out of date, but saving money and waiting to purchase big items like a house or car can protect you from the burden of slavery to debt and give you freedom millions of Americans do not enjoy. Today, seek to be different. If you have debt, communicate with your spouse and come up with a plan to pay off all debt and to not acquire any new debt. If you do not have any debt, avoid it at all costs. You are free indeed.

> *Heavenly Father, teach me the wisdom of proper financial stewardship and the freedom in not being slave to the lender. Amen.*

The rich rule over the poor,
and the borrower is slave to the lender.

PROVERBS 22:7

Gaining Wealth Is Not Evil

Some folks will tell you that if you are rich, then you are evil. This is far from the truth. It is the *love* of money that is the root of evil, not the possession of money. If you have excellent business aptitude, consider saving and investing, as long as it does not interfere with your duties. Invest your money wisely and accumulate wealth but do it for the right reasons. Doing any of this for the simple love of money will lead you down an evil and dark path.

Still, do not allow a goal of gaining financial wealth to cause you to wander from your faith or become encompassed with immorality. The key to acquiring wealth is giving because it ensures that your heart remains pure of greed and that your love is not for money but for God. Keep your heart right and your pursuit pure, and your acquisitions will take care of themselves.

> *Heavenly Father, I know my family has needs, and they will have needs in the future. I also know I will need to retire one day. Please give me the wisdom from your Word as it pertains to building wealth the godly way, beginning with giving. Amen.*

For the love of money is a root of all kinds of evil.
Some people, eager for money, have wandered
from the faith and pierced themselves with many griefs.

1 TIMOTHY 6:10

January 24

The Power of Giving

It would be foolish to believe your entire life revolved around your duties at work or that your influence ended where your jurisdiction begins and ends. Your influence can span this globe because of giving, and the benefits are not only good for your heart and soul, but they can also help you in many other ways. Honoring God with your wealth may sound old-fashioned and out of date, but it is one of the best ways to keep your heart aligned with his and ensure you stay far from greed.

The power of giving is deeper and wider than giving to receive more in return. The power of giving is the freedom found in covenant with the Father through his Word. No other financial system will reward you or provide you with security, both short term and long term, the way God's financial system will. Tap into the power of giving, first locally with your home church and then with missions, and watch God's power expand in your life.

Heavenly Father, I give you all that I possess because it is yours. It is not mine. I am merely a steward over it. I submit to your ways and ask for your blessings on all I put my hand to and all I give. Amen.

Honor the LORD with your wealth,
with the firstfruits of all your crops;
then your barns will be filled to overflowing,
and your vats will brim over with new wine.

PROVERBS 3:9–10

January 25

Be Thankful for What You Have

To everything, there must be order. Imagine if a new private was assigned to be the duty NCO (Non-Commissioned Officer) for the night. Because a private is not ready for such responsibilities, the results could be disastrous on many levels. For some, patience to achieve their goals runs thin, and ambition tends to put the goals before the process. However, if we will simply focus on being thankful for where we are, where we have come from, and what we have, our perspectives will shift to a much healthier vantage point.

If we cannot be entrusted with authority over our AO (Area of Operation), we cannot be entrusted to lead in larger responsibilities. If we cannot be trusted with little, then we cannot be trusted with much. It is a simple principle. Learn to cultivate the heart of a giver, live from a place of perpetual thankfulness, and watch your fields flourish. Thankfulness is a great virtue to have in your heart and a wonderful place from which to live.

Heavenly Father, life is not always perfect according to the standards others set. But I have all I need, and I am thankful. Remind me to come to you daily with a heart of thankfulness and not as a spoiled brat. Amen.

Whoever can be trusted with very little can also be trusted with much, and whoever is dishonest with very little will also be dishonest with much.

LUKE 16:10

January 26

Think Outside the Budget Box

If you have made some bad financial decisions and your credit record, score, and bank account have the scars to prove it, then you may need to think creatively as it pertains to addressing your situation. There are many plans and ideas when it comes to setting finances in order, but at the end of the day, the key is to spend less than you bring home in your paycheck. If you have since overextended yourself in financial obligations, it may be time to put some creative ideas to work so you can eventually get to a working budget.

Your family needs the peace of mind of knowing you can not only lead them but also manage the finances and pass on the lessons so your children do not make the same mistakes. With the wisdom gained from God's Word, the lessons learned from others who have mastered finances, and your hard work, sacrifices, and creative ideas, you will have things rolling in the right direction in no time. It's time to think outside the budget box, get creative, and put those ideas to work.

Heavenly Father, I know you did not create me to live under stress, bound in debt to lenders. Give me creative ideas and strategies for getting all of my debt paid off in a legal, ethical, and holy manner. Amen.

All hard work brings a profit,
but mere talk leads only to poverty.
PROVERBS 14:23

January 27

Testing God

The topic of tithing is one that many people debate. However, I am of the belief that everything I have belongs to God, and it all came from him because he is my ultimate provider. Giving ten percent is not a difficult thing to do. Not only does it keep our heart aligned with God, but it also reminds us where our provisions originate from. Our nature is often to be self-reliant and self-sustaining, and there's nothing wrong with that. But at the same time, we must remember God is the source of all that we have received.

I am issuing you a challenge today, much like the challenge we read in Malachi 3:10: Test God in the tithe. Be consistent and give from a pure, joyful heart. Do not give with an anticipation of receiving. Instead, give with thankfulness for all you have been given. Your life, your family, and your career will never be the same.

Heavenly Father, you are the provider for all the needs I have in life, and all the provisions I have come from you. I commit to living out my thankfulness to you by giving back to you ten percent of what is already yours and watching you meet every need. Amen.

"Test me in this," says the LORD Almighty, "and see if I will not throw open the floodgates of heaven and pour out so much blessing that there will not be room enough to store it."

MALACHI 3:10

The Art of Balance

What a wonderful opportunity you have in life, to serve your nation. Finding the balance in life as a service member, regardless of the branch you serve with, is a challenging task. It is essential, however, if you want to achieve a certain level of success in your career and, if married, in your family. This means you must live in a way that not only addresses conflict with others but also keeps your life free of unnecessary strife and drama. Find the balance between career and family, and you find a place few ever discover.

With proper time balance and an understanding family, you will face less strife and division. But if you fail to communicate and make your family a priority, you will find that the cost of overtime is beyond the price you are willing to pay. It may be time to cut some expenses so you do not lose the reason you work. It's better to have less or nothing and have peace than to have it all and live with strife.

Heavenly Father, thank you for the wisdom of knowing that less is more. Help me to number my days, to place my relationship with you and my family above my career, and to seek you in all I do. Amen.

Better a dry crust with peace and quiet
than a house full of feasting, with strife.

PROVERBS 17:1

Investment Officers

In a 2006 poll taken by the Consumer Federation of America and Financial Planning Association, twenty percent of Americans said they were depending on winning the lottery as their retirement plan. While winning the lottery would hardly be considered dishonest, the number of lives destroyed by lottery winnings is staggering. At the end of the day, we could hoard more money than any major country, but if we don't know how to manage it, we are wasting our time and energy.

Putting together a solid plan for your future means you have a plan for giving, a budget for expenses, and plan for saving. Dishonest money dwindles away because the heart is the issue, not the money. The one who gathers money little by little has established self-discipline and put forth hard work. Take time to think about your future today. What are you depending on for retirement? If you don't have a budget or you are not saving or giving, today is a great day to begin a new life.

Heavenly Father, give me wisdom above all things as it pertains to finances and accumulating wealth. Amen.

Dishonest money dwindles away,
but whoever gathers money little by little makes it grow.
PROVERBS 13:11

January 30

Stay Focused on Your Goals

The key to reaching your goals, whether they relate to health, relationships, finances, or career, is consistency in executing a well-thought-out plan. However, you may find yourself facing distractions along the way as you encounter growth phases. These are times when it is critical to remain focused on your goals, keep your eyes on the prize, and remain consistent. Anyone can do something for a day, but those who are focused and consistent win the prize.

What are you willing to do to have abundance in your life? Are you willing to plan, sacrifice material things, work hard, and be a committed follower of Christ? If so, then you have the characteristics of a champion, and it is time to put your hands to work. Like you do on many of the days you experience in your duties, staying focused and consistent in your goals in life isn't always easy, but it is necessary those goals are part of being a champion in life. You have what it takes—your family needs it, and you can deliver. Stay focused!

Heavenly Father, when wild ideas cross my mind, teach me to test them and see their value before pursuing them or entertaining them. Give me wisdom and strength to endure and to be consistent and the spirit to remain focused amidst distractions. Amen.

Those who work their land will have abundant food, but those who chase fantasies will have their fill of poverty.

PROVERBS 28:19

January 31

Primary Command

When we consider the greatest command that we could issue to an individual, there are many options to choose from. Some may suggest we command others to travel safely, while others may suggest we command others to be vigilant. We all have experienced commands from a superior, and we know what it means to carry out those orders. We do this because of established policy and procedures that tell us how we are to do so.

Much like the SOPs (Standard Operating Procedures) we have at work, God's Word spells out how we should respond to various challenges and situations in life. At the end of the day, the greatest command is to love God and love others. It sounds simple, but it is often complex. Loving someone who loves us back is an easy and almost an automatic task. But loving someone who doesn't love us back is difficult. To carry out that command, we must fear God and keep his commandments. Do these things, and you will be on your way to a fruitful life.

Heavenly Father, thank you for loving me before I ever took the step to love you. I pray that you will keep watch over me as I serve your people. Guide my steps to honor your word and keep your commandments. Amen.

Fear God and keep his commandments,
for this is the duty of all mankind.

ECCLESIASTES 12:13

February 1

Armed with Wisdom

Maybe you have heard combat veterans not trusting teammates with reckless courage. You know someone like that, I'll bet, someone with no fear, no strategy, who just lays it all on the line and goes in guns blazing. I'm not suggesting there are never times we must go into harm's way without hesitation, but we need to have the proper training and mindset if we do. After basic training, a person's mindset is such an overlooked and rarely discussed tool. The best thing you could ever do is learn to think, know when to speak, and know when to act.

King Solomon remains heralded as one of the wisest men to have ever lived. He is famous for his wealth and possessions, but few know of his mistakes. Why? King Solomon sought God for his wisdom instead of asking for stuff. Solomon knew the importance of wisdom and its value over all other things a person could attain. It's not a matter of *if* you will encounter danger but *when* you will encounter it. When you do, having supernatural wisdom gained only from God can guide you to victory or help you know when to retreat.

Heavenly Father, grant me your wisdom above all else. I understand the fear of you is the beginning of true wisdom, and I submit this day to your will. Amen.

The prudent see danger and take refuge, but the simple keep going and pay the penalty.

PROVERBS 22:3

February 2

Prudent Troops

You are expected to be aggressive yet professional in all you do as a warrior. Acting with consideration for innocent civilians means knowing when to decide how to engage the enemy. Prudence is wisdom looking forward, not only thinking about the here and now but also how your current decisions will affect you and those around you in the future. You have undoubtedly heard the phrase "risk versus reward" in your training. Think about your decisions. Will they honor God, your unit, and your nation?

Shunning evil is not something you have the liberty to do. Your job is to confront it, save lives, crush the enemy, and protect the innocent. But doing so in an even-tempered manner is critical to your reputation. Don't be known as someone who loses his or her temper quickly over minuscule things. Your demeanor can escalate or de-escalate a situation and have a permanent impact on the lives of other people. Live as a person who fears God, seeks his wisdom, and makes decisions with the future in mind, not only the here and now.

Heavenly Father, give me discernment today in all the decisions I will be asked to make. Help me make the best decisions for the people I serve. Amen.

The wise fear the LORD and shun evil,
but a fool is hotheaded and yet feels secure.

PROVERBS 14:16

February 3

Unwavering Faith

At some point in your career, someone who was unethical in his or her duties or even someone who committed criminal acts has probably affected you. This type of negative behavior brings a great deal of criticism within our ranks, even though those who are responsible make up a small percentage of the entire military. When we condone or commit crimes or unethical behavior, we are complicit in tarnishing the uniform. Each of us is held to a higher standard because of the authority we have.

Maybe it didn't begin as a big deal. Maybe it was just an innocent lie or some other seemingly innocent action, but before you knew it, you found yourself on the other side of character and what is right, and maybe you even lost your reputation or career. There are always consequences to our actions. Hold yourself accountable, but don't forget you are also responsible for your teammates if you have knowledge of improper behavior or activity. Don't muddy the waters and don't give way to the evil you confront.

Heavenly Father, give me strength in the face of temptation, strength to stand, and wisdom in difficult circumstances. Amen.

Like a muddied spring or a polluted well are the righteous who give way to the wicked.

PROVERBS 25:26

February 4

Serving the Persecutor

If you have ever been formally written up, the frustration associated with that can be detrimental to your development. Concern for your future may linger in your mind while you await a decision. It has been said that those who are best in the field will be more likely to get in trouble in garrison. You will, over the course of your career, find yourself having to answer for poor decisions or simple mistakes as you learn and grow. The question is whether you will let these moments set you back or learn the lessons and grow from them.

Don't allow these setbacks to create bitterness and resentment in your heart. It is easy to hate and withhold forgiveness, and it is not easy to love those who are hard to love, even those responsible for discipling you within the ranks. Loving our friends and family is easy, and it comes naturally in most cases. But Jesus said love includes loving those who hate and persecute us. It is perfectly normal to find loving our enemy a difficult task, especially within our own strength. But through the new life found in Jesus Christ, we are not only empowered to love those who persecute us but also expected to love them. Jesus commands us to love our enemies and pray for those who persecute us. Complaining does no good, but praying will change the circumstances.

Heavenly Father, thank you for empowering me to love not only those who love me but also those who hate me and persecute me. Remind me of the power of praying for those who seek to harm me. Amen.

You have heard that it was said, "Love your neighbor and hate your enemy." But I tell you, love your enemies and pray for those who persecute you.

MATTHEW 5:43–44

February 5

Pain Tolerance

On occasion, you may find yourself wondering if God has forgotten you. When you are consistently serving others, it is easy to forget about taking care of your needs. Years of working at high levels of stress preparing for or experiencing the hardships of war will take a toll on any human soul. Through all the training we have experienced, seldom do we address pain management from an internal perspective. After all, we aren't supposed to talk about those things. But past pain, if not properly addressed, is a weapon the enemy can use to bring us defeat and thwart our God-given purpose.

God records every single moment of pain you have ever experienced or witnessed. He sees all and knows all. We have all wondered why God "allows" terrible things to happen. The answer is simple: we live in a fallen world, and sin has consequences. Our hope of healing spans beyond this life, and our impact goes far beyond our military careers. If you need pain management, God's eyes are not passing you by. In fact, he is the solution to your pain. Much like you have to document everything you do on duty, so God has a record of your life.

Heavenly Father, help me to find healing from the things that bring me pain and misery. Help me to realize I am a human being and will have more positive impact when I operate in total healing. Amen.

Record my misery;
list my tears on your scroll—
are they not in your record?

PSALM 56:8

February 6

Through the Valley of Death

Whether you are working endless hours to provide essential battlefield life support or are the point man on a patrol through an IED (Improvised Explosive Device) infested route, you are never alone. It can seem as though you are by yourself at times, but having the promise of an eternal partner will give you the confidence you need to be successful and safe on every assignment. Your training has completely prepared you for the steps you should take to safely, successfully, and securely conduct your duties, but peace that God is with you is a confidence we all need.

At the end of the day, you need to know you will never be alone. There are men and women who are completely willing to serve by your side and are fully equipped to do so. However, there may be times when you still feel alone for what seems to be an eternity. There is a strength within you that, when called upon, will not fail. You must do your part, and part of that is to properly train and prepare, which includes engaging in regular prayer. The other part is to call on God in these times of need. God will not fail you.

Heavenly Father, gently remind me that you walk with me even when I feel like I am alone. I acknowledge you are the sole source of my strength. Amen.

Even though I walk through the darkest valley,
I will fear no evil, for you are with me;
your rod and your staff, they comfort me.

PSALM 23:4

February 7

The Hands of Justice

For everything with a beginning, there is also an end. The end may not be in sight to you or anyone else at this point, but the end is already established. However, now may not be the "proper" time for something or someone to come to an end. Proverbs 16:4 is a great reminder that even the wicked have an established end to their plans and actions. Your service, without a doubt, will deter evil actions from taking place today. Your courage, wisdom, experience, professionalism, and readiness will make those who plot terror think twice about the consequences they might face.

To this end, you are marked as the hands of justice, protecting the innocent and removing wicked and evil people from this world. If you have felt discouraged by the outcomes of trials in the past, remember your job is not to prosecute or judge but to enforce justice on evil to protect the innocent. Focus on doing your job with excellence and bringing an end to the plans of those who bring pain, frustration, and disaster to the lives of innocent and helpless people.

Heavenly Father, reinforce my training and your promises and surround me with your protection. Position me to be the "proper end" to the wicked plans of evil people today. Amen.

The LORD works out everything to its proper end— even the wicked for a day of disaster.

PROVERBS 16:4

Miraculous Moments

There are opportunities for us to be a miracle to someone today if we look for those opportunities. When we are on duty, we can deliver comfort and peace, restore order, and give back life to those who have lived through what could be described as hell. Through your service, you can take what the enemy intended for harm against the innocent and help bring comfort and healing. Your interaction with individuals can be life-altering for the good.

What is the value of adversity? It is whatever good we allow to come from it. If we choose to complain, we dig deeper in negative, poisonous living. If we choose to believe God can take whatever comes against us and use it for good, then that is where we will find ourselves. Life isn't a magic fairy tale. Rather, it's the result of maintaining faith, remaining consistent in relationship with Christ, treating others right, forgiving, and remaining strong through adversity. God will take the difficult times and use them to elevate us to a place of empowered living. Look for the opportunities for the miraculous.

Heavenly Father, help me see the opportunities where I can be used by you in the lives of other people to demonstrate your love and kindness. Thank you, Father, for turning into good what was meant to harm me.
Amen.

You intended to harm me,
but God intended it all for good.
He brought me to this position
so I could save the lives of many people.
GENESIS 50:20 NLT

February 9

Prepared to Engage Evil

As you engage the enemy, it seems their attacks are relentless and unstoppable. A barrage of attacks starts to overwhelm you before you realize what you are capable of as an individual and as a team. Something rises up inside you, your heartbeat increases, and your focus becomes clear. This is time for war, and you were trained for it. Not only physically but also mentally, emotionally, and spiritually. You are prepared to engage evil with superior, righteous violence.

The difference between good and evil is the fact that evil people want to move quickly without considering others. Evil is not logical or rational. Those who pursue evil schemes, whether violent or nonviolent, will face the consequences. They will eventually have to pay for their wrongdoing if their schemes were criminal. When that day comes, you may be the wall of reckoning. When you have to deal with evil, deal firmly, fairly, swiftly, and justly. Do not succumb to the demands to surrender to evil. Evil may attempt to elude you, but you are prepared for this day.

Heavenly Father, make my feet swift, give me the strength and endurance needed to pursue the evil of this world physically, and spiritually protect me every step of the way. Amen.

Their feet rush into sin;
they are swift to shed innocent blood.
They pursue evil schemes;
acts of violence mark their ways.
ISAIAH 59:7

February 10

Defending the Righteous

Part of your service is protecting those who cannot defend themselves. It is an honor to stand between their well-being and the evil that lurks beside them. It is reassuring to know God will rescue those who are his, but he is also a just God who will give protection to those who have no way of knowing right from wrong. Life is full of difficult questions, many of which no human, regardless of scientific, philosophical, or theological degrees, can answer.

We can rest in knowing that God will rescue the godly in their time of need. Those who seem to go unpunished for their sins will pay for their evil deeds. Stand up for what is right, moral, true, and good. Most of this world has surrendered their convictions in the name of political correctness, and the least we can do is hold the line of righteousness and justice. God will not turn a blind eye to good or evil.

Heavenly Father, thank you for the task of defending the innocent, helpless, defenseless, weak, and oppressed. Thank you for the opportunity to reflect who you are to the world around me. Amen.

If God did not spare angels when they sinned, but sent them to hell, putting them in chains of darkness to be held for judgment; ...if this is so, then the Lord knows how to rescue the godly from trials and to hold the unrighteous for punishment on the day of judgment.

2 PETER 2:4, 9

February 11

Everything in Love

February is, for many people, all about love. This month can be rewarding or depressing. For some couples, this month is one of the rare moments where they express love and affection. If someone gives a card or gift out of tainted motives, it ruins the potential reward for the giver. It's all in the attitude and motives, which are found in the heart, which is, by nature, corrupt. For those of you who are like me, talking about "love" makes you think back to the last time you were at the range slinging lead at targets. I get it. But if you are a believer, 1 Corinthians 16:14 makes it clear. We have received a clear-cut command. It is not an easy command, but it is clear: "Do everything in love."

Maybe expressing truth or communicating in love is something you find difficult or, at the very least, not natural. Most of this month has focused on how you deal with adversity, persecution, or other on-the-job issues as they relate to love. Will you accept the challenge today to be intentional with expressing love to your family? If you are married, remember your spouse is not the enemy, and your children do not want to be interrogated. Serve in love, both in and out of the uniform.

Heavenly Father, fill my heart with your love and help me be a vessel of your love. Amen.

Do everything in love.

1 CORINTHIANS 16:14

February 12

Death Is Not the End

The pain we feel when we lose someone we love is unexplainable. It's like a part of our life dies with them. Death is a painful and sorrowful experience for the loved ones who remain, but should it be? We know sin entered the world through Adam in the garden of Eden, and because of such, we were all exposed to death. But because of Jesus, we have received an opportunity for eternal life. While we will all face physical death, we can live eternally with Christ.

When we approach life and service through this angle, no weapon can harm us. This is no excuse to be careless, reckless, or foolish, but it should give us relief in knowing there is nothing any person can do to harm our eternal souls. The threats and dangers in this world are real, but death is not the end of the story. Be encouraged in knowing that you are more than a victor, more than a conqueror, and more than a peacemaker. The Father created you to have an eternal impact on humanity for the kingdom of God.

Heavenly Father, thank you for the gift of eternal life through your Son, Jesus. Thank you that death has lost its sting, and I can rejoice in life eternally with you. Amen.

Just as sin entered the world through one man,
and death through sin,
and in this way death came to all people,
because all sinned.

ROMANS 5:12

February 13

Unconventional Warfare

We are living in unprecedented times, which call for unconventional methods of addressing the global threat to our nation. We will not fight all wars with traditional means we have known from years past. But how would you feel if you were David, having received an answer from God about a surprising and unusual battle strategy? Sometimes, our approach to the strategy of the enemy is not going to be direct or head on. There may be times when God gives us instructions that are contrary to our own desires or man-made plans. In these times and all others, obedience is key to victory.

Today, if you find yourself in a place of adversity and warfare, remember to seek out methods that you may not have previously considered. When you've done all you know to do, your next steps should be to seek the wisdom of God. As God said to David, "Do not go directly after them, but circle around them." It's time to circle the wagons, dear warriors. It is time to gather what is left, prepare your hearts for battle, and not to limit this warfare to the ways you have known. God will go before you, and he will grant you victory in this battle. Rise, warriors!

> *Heavenly Father, your wisdom is key to my victory. I seek your wisdom in this life, in every battle, in all things. Go before me in this battle and all others. Grant me victory, I pray. Amen*

Once more the Philistines raided the valley; so David inquired of God again, and God answered him, "Do not go directly after them, but circle around them and attack them in front of the poplar trees. As soon as you hear the sound of marching in the tops of the poplar trees, move out to battle, because that will mean God has gone out in front of you to strike the Philistine army."

1 CHRONICLES 14:13–15

Inside the Enemy's Playbook

There are people who want to end your life simply because of the nation you represent. It doesn't matter what your name is or your skin color, family status, social status, or financial situation. What matters to them is the fact you are the enemy of their motives. You and everything you stand for are deterrents and obstacles to their evil motives and agendas, and there would be nothing else to stop them from taking over.

John 10:10 tells us that the enemy comes to steal, kill, and destroy. We have seen the living proof of this in ravaged families and individual lives across our nation. But as ambassadors for Christ, we are to interrupt those plans and stop those attacks when possible. When we know the plans of the enemy in our profession, it makes our jobs of strategizing to counter the attacks easier. The enemy is the same, regardless of nation, religion, or ideology. Today, be wise and know and understand the plans of the enemy. Give life to those you encounter and relentlessly pursue and eliminate the evil of this world.

> *Heavenly Father, thank you that your Son came to give me life and life to the full and that you have fully equipped me to overcome the world and the schemes of the enemy. Amen.*

The thief comes only to steal and kill and destroy;
I have come that they may have life, and have it to the full.

JOHN 10:10

Supernatural Protection

Many of you have experienced or know someone who has experienced something unexplainable. Whether it was divine intervention, wild coincidence, or what some might call a form of fate or destiny, a moment when any other person would have been seriously injured or killed, you survived unscathed. While it is certainly not doctrinally sound, I believe God uses everyday people to provide divine intervention in times of dire need. Some call it being in the right place at the right time, but I call it supernatural intervention.

Today, you may be the angel that someone has been praying for. When a child in a small village in a foreign land faces true oppression or parents who have lost not only their freedom but have also had their children torn from their arms, you could be the answer to their prayers. God's Word tells us that he has heavenly messengers encamped around those who fear him, but he also uses people to meet the needs of those who call on him. When we are aligned with God's plan, we become part of the answer to prayer. When we realize that, we realize the power of supernatural protection. It's all around us.

> *Heavenly Father, I ask for you to use me as you will, as your messenger, to deliver those who are oppressed and victims of evil. As I fear you, encamp your heavenly angels around me and those who serve with me. Amen.*

The angel of the LORD encamps around those who fear him, and he delivers them.

PSALM 34:7

The Enemy's Schemes

The range instructor stood before the group of warriors and demonstrated the proper standing position for firing a weapon. One young man couldn't seem to grasp the concept. "No, place your foot here," the instructor demonstrated. "Good, now place your right hand here." The young man seemed to have difficulty standing in proper position because of his cumbersome armor. As difficult as it may be, it is necessary to train with body armor because it is there to save our lives, and we must get comfortable wearing it and operating in it.

The armor we wear is to protect us from the attacks of the suspects who would try to end our lives. In the same manner, the armor of God is to protect our spirit so that we are fully equipped to stand against the attacks of the enemy. Just like when we are on the range, however, we ought not be careless with our armor, our weapons, or our skills. Rather, we should take care of them, stay prepared and trained, and be ready to do battle against the schemes of the enemy.

> *Heavenly Father, thank you for equipping me with the full armor of protection spiritually and for the wisdom and common sense to wear my armor every day.*
> *Amen.*

The God of our Lord Jesus Christ, the Father of glory, may give to you the spirit of wisdom and revelation in the knowledge of Him...that you may know...what is the exceeding greatness of His power toward us who believe.

EPHESIANS 1:17–19 NKJV

February 17

Sustaining Power

When a natural disaster, such as a tsunami, hits one of our foreign neighbors, the world often calls for the aid of the US military. Such humanitarian efforts involve endless hours and days without breaks, bringing on physical fatigue, mental stress, and often emotional heartbreak from the tragic loss of life and economic destruction of good people. Through all the difficult times, long hours, and exhaustion, there's good news: difficult times don't last for you or those you serve. You are equipped to sustain and are surrounded by people who will support you and lift you up through the tough times.

Second Thessalonians 3:3 starts off with a wonderful reminder, "The Lord is faithful." Even when we feel like we have reached an empty tank, we have nothing left to give, our faith is depleted, and we cannot go on, he promises to sustain, strengthen, and empower us. When we choose to lean on his promises, we find strength and hope that the world cannot offer. It is our faith in Christ that sustains us, protects us, and propels us to the finish line every time.

Heavenly Father, thank you for the power to finish well. Thank you for strength to endure difficult times and adversity and to be more than a conqueror. Amen.

They are new every morning;
Great is Your faithfulness.
LAMENTATIONS 3:23 NKJV

February 18

The Devil's Playground

We live in a world under the control of evil, and the only thing holding evil back from having total rule is the mercy of God. We live and operate in the devil's playground. Despite how it looks, people are not the enemy. In Ephesians, Paul had a way of showing us who the real enemy was: "Our struggle is not against flesh and blood, but against the rulers, against the authorities, against the powers of this dark world and against the spiritual forces of evil in the heavenly realms" (Ephesians 6:12).

If we are not clear about who we are at war against, then we will not be effective in battle. It is essential to know your location, and this is all the truer in these times in which we live. It would behoove you to equip yourself with high-quality training, equipment, and a proper mindset but also daily prayer and fellowship with God. With these steps, you will be prepared to face the plans and dangers in a world laced with danger, and you will be equipped to give peace to a world that seeks answers only God can give.

Heavenly Father, thank you for victory, protection, and a prosperous career. Place a shield of protection around me and those who serve with me. Grant me favor in your sight and in the sight of those I serve with. Amen.

We know that we are children of God,
and that the whole world is under the control of the evil one.

1 JOHN 5:19

February 19

The Altar of Freedom

What happens when the day comes and one of us pays the ultimate price on the battlefield? We stop at nothing short of exhausting all resources and manpower and even go at great personal risk to rescue others, recover them, and get them to life saving medical attention, but despite all efforts, we couldn't save them, and it was their time. Since 1775 nearly three million American warriors have laid their very lives on the altar of freedom, and it will happen again.

At the end of the day, even the strongest believers in Christ may have questions after losing a teammate in combat, but knowing we can rest in the peace found in Jesus gives us hope and strength to continue. It takes a different breed of people to place themselves in harm's way to defend those they don't even know. But to those who violate humanity and all that is good, those who take the lives of our brothers and sisters or any other human being, we are all committed to bringing them to justice.

Heavenly Father, thank you for allowing me to live the life of a warrior. Preserve my life as I walk in the midst of trouble and danger. Guide my feet and give me discernment as I serve. Amen.

Though I walk in the midst of trouble, you preserve my life. You stretch out your hand against the anger of my foes; with your right hand you save me.

PSALM 138:7

Cream of the Crop

Regardless of your job, not everyone who set out to do what you do in the military made it. In fact, you were likely selected from a large pool of applicants in recruiting, endured basic training, and made it through advanced schools for your occupational specialty. You endured rigorous testing and training and eventually made the cut. In the end, it was worth it. The citizens of our nation are thankful that they do not have the bottom of the stack responding when they need them the most. The world gets the very best when they get the men and women of the United States military.

In the same way, Father God did not send a cheap substitute to rescue us from this present evil age, a world dominated by evil. No, he loved us so much that he sent his only Son, Jesus, to rescue us from our own destructive living. There's nothing wrong with striving to be excellent in all we do. After all, the Father set that example a long time ago. We should do our best in all we do. And at the end of the day, he gets the glory for the work we do, for the lives we impact, and for the evil we apprehend.

Heavenly Father, thank you for sending your Son to rescue me from my own destruction. Thank you for empowering me to overcome and conquer this world. Amen.

The Lord Jesus Christ...gave himself for our sins to rescue us from the present evil age, according to the will of our God and Father.

GALATIANS 1:3–4

February 21

Specialty Rescue Team

Difficult times often challenge our faith. It's easy to be strong in our faith when everything is going well, but how we respond when things don't go well is a true testament to our character in Christ. Military members will lose their lives on the battlefield, and many will be faithful Christians. These bodies we live in will not last forever, and at the appointed time, we will leave for eternity. Our lives as believers do not end when our physical bodies cease to function. In fact, life only *begins* at that moment.

Second Timothy 4:18 says God will rescue us from this life. He will rescue us from a life where we intimately know pain, hurt, sorrow, and disappointment. Our perspective has always been that all the chips are on the table when we choose to serve. But that is far from the truth. When we shift our thinking and living to the eternal instead of the things of the earth, we begin to think with the mind of Christ, and our service as warriors becomes exponentially more effective.

Heavenly Father, thank you for giving me abundant life. If it is your will, give me a long and prosperous life and give me favor. When my time comes to leave, may I leave having fulfilled the purpose and mission you set before me. Amen.

The Lord will rescue me from every evil attack and will bring me safely to his heavenly kingdom. To him be glory for ever and ever. Amen.

2 TIMOTHY 4:18

February 22

Our Shield and Protector

This life is temporary. It is like a blip of time on the radar of existence. It's over before we know it. Our lives are part of a significantly bigger plan, so our job is to make sure we are doing our part by being involved in the plan, reaching others with the message of the love of Jesus Christ.

When we are afflicted with pain or injury, know that God did not send those struggles to punish you. He is not waiting for you to mess up so he can punish you, but he loves you with an everlasting love. In all things, whether we are serving or resting, he will watch over us so that we are not taken before our appointed time. As his servants, he will protect us as we trust him, follow his guidance, use wisdom, and obey his commands. His mercy will keep us, even in our errors and foolishness, but only for a season. Therefore, follow the leading of the Holy Spirit as he guides you.

Heavenly Father, thank you for peace, even in the face of death. Thank you that I have eternal life because of your Son. Grant me wisdom and discernment and keep me from foolish decisions that would cost me. I trust you, Father, and give you my life. Amen.

The LORD will keep you from all harm—he will watch over your life; the LORD will watch over your coming and going both now and forevermore.

PSALM 121:7–8

Cover and Concealment

If we approached a compound and someone began firing shots at us, as trained warfighters, we know what would provide adequate cover and what would not. It is important to quickly find a place that will protect you and keep you from being struck. *Take cover* is a phrase that movie characters use a lot, but we know the real-life application of cover and the proper time for concealment.

When we say, "God is our hiding place," it does not mean we are cowards. Rather, it means we have enough wisdom and common sense to know when to take cover from attack. Concealment is the life we used to live, going through the motions. Maybe that included going to church and maybe reading the Bible. We were inconsistent, with no passion and no enthusiasm. But when our focus in life shifted from the problems of this world to our eternal significance, we realized the power of refuge found in Christ. He will truly protect us from the attacks of the enemy. Lean on him, and he will come to you.

> *Heavenly Father, I am placing myself under your protection, at your mercy, and I ask for your direction and leading. I cannot do this without you. Thank you for your divine power to accomplish what you have placed me here to do. Amen.*

You are my hiding place; you will protect me from trouble and surround me with songs of deliverance.

PSALM 32:7

February 24

Know Your Limits

We all have a breaking point because we're human beings. It's basic biology. At some point, if we don't recognize our limits and operate within them, then our limits will let us know where they are and will issue warnings. But what will you do when you encounter your giants? Will you cower down and flee? Will you abandon your teammates to fight alone?

We must be excellent ambassadors for God as representatives of his great name and, as such, we should never run as cowards. He will give us strength to fight, and he will deliver us from those who are our enemies. Most of you don't have a problem with fear. In fact, most of you have zero issues with fear. On the contrary, the issue is knowing your limits. Yes, we serve a faithful God who will be with us through every battle. But at the same time, we must not bring reproach to his name through our actions. Today, work within your limits, but serve in such a way that those who serve alongside you want to know more about this Jesus you proclaim. After all, what more powerful testimony is there than the transformed life?

Heavenly Father, thank you for giving me the eyes to see, the mind to know, and the heart to understand my physical limitations. Give me the will to work within them and the power to overcome them when absolutely necessary. Amen.

I called to the LORD,
who is worthy of praise,
and have been saved from my enemies.

2 SAMUEL 22:4

February 25

Ambushed and Attacked

One of the greatest challenges in this life is how we respond to tragedy, adversity, hatred, and evil. Sure, it's easy to talk about faith when the living is easy, but we exercise faith when we put it to work, such as at the hospital bedside of a loved one, grieving the loss of someone close to you, facing hardship, in difficult, trying times. I believe 2 Corinthians 6:6 gives us a precise and effective prescription from God's Word for how we should respond in these times: "in purity, understanding, patience and kindness; in the Holy Spirit and in sincere love."

As ambassadors for Christ, it is important to remember that everyone will see our mistakes and that when we do sin, it will be highlighted for many to see. No matter the circumstances, we should always strive to be professional but also kind, patient, and understanding, knowing everyone we meet is enduring different circumstances. How will you represent Christ to your community today?

Heavenly Father, help me be a living example of what your Word does when it transforms a person. May those who know me see the change you have made in me through your mighty Word. Amen.

We commend ourselves...in purity, understanding, patience and kindness; in the Holy Spirit and in sincere love.

2 CORINTHIANS 6:6

A Mighty Defender

The views we have of God as children often change drastically as we age based on our life experiences. As children, we may have seen God as a mighty warrior and a great defender of people, but as we aged, life happened and bad things occurred, shaking our faith. We began to doubt, and because of this, we began to see God as one who punishes us for our mistakes or as someone or something that doesn't exist at all. The truth is that he does exist, and he has never changed.

The same God we saw as a mighty defender and shield in our lives, the same God we used to believe could and would do the impossible, still exists and still can do those things. The trials you face may shake your faith to the core, but hold firmly to the promises in his Word. As you do, the love of God will wrap around you as a reminder that he exists. He will prove himself mightily in your life again, if not today then very soon.

Heavenly Father, if there is any unbelief in me, please help my unbelief. If there is any doubt in me, please help my doubt and take it from me. I give it to you. Heal my perspective of you as God, as my heavenly Father, and as my Mighty Defender. Amen.

You, LORD, are a shield around me,
my glory, the One who lifts my head high.

PSALM 3:3

Skilled Warrior

Learning the skills, the craft, and the necessary arts of being a warrior requires more than mere physical training. It also requires us to be totally in tune with our bodies, knowing our physical limitations and having the mental power and strength to crush them when needed. David wrote Psalm 144:1 as a declaration of confidence in the skills God had given him. Once you've defeated giants, you know your victories are beyond your own human strength. You know it was not totally up to you, that you are only the vessel, and if you are willing, God will provide all you need for battle.

The difference is in where we are today and where David was with his confidence in God. As Americans, we complain at the slightest of discomforts, but he slayed bears and giants. You are a skilled warrior, but are you where you could be if God sharpened you to become a precision instrument? Today, know you can place your confidence in his Word. We can learn much through our instructors, mentors, and leaders, but the lessons God gives us are even more valuable, even invaluable.

Heavenly Father, thank you for training my hands, for giving me the necessary skills for battle in combat and on my knees in prayer, and for total victory wherever I may go. Amen.

The LORD is my rock, my fortress, and my savior;
my God is my rock, in whom I find protection.
He is my shield, the power that saves me,
and my place of safety.

PSALM 18:2 NLT

February 28

The Way to Victory

Working long military hours, field training, and deployments can make attending worship services difficult. But the place of worship isn't as important as your heart and the nature in which you worship. If military life prevents you from attending worship services regularly, then you need to be more intentional with fellowship and your personal worship time. It gives you more reason to make time to study the Bible and pray individually, with friends, or with your family at home.

Make a commitment to worship God in all you do, from the time your eyes open to the time you lie down for bed. This is not a call to live a life of rigorous legalism, by which we base our relationship with Christ solely on our performance; rather, it is a call to diligently pursue fellowship with him through his Word and prayer and the way we treat others. Our lives have tremendous potential to reach others for his kingdom. With the right heart, we can demonstrate the love of God to those who may have never experienced his love before, giving us the opportunity to lead others to victory. Worship is a powerful weapon in our arsenal. If we are consistent in worship of the Father, it can be life-altering.

> *Heavenly Father, cleanse me of all sin, of all wrongdoing, and accept my worship. May my thoughts, words, and deeds bring you glory in all I do today. Amen.*

God is spirit, and his worshipers must worship in the Spirit and in truth.

JOHN 4:24

February 29

No Time for Talking

There is no doubt you have a high degree of intellect, or you wouldn't be able to perform the number of complex tasks required of you. Take, for example, your ability to de-escalate a situation by talking to local nationals. You possess skills and abilities that not only help you think about what to say and how to say it but also to act on those thoughts. Your faith and action make you a powerful force for good. If you were to have zero communication with the locals in a new AO (Area of Operation), the results could be disastrous.

In our spiritual walk, we lack power when we hold faith dear to our heart but never exercise it in action. Much like our spiritual walk, there is a time to move from talking to "exercising" our faith as warriors. It is always great when we can solve a situation with words, but if we must handle business, then we must do it swiftly and with excellence. Our lives as believers are empowered when we take the faith we have in God and use it in action for his glory. What marvelous results we see when we do.

Heavenly Father, thank you for the heart to serve your people. Thank you for faith and the guts to take action on that faith. Show me the line in the sand when it is time to quit talking and act. Amen.

You see that a person is considered righteous by what they do and not by faith alone.

JAMES 2:24

Distractions Lead to Defeat

The hysteria people dive into anytime a major storm is approaching usually causes more harm than good. Their focus is on the storm, on the negative, and on the destruction, usually due to a lack of preparedness. If our focus is on the right fog line of the roadway, guess where we will end up? The same principle applies in life with our thoughts. You may be facing difficult circumstances, but do not let this distract you from your ultimate purpose.

Most of the time, the things that go wrong are nothing more than a small part of your life. God does not send storms. We live in a fallen world, so sickness is part of life. It's all part of the package. But because of Jesus, we are more than overcomers. The relationship problems, difficult coworkers, professional challenges, and financial issues are not the enemy. The enemy is not of this world. You cannot fight spiritual battles with the weapons you wear on your duty belt. But tunnel vision can still cause you to be defeated. Focus on Christ today.

Heavenly Father, keep my focus on you. Keep my eyes on you. Help keep my focus off the problem and remind me of the weapons of warfare to use against the enemy. Amen.

The weapons of our warfare are not carnal but mighty in God for pulling down strongholds.

2 CORINTHIANS 10:4 NKJV

An Inferior Force

Imagine a breaking news report of a small class of kindergarten students taking a team of Special Forces operators hostage. Unbelievable, yes? Indeed, it is! You would never see that happen in the United States, but think about this illustration on a spiritual level. God owns and orders your mind, body, and steps as you have surrendered your life to him and him alone. You died with Christ, and the elemental spiritual forces of this world are no longer in control of your life.

Your authority comes from a higher place. It is a better way of life, and no, a kindergartener is not going to take you hostage. Today, look at the challenges of this life through a different perspective. Know there is a weaker, elemental spiritual force vying for your life and your family. Once you see the truth, you know the battle that you must address. Today, you have received a clear lens and perfect vision to proceed. Never again will you submit to the rules of the weaker spiritual force.

Heavenly Father, thank you for giving me a clear lens to see through and perfect vision with immaculate focus. Amen.

Since you died with Christ to the elemental spiritual forces of this world, why, as though you still belonged to the world, do you submit to its rules?

COLOSSIANS 2:20

March 3

What's on Your Mind?

When negative people, negative words, and negative influence constantly surround you, you need to have a strong mindset to battle those so you do not begin to display the same attributes. The natural draw is toward the negative, toward the poison. But we should dwell on God's Word and on what he has established in heaven, not on all that is wrong here on earth. If our entire mindset is on the earthly, we lack the appropriate power to be fully equipped as overcomers and more than conquerors. Focusing on the wrong thing allows the enemy an opportunity for a blindside attack.

As you begin your day, think about *what you are thinking about.* This is not to suggest you become weird or alienated from your relationships, but do not become so entangled in the things of this life that you forget about the reward that awaits you in eternity. Jesus taught us to pray "on earth as it is in heaven." That is what we should be living. We should have our focus on how God intended this world to be in the beginning and live in the reality that he has called us to be fully empowered men and women who are focused on him, watching for the miraculous to occur.

> *Heavenly Father, thank you for the power to focus on the solution, which is the reality you have given me. Amen.*

Set your minds on things above,
not on earthly things.
COLOSSIANS 3:2

March 4

Prepare Your Shields

Flaming arrows used to be a thing of the past until Molotov cocktails became popular. Now people use them in riots and protests here at home and around the world. There are times in the military when you may have to provide security or de-escalate these situations, using the proper gear and equipment to protect yourself. When you have the proper equipment, the proper mindset and focus, a solid team on your side, and strong faith and support from family, then there's nothing you cannot face without being totally victorious.

Having your shields ready at the right time is essential to stopping the enemy's attacks. If you have a shield by your side but not positioned where it can stop the incoming projectile, it is useless. Likewise, if you hold the shield in front of your face for hours and exhaust yourself five minutes before the attack, it was for nothing. Patience, strategy, and preparation are all keys to defeating the enemy's attacks, both in a heated protest or in our lives spiritually. Today, take up your shield of faith. Prepare yourself and be on guard against the attacks the enemy will launch your way. We will not be defeated because we are prepared and focused.

Heavenly Father, show me the power of taking up my shield of faith and the importance of it, and give me understanding of this Scripture. Amen.

Above all, [take] the shield of faith with which you will be able to quench all the fiery darts of the wicked one.

EPHESIANS 6:16 NKJV

Keep Your Feet Moving

I once had a pastor who told his philosophy of traveling in inclement weather: "It doesn't matter how bad it gets; just keep your vehicle moving." The same is true when running: no matter how slow my pace, as long as my feet kept moving, I will reach the finish line. As a competitor, that hurt my pride, and it may affect you in the same way. But I would rather finish than fail.

This is what enduring to the end is all about. It means you stay in the race and don't throw in the towel when things get tough. It sometimes means that you may have to carry a brother or sister to the finish line. Whatever you do, keep your feet moving. Don't stop where you are and focus on the problems of today because things get tough—this is not the end. If things haven't gone your way or if life has been difficult, know that if you keep digging in, trusting God, and focusing on the finish line, you will reach the end, and you will receive your reward. Enjoy the race.

Heavenly Father, help me to endure through difficult times and not always place my focus on the negative. Show me the good in life so I can celebrate and be thankful and get an extra breath to finish my race. Amen.

He who endures to the end shall be saved.
MATTHEW 24:13 NKJV

The Point Man

There's always been someone to blaze the trail, a person who has the guts to stand up and be the first to go in. Maybe that's you. When clearing a building or making an entry to search a building for enemy combatants, one person typically leads the way, and he is usually referred to as the point man. That person has a dual responsibility of both eliminating threats and leading the way forward. Many times, we are leading the way in the lives of our children, families, and communities, and we don't even realize it.

The first in our faith was Jesus, who was the author and finisher of our faith. He went in first, eliminating the threats and providing a shield for us as we followed so we no longer have to fear what was to come. Today, as you go about your life, even if you are handling business on duty, think about how those who have gone before you led the way, how you can lead the way for others coming behind you, and how a legacy of faith can change the world in which you live.

> *Heavenly Father, thank you for faith that leads me, guides me, and sustains me. Amen.*

Looking unto Jesus, the author and finisher of our faith, who for the joy that was set before Him endured the cross, despising the shame, and has sat down at the right hand of the throne of God.

HEBREWS 12:2 NKJV

March 7

One Shot

Whatever you do, do it with excellence and do it with all your might. Don't do it halfway. Only a lazy person would expect to put in half the effort and get the full reward. Life here on earth only comes around for us once. We get one shot at this. That's it. So why should we waste our time worrying, winging our way through our days, and halfway completing what we're put here to do? Think about how our world would look if everyone got a hold of the vision behind Ecclesiastes 9:10.

If we go through life with apathy, we will never experience the best God has for us as a person or as a warrior. After all, once we enter eternity, there's no coming back for second chances, do-overs, or retakes. Most of the time in the military, you only get one chance to make a good first impression, to have a good career, and to have a positive impact. Start well, keep your mind in the right place, and stay focused. Do whatever you do with excellence, no matter how minor or insignificant it may seem at the time.

Heavenly Father, thank you for this life. I ask you to give me wisdom to navigate it and the passion to do all I put my hands to with excellence for your glory. Amen.

Whatever you do, do well. For when you go to the grave, there will be no work or planning or knowledge or wisdom.

ECCLESIASTES 9:10 NLT

March 8

Invaluable

You are highly valued, not just in the eyes of God but in the eyes of those who decided to recruit you, train you, equip you, and put you in the uniform. After all, God gave everything so that we could have eternal life. But for your military career, have you considered the cost of training you? While the starting pay, benefits, and other variables may not seem like a lot to you at times, it is safe to say it is a tremendous investment to make civilians into military professionals and then to keep them well trained and mission ready. That's a statement from people who are placing tremendous value on you and your ability to serve our nation.

We cannot put a price tag on a life because it is invaluable. We were bought at a high price, the price of the life of Christ, which no person can number. It was the price of his blood shed for our sins. If our focus is not on who he has called us to be, who God said we are in his Word, then we begin to lose sight of this and fail to glorify God. Take care of your body and your spirit by taking time to rest, exercise, and honor God in all you do.

Heavenly Father, let all I do with my body and in my spirit honor and glorify you. Amen.

You were bought at a price;
therefore glorify God in your body and in your spirit,
which are God's.

1 CORINTHIANS 6:20 NKJV

March 9

For Those Left Behind

Since September 11, 2001, more than 7,000 Americans have been killed in military operations associated with the War on Terror, according to the Pentagon.[1] These valiant heroes who have given their lives for another person, whether it was a stranger or their fellow warrior, remain the greatest demonstration of love on earth. God will call us all home one day, and we have a choice to make, right here and right now. We can choose to focus on the mess this world is in and all the negative things, or we can focus on the promises God has given us, like we see in Philippians 3:14.

Many of your teammates are fighting silent battles because of losing a friend. Do not let these fellow warriors fight this battle alone. Instead, help them in their own race because it should not be a race we run alone. We know the medals we earn here will never compare to the rewards God has for us in heaven. We should not focus on rewards and accolades here, but knowing that those who paid the ultimate sacrifice are honored for their heroism should encourage us all in our pursuit.

> *Heavenly Father, help me to be mindful of those around me who may be silently battling. Amen.*

I press on to reach the end of the race and receive the heavenly prize for which God, through Christ Jesus, is calling us.

PHILIPPIANS 3:14 NLT

---

1   "Defense Casualty Analysis System - DCAS Timeline View." DCAS. Defense Manpower Data Center (DMDC). Accessed May 24, 2020. https://dcas.dmdc.osd.mil/dcas/pages/timeline.xhtml.

March 10

Reckless Anger

Even the animals in the wild know the power that comes with bridling anger. Take, for example, the lion. Soon enough, everyone will know it is present and will feel the power of *who* the lion is. It would make a fool of itself if it made a scene, scaring the prey off before apprehending it. Much in the same way, if we were to unleash our anger or rage in an undue fashion, what profit would there be? Surely there is a season when righteous anger is justified, but unbridled anger is reckless and foolish.

For some, approaching conflict like an unbridled wild animal is all they know. They scare off everyone in their path, including their family, friends, and anyone with whom they could develop a relationship. Today, whatever the root of your anger is, don't allow yourself to become prey. Bridle those emotions, use them as fuel, flip the tables, and do not give the enemy any margin in your life to take authority over you. A bridled passion and a controlled anger managed properly and used sparingly can have a positive impact on the world.

> *Heavenly Father, thank you for the power to overcome my emotions—even anger. Thank you for teaching me to control my emotions. Amen.*

"Be angry, and do not sin":
do not let the sun go down on your wrath,
nor give place to the devil.
EPHESIANS 4:26–27 NKJV

Called to Speak Life

Any warrior who has experienced combat, a deployment, or the general trials of life knows the weapons we face are not always physical. Sometimes we create weapons against ourselves with negative emotions or thoughts without even knowing it. In fact, psychological attacks of the enemy are common, as are spiritual attacks. No weapon the enemy can use to attack you in those areas will prevail either, if you stand on Isaiah 54:17.

When you read the line in this verse, "you will refute every tongue that accuses you," the first thing to come to your mind might be the false accusations of others. However, what we speak over our own lives, situations, and circumstances are sometimes things that oppose the faith we claim to possess and the words God has for us. When we live in opposition to what he has for us, then we experience undue friction and resistance. All we must do is to realize that sometimes we are our greatest weapon, and it is often our own minds and our own tongues fighting against ourselves. Remain cool under pressure and stop sabotaging yourself with your thoughts and words. Speak life, walk in faith, and live victoriously.

Heavenly Father, forgive me for opposing the words and plans you have for my life through my negative thoughts, words, and actions. Amen.

*No weapon forged against you will prevail,
and you will refute every tongue that accuses you.*

ISAIAH 54:17

March 12

When "Rights" Aren't Enough

Society has drastically changed over the past twenty years. Americans have always been passionate about their rights, but for some reason, it seems that with the presence of social media, some folks don't even take time to educate themselves on what their rights are before they take a stand. You have the right to jump off a second story balcony. You probably shouldn't, but you can. Why can you? Because it's your right. Why shouldn't you? Because everything you have the right to do is not in your best interests.

I could list examples of things we have rights to do, but just because we have rights doesn't make them constructive or beneficial. There are times when we should step aside from the platform of our "rights" and look through the lens of what is good and constructive for everyone who will be impacted by our decisions, not just ourselves. When our focus is limited or narrow-minded, it can lead to negative outcomes. Consider the weight your decisions have on those around you and if they are beneficial to all involved.

Heavenly Father, grant me the capacity to see not just through the lens of my rights but also the impact my decisions have on those around me. Amen.

"I have the right to do anything," you say—
but not everything is beneficial.
"I have the right to do anything"—
but not everything is constructive.

1 CORINTHIANS 10:23

March 13

On the Firing Line

Any moment of any given day can bring unique challenges, distress, and life-altering battles. Most people do not begin their day with the thought of getting into a gunfight or having to fight for their lives. Think about how different your mindset must be from the rest of the world and how that affects your interaction with others. It's not uncommon for us to focus on the thing or person attacking us and completely forget about our heavenly help or others around us. It is nearly impossible to focus on two things at once.

If we take the time to cry out to God in our time of need, he will hear us and grant us favor and protection. Pursue a relationship with Christ and combine it with your skill set and training, so when the day comes, you can call on him. If there are two people opposing each other who are equally skilled in battle, the only advantages available are willpower and the favor of God. May God answer you in *your* time of distress and protect you in all you do.

> *Heavenly Father, thank you for favor, even on the firing line. I ask for your divine intervention in distress, protection on the battlefield of combat and life, and protection for my family and those who serve with me. Amen.*

May the LORD answer you when you are in distress;
may the name of the God of Jacob protect you.

PSALM 20:1

Maintain Focus, Warrior

Where your eyes focus, your feet will follow. If you are always looking to the right or left, your feet will take you in that direction. The same applies with driving a vehicle. This is not to suggest that we should compromise our situational awareness, but in our spiritual walk, it is different. With a warrior mindset our eyes are always moving, and we are always on guard against complacency and tunnel vision, but in our pursuit of Christ, we should look neither to the left nor to the right but look straight ahead.

Think about standing at attention. You know there is someone in charge, and others who are watching you generally surround you. There's no need to look to the left or right because you know the orders are to look straight ahead. This is so that you will not focus on worthless things and will listen clearly to what whoever is in charge has to say. Fix your heart's focus on pursuing a relationship with the Creator and do not veer to either side. Keep your eyes fixed on what he has called you to do to fulfill your purpose in life and live as more than a conqueror.

> *Heavenly Father, help me to keep my heart fixed on you, to keep my eyes set on the goal of having a relationship with you. Keep me from being distracted by worthless things. Amen.*

Let your eyes look straight ahead;
fix your gaze directly before you.
PROVERBS 4:25

March 15

Promotion Power

Tests are a part of life and part of completing basic training and earning the right to don the uniform of the United States military. A problem occurs when we are taking a test we have not prepared for. Most of the time, before we take a test, we have time to prepare, to study, and to rest. But life isn't always like a classroom. Sometimes the test is laid in front of us before we think we're ready. One resource shows that the Greek meaning for the word *temptation* in 1 Corinthians 10:13 also means *tested* or *test*.[2]

Think about some of the moments in your life when you faced tests without prior notice. Maybe it was a potentially compromising situation with someone you were attracted to or a with a large sum of money. When we are in these situations and pass these tests, we ultimately find great rewards on the other side. Be aware of these tests in life and live in a way that, at any time they present themselves, you will pass and be promoted.

> *Heavenly Father, thank you for your faithfulness to me through tests in life. Amen.*

Let no one say when he is tempted, "I am tempted by God";
for God cannot be tempted by evil, nor does He Himself tempt
anyone. But each one is tempted when he is drawn away by his
own desires and enticed. Then, when desire has conceived,
it gives birth to sin; and sin, when it is full-grown,
brings forth death.

1 JAMES 1:13–15 NKJV

---

2 "Peirazó," *Bible Hub*, https://biblehub.com/greek/3985.htm.

March 16

Heavy Duty Hope

Anytime we think of the word *drunk*, we often relate it to excessive alcohol consumption. If you have spent any time living in the barracks you likely have witnessed the drunken stupor of more than one young warrior who surpassed their limit of alcohol. But there are many other things that can cause impairment. For example, lack of sleep is a dangerous silent monster that will sneak up on us if we are not careful. It is in our moment of weakness that the enemy will strike the hardest and do so relentlessly.

Will you remain sober in your heart, spirit, and flesh? It is impossible to keep our focus on the promises of God's Word when our own anxieties leave us burdened, which is one of the enemy's greatest strategies. He knows if we can remain distracted, beat down, and exhausted, we won't be able alert to his traps and lies. Pull up your armor, gather your might, and call out for the assistance of the Holy Spirit. The duties and burdens in life are indeed heavy, but the power of Christ in our lives empowers us all the way.

Heavenly Father, help me remain sober in mind, heart, body, and spirit, not only in vigilance against the attacks of the enemy but also in watching for the return of your Son, Jesus. Amen.

Take heed to yourselves, lest your hearts be weighed down with carousing, drunkenness, and cares of this life, and that Day come on you unexpectedly.

LUKE 21:34 NKJV

Hidden Assets

The hell you've endured would've destroyed most people. You had the heart to endure, the "it" factor, the resiliency to press, be pressed, and press back. It requires more than just physical strength to successfully complete the training you've endured. It requires more than just intelligence, willpower, and desire. It's a matter of the heart. Warriors aren't born. They are developed. They are molded, created, built. But they must have the heart.

David often asked God to search his heart, which is a bold request. If we're honest, there have been times when we wouldn't want God searching our hearts, minds, or anything about us. Since he's God and he knows all about us anyway, that's not going to be something we can control. While others may focus on temporary things today, focus on what pleases God. Ask him to search your heart. When we set our focus on him, we find favor in his sight.

> *Heavenly Father, I ask you to give me a clean heart, to wash me, forgive me, and purify me. Search my heart, Lord, for any offensive thing, any hidden sin in me. Make me clean before you. Amen.*

You have searched me, LORD,
and you know me.

PSALM 139:1

Life of Peace

There are some folks in this world who won't settle until they've created havoc and chaos. An offer for peace won't do. In those situations, your training will tell you what to do. But when at all possible, leave the ball in the other person's court. Make all efforts to live at peace with others, as much as others will allow. You cannot force people to adhere to this, which is why we have laws, police officers with arrest powers, and people working in jails and prisons. When it is possible, navigate relationships and situations in a way that peace is dependent on the other person. You've done all you can do, so now it is up to them.

When our relationships are in turmoil, whether professional relationships or personal ones, it can be difficult to focus on what we are supposed to focus on, such as our duties, assignments, spiritual walk, family, and the safety of those around us. Today, focus on mending relationships and keeping peace, and maybe it is time to remove the weeds of bad relationships of people who just won't allow peace.

Heavenly Father, thank you for the power to make peace in relationships, for restored relationships, and for the will to move on from those that will never heal. Thank you for wisdom and discernment. Amen.

If it is possible,
as much as depends on you,
live peaceably with all men.
ROMANS 12:18 NKJV

Walk the Talk

In the garden of Eden, Satan did not appear with a pitchfork and horns on his head. No, he slithered in as a serpent. His subtle suggestions were just slick enough to throw all mankind into a destiny of despair, but for Jesus. Those are the threats to be cognizant of, warriors. It is not always the boisterous threats we must beware of, but often it is the one that woos you in only to choke you out. Keep your focus, keep your vigilance, and remain on guard with your eyes on the Great Shepherd.

When we take time to focus on the situation, having confidence in our training and our faith in God, we will be prepared for any situation we may face. There are times, however, when the behavior is not due to the individual being "wicked" but rather to his or her mental condition, whether it is a mental disorder or is caused by a substance. Either way, when we take time to *think*, we take time to *focus*. And when we focus, we gain clarity and power over the situation.

Heavenly Father, thank you for the power to think, for clarity of thought, for wisdom, for discernment in dangerous situations, and for the ability to make split-second judgments. Amen.

The wicked put up a bold front,
but the upright give thought to their ways.
PROVERBS 21:29

March 20

To the Great Commander

If you find yourself worrying about things but you just can't define the true source of the issue, you are not alone. According to Harvard Health, unaddressed worry can lead to more serious issues, including something known as GAD (generalized anxiety disorder), along with serious health consequences like high blood pressure, depression, and addictive behavior.[3] It is safe to deduce that warriors lose their strength and power if they live in a constant state of worry, as worry disempowers, destroys, and debilitates the individual.

What freedom we have, what peace is available, knowing we can give our worry to God. In reality, we cannot control most of the things we worry about, and if we're worrying, we're not positioned to be a warrior. From worry stems deep anger and wrath, the seeds of Satan. There is an antidote to this issue of the heart: giving it all to Jesus. Whatever you worry about, he controls, he knows about, and he cares about.

> *Heavenly Father, you know the things that keep me up at night and the things on my mind that strip me of strength and power. Today, I lay them at your feet and ask you to take control, to help me deal with thoughts of worry and anxiety. Amen.*

Refrain from anger and turn from wrath;
do not fret—it leads only to evil.

PSALM 37:8

---

3   Harvard Health Publishing. "When Worry Becomes a Problem." *Harvard Health*, January 2018. https://www.health.harvard.edu/mind-and-mood/when-worry-becomes-a-problem.

Yes, I Hear You

It's hard to communicate with someone who isn't really listening to you. Just because someone hears words does not mean he or she understands what you are saying. This can be detrimental at a professional level or on a personal level. Often, we can swiftly resolve a conflict by actively listening to the other person communicate his or her concern, no matter how upset or emotional he or she may be. However, if we are quick to speak or respond in anger, it removes the opportunity to make peace or calmly resolve the situation.

For some, actively listening requires intentional effort and hard work. This may mean we have to put our smartphones down, look the other person in the eye, and verbally respond to his or her words. Our words and tone of voice have tremendous power, and it takes focus to keep them in line. However, when we make this a common practice in our everyday life, it becomes part of our behavior. Focus on actively listening to those you interact with today and respond with intentionality.

Heavenly Father, may my ears be open, not only to hear but also to listen to those who speak and communicate with me. May my words be covered with love and grace. Amen.

*My beloved brethren,
let every man be swift to hear,
slow to speak, slow to wrath.*
JAMES 1:19 NKJV

March 22

Change of Duty Station

Whether it is a permanent or temporary change of duty stations, the need to have continuous coverage in your AO (Area of Operation) is essential to mission success. As you are already aware, there are times when you are required to remain on duty after your shift has ended until the oncoming shift arrives to relieve you. This is part of your commitment to your service and success of your mission.

I liken this to the old law in the Bible and the atonement we received through Jesus Christ. In a similar fashion, the laws of God found in the Old Testament acted as a guardian until Christ came, providing us with the coverage of our sins until his perfect atonement. When we needed it most, we received relief for our souls, and not just for our souls but for our bodies and minds too, for the abundance of life on earth. There's never been a moment when you've not been covered. Place your focus on the power of a God who is ever present, always on time, and knows just what we need and when we need it.

Heavenly Father, thank you for sending your Son to fill the gap between you and me permanently. Amen.

The law was our guardian until Christ came that we might be justified by faith.

GALATIANS 3:24

March 23

For the Flag

The generation before ours knew the meaning of honor, loyalty, courage, and commitment. They knew what it meant to live in a way that brought honor to their superiors, God, and their country. Today, it often seems like many have thrown these principles to the side. Sometimes, even when we may be justified in venting our feelings, it would dishonor our superiors, pastors, family, God, and fellow warriors. Therefore, it is better to keep silent.

While there may be temporary reprieve in venting about something today, think about who your actions would honor if you chose to hold back on those words. As military warriors, we know the importance of honor, and we should always strive to bring honor to our profession, to those who are in leadership, to those who have gone before us, to God, and to our families. A culture that focuses on honor will be a culture that knows great peace.

Heavenly Father, help me today to see the value and path of honor in all I do, especially when I feel like venting my feelings. Amen.

A fool vents all his feelings,
but a wise man holds them back.
PROVERBS 29:11 NKJV

March 24

Subduing Conflict

If our lives were free of responsibility, then the issue of patience would not be as critical as it is in the military. You may be dealing with an armorer who won't accept your weapon for lack of cleaning or the traffic signal on the way to morning PT that is taking too long to change. Nevertheless, having patience can be a powerful weapon we use to our advantage, but impatience often works against our favor. Typically, the issues that trigger our tempers relate to impatience, but they are rooted in goals, deadlines, schedules, or in our idea of how long a specific event or service was supposed to take.

Throughout life, we often face choices, and we often have the choice to take control of our emotions when it relates to patience. As Proverbs 15:18 states, we have the power as a patient person to calm a quarrel with our temperament, words, presence, and attitude. But when we are quick to argue or hot-tempered, we escalate a situation that peace could resolve.

Heavenly Father, help me in my moments of impatience and let my words bring peace to chaotic situations. Amen.

A hot-tempered person stirs up conflict,
but the one who is patient calms a quarrel.

PROVERBS 15:18

March 25

Dropping Empty Magazines

We've all been hurt by someone, and we all have handled it in different ways. Some internalize the emotions until they are so buried inside that the pain is numb while others project onto everyone they encounter the pain they experienced at the hands of someone else This is often the result of unforgiveness, which I like to compare with carrying around empty magazines on our kit in a gunfight. They. Are. Useless.

Unforgiveness is hurting only *you*. It is holding no one back but *you*. In fact, even if you weren't wrong and the other person was, when he or she doesn't make the first step to forgive, then your expression of forgiveness is a major extension of peace and can do remarkable things to maintain, heal, or restore relationships. Today, I challenge you to rid yourself of any empty magazines that you may be carrying. Until you have reloaded with the grace and mercy of God, his forgiveness, and your forgiveness toward others, you will remain stuck and burdened with those pains.

> *Heavenly Father, help me to take the first step, even when it is not my place to forgive, in order to live in peace. Amen.*

*Bear with each other and forgive one another
if any of you has a grievance against someone.
Forgive as the Lord forgave you.*
COLOSSIANS 3:13

God-Approved Plans

Whenever the time comes to execute an operation, generally a senior officer is required to approve the plans or strategy, or at least to be aware of them. This is not to micromanage those carrying out the plans but rather to ensure there is nothing overlooked or simply to have another set of eyes review the strategy. There are several reasons this is beneficial, both tactically and legally, for you, those involved, and your unit.

When we try to go our own way and create our own plans, we often find ourselves in difficult situations. However, as we seek God's wisdom, it is easier and more beneficial to commit our work to him from the beginning, and then our plans will succeed. Another way to put it is that your God-approved plans will lead you to reach your goals, causing you to experience fulfillment and joy in life. Today, stop trying to do it all on your own and surrender to God's plans. Give it a try and watch what he does with your life.

Heavenly Father, I commit to you my work, my family, and my life. I ask you to take it all and establish the plans in my life, making them yours. Amen.

Commit to the LORD whatever you do,
and he will establish your plans.

PROVERBS 16:3

March 27

Live God's Word

Ignorance is no excuse for violating the law. Take, for example, someone who does not know the speed limit but blatantly and recklessly races down the highway. For them to say, "I did not know the speed limit" does not justify unsafe driving. In the same sense, many *know* the law but continuously violate it (see FBI statistics on theft, burglary, robbery, etc.). We can study the law our entire lives and remain immoral, criminal, and useless to society if we fail to adhere to it. The same applies to the precepts of God's Word.

Think about how many church services people sit through, collectively, throughout America in a year's time. All too often, we associate performance or attendance with right standing with God when his commands tell us that obedience is the only satisfactory requirement. Do not conform to the rest of the world. Do not settle for merely hearing God's Word or knowing to do good but obey his Word. Put good works to action. When we shift our focus from knowing and acquiring to doing and serving, we become world changers.

> *Heavenly Father, thank you for equipping me with the knowledge and understanding of your Word. Give me the will and strength to obey and live your Word. Amen.*

*It is not those who hear the law
who are righteous in God's sight,
but it is those who obey the law
who will be declared righteous.*

ROMANS 2:13

March 28

The Duty of the Sheepdog

Our culture often associates the term *ministry* with a vocational full-time pastor whose total responsibility lies within the church and its people. While this is partially true, the work you do as a military warrior can be ministry, especially considering your role as a sheepdog. You are responsible for keeping people safe and upholding what is just and good, which requires you to be held to a certain standard, above reproach and blameless. If you think about the characteristics of the breed of dog known as a sheepdog, it is similar.

The temperament of the wolf is violent, but you are not quick-tempered nor do you pursue dishonest gain. While Titus 1:7 was written for the elders or overseers of the church, it can apply to the positions you hold in authority. You are required to live above reproach, both professionally and personally. Take time today to focus on the calling God has on your life. Be thankful for what you do. And take good care of your flock.

Heavenly Father, thank you for entrusting me with the care of your people. I ask you to keep me in good standing in your eyes and in the sight of others. Amen.

Since an overseer manages God's household, he must be blameless—not overbearing, not quick-tempered, not given to drunkenness, not violent, not pursuing dishonest gain.

TITUS 1:7

March 29

A Time to Rest

There is a time for everything under the sun. While it may be tempting to worry when you lie down in bed to sleep, let your heart rest assured that God is in total control. For some, the only time their minds can think clearly is when they lie down in their beds to sleep. This is one of the biggest reasons why people find it difficult to get adequate sleep each night. Taking a few moments to pray or meditate before going to bed will allow you time to clear your mind. You can write your thoughts down if that helps.

There is a time and necessity for rest. You are not invincible, as much as you and everyone else wish you were. Take time today to take care of your body and mind. If you do not have good habits before bed, ask your doctor if he or she has any suggestions for you to create new healthy habits to ensure better, consistent sleep patterns. Before you go to sleep tonight, focus on the things you should be thankful for, for the good in your life, and for the blessings you have.

Heavenly Father, I ask you, in my time of rest, to relax my mind and body. Allow me to recharge and reset to prepare for the next day. Amen.

Tremble and do not sin;
when you are on your beds,
search your hearts and be silent.

PSALM 4:4

March 30

The Champion's Salute

While everyone around you is bickering and in an upheaval of chaos, you can either choose to participate in it or remain focused on your work. Champions do not allow the little things to throw them off course but remain disciplined to their path, pressing forward toward the prize before them. You have a choice as a warrior: you can go in every day and do just enough to get by, get your check, and go home, or you can focus on finishing strong while looking at the bigger picture.

If you allow the actions of others to affect your performance on duty in a negative way, then you have allowed them to take a little bit of your reward, a reward they did not earn. Whether you ever verbally share the good news of God's love, mercy, and grace to anyone or if your life reflects it, live in a way that others see the handiwork of God in your life. Stay focused on finishing well. Follow through, be consistent, and live with passion.

Heavenly Father, my life is nothing to me unless it glorifies you. Strengthen me to serve you, to serve others, and to live in a way that shares your message. Amen.

I consider my life worth nothing to me; my only aim is to finish the race and complete the task the Lord Jesus has given me— the task of testifying to the good news of God's grace.

ACTS 20:24

March 31

Listen to Their Words

There's nothing quite like interviewing a local national while on patrol and *knowing* without a doubt that they are lying to you. It's like parenting, really. I've always told my kids that if they were honest with me when they were in trouble, the consequences (if any) would be significantly less than if they lied to me. Many of us received training in numerous ways to detect indicators of potential deception in either verbal communication or body language. Empty words are powerless and meaningless. They waste time, manpower, and other resources.

Let's call them what they are: empty words are lies. We can say they are "little white lies" or "half-truths" or whatever else makes us feel good at the time, but at the end of the day, these things do nothing to help us in the moment, whether we are the one telling the lie or the person being lied to. Today and every day, focus on the suspect's hands. They can lie to you, but their words cannot kill you. Watch their hands, listen to their words, and do not be deceived.

Heavenly Father, may all I think, say, and do be done in honesty and truthfulness. Help me to detect dishonesty in those I interview. Amen.

Let no one deceive you with empty words,
for because of such things God's wrath
comes on those who are disobedient.
Ephesians 5:6

April 1

Courage to Face Fear

With one echoing boom after another, the volley of a twenty-one-gun salute rang through the air on a cloudy winter day. In full dress uniform, his brothers and sisters held their salute with tears running down their faces. Later, when I returned home from attending the out-of-town funeral, I hugged my wife and kids a little firmer than usual. It took all I had to emotionally hold it together that day, but inside I was a wreck.

We learn through training to control our emotions in even the most volatile situations, and suppressing our emotions often bleeds over into other areas of our lives. The reality of military life is danger, fear, and the potential for injury or death. There is also the reality that our careers can affect us in numerous ways, including PTSD, anxiety, alcohol abuse, and relationship issues. Thankfully, that is not the end of the story. As you face the realities of your duties today, including grief, know that you are fully empowered, fully prepared, and fully equipped to carry out the duties of your calling.

Heavenly Father, give me the courage to face the fears
I will encounter, guide my steps, and place a shield
of protection around me and those serving with me.
Amen.

Have I not commanded you? Be strong and courageous.
Do not be afraid; do not be discouraged,
for the LORD your God will be with you wherever you go.

JOSHUA 1:9

Truth Creates Conflict

At some point in life, we face painful truths. Often, the confrontation with truth creates conflict that is the foundation for many of the calls you answer daily. It's not always easy to be the messenger or the recipient of truth. If everyone in the military was asked why they serve, many of the answers would sound different, but all would come down to the same root reason: commitment to truth. Our relationship with Jesus is based on our consistent commitment to him.

Our duties are carried out because of our commitment to truth and our nation. When the commitment fades, the motivation to serve will fade too. The reason why any of us serve boils down to our commitment to the cause. It is a high calling to serve something bigger than ourselves. While everyone you encounter will not want to adhere to truth, they will be held accountable for their response to it. Whatever your assignment, be a good steward of the truth today.

Heavenly Father, help me keep my focus not only on the reason why I began my military career but also on you. Protect me from the attacks of the enemy, both spiritually and physically. Amen.

Jesus answered, "You say that I am a king. In fact, the reason I was born and came into the world is to testify to the truth. Everyone on the side of truth listens to me."

JOHN 18:37

A Righteous Risk

Every day that you head out to do your duties, you accept the unknown risks. While others tell you how hard your job is and how they could never do it, you carry out your duties without hesitation. One distinguishing difference between what some call a job and what others refer to as a calling is the amount of risk they take to accomplish their duties. I can think of few professions where you can carry out the acts of faith as truly as in the military. Risk requires faith, and we strengthen our faith by addressing risk.

Today, allow the voice of God's promises to ring true in your heart. Just as you make instant decisions based on extensive training and experience, you can also listen closely to his words for discernment and direction. Today may bring previously unconquered challenges and leave you asking questions. But know this: you have been appointed to face these risks as an authority under God's command. You are well trained and conditioned to respond to and address each issue you face. As you cling close to the leading of his Word, you will find protection and wisdom to face every risk you encounter.

Heavenly Father, guard me against unseen risks. You alone are the one giving me the courage to face this day, and I thank you in advance for courage, freedom, and protection. Amen.

You will not fear the terror of night,
nor the arrow that flies by day.

PSALM 91:5

April 4

The Audacity of Obedience

It's natural to have apprehensions when faced with certain situations. When we face great danger, fear, pain, or sorrow, our instinct is often to attempt to elude those negative reactions and instead find a place of comfort. One of the biggest differences between you, those with whom you serve, and the rest of society is the moment before a response to danger. Obedience to your call is your priority, and it requires audacity to confront the kinds of realities that you face.

Consider the emotions Peter felt when Jesus stood *on the water* and commanded Peter to get out of the boat and walk to him. Most of us would call for assistance. It is easy to become distracted, lose focus, and falter in life when we focus on what is around us: storms, circumstances, criticisms, and finances. But when we keep our eyes on Jesus and our focus on his Word, and when we live in a way that honors him, we will make our way to him every time.

> *Heavenly Father, thank you for the faith to step out of the boat. Thank you for the audacity to obey, to overcome fear, and to serve my family and my nation. Amen.*

Peter got down out of the boat, walked on the water and came toward Jesus. But when he saw the wind, he was afraid and, beginning to sink, cried out, "Lord, save me!"

MATTHEW 14:29–30

April 5

A Perfected Love

It seems like at every corner, you face criticism. There is no doubt that our society's opinion of the military has drastically changed over the past decade. One thing that remains unchanging, however, is God's love and the power he gives us to deal with a hateful world. We could easily fall into the trap of being negative and cynical and of living in fear, but those are not the fruits of love.

While 1 John 4:18 refers to the genuine love a believer possesses in Jesus Christ, which is a sign of salvation, we can also see a figurative parallel to the power of serving in love and the freedom we have from fear. When we know the love of God and allow his power to save us, then we no longer fear his judgment. Therefore, there is no fear in love. May love be used to drive out fear in practical ways, and may love cause you to be the tool God uses to drive out fear in the lives of others. Watch his Word come alive as you study it.

Heavenly Father, thank you for the life-changing love you have shown me. Fill me with your love and empower me to live in a way that casts out all fear and exudes love in all I do. Amen.

There is no fear in love.
But perfect love drives out fear,
because fear has to do with punishment.
The one who fears is not made perfect in love.

1 JOHN 4:18

April 6

Destined for Victory

If we're not careful, especially considering our chosen profession, then we will develop a cynical, pessimistic attitude toward the world. It is strange that we work so diligently to give peace and security to others, but in return we often find ourselves in a state of internal distress. This occurs when we allow the world to overcome us instead of us overcoming the world. To put it simply, we were created and equipped by God, through his Son, to overcome the world, not to be defeated by life.

You are more than a conqueror, and nothing can pin you down for long. Not sicknesses, relationship problems, financial issues, career issues, depression, or anxiety. Nothing can keep you from the victory God has set for you if you will accept the path to peace laid out by Jesus. In this world, we will have trouble, but in Jesus we will have peace, and thankfully he intercedes on our behalf. Today, ask God to reveal your identity as one who is "more than a conqueror" in Christ. When you see yourself as God intends, the troubles of life won't stand a chance.

Heavenly Father, thank you for giving me the power to overcome this world, for power to overcome my own emotions and to be victorious in life. Amen.

But thanks be to God, who gives us the victory through our Lord Jesus Christ.

1 CORINTHIANS 15:57 NKJV

April 7

Never Stand Alone

There are always going to be some negative views and opinions about the military —from activists, politicians, or the media. It is an absolute certainty that there will always be someone to complain about your performance. At the end of the day, however, their complaints are indicative of the positive impact you have this world. But if you remain united in solidarity, unwavering as one body, then nothing will shake you.

Romans 8 tells of the sufferings of God's people. Many of us do not know *true* suffering because of our faith. We may face economic and social consequences, but many of us have never witnessed someone losing their life because of their Christian faith. If we can remember in times of trouble the power of one, the power of unity, and how we have all we need when we have God with us, then we will come out on the other side victorious. Make your own personal resolution to ignore what others say about you or your professional work. Focus on the goal and do not let foolish things bring division in your service.

Heavenly Father, thank you for unity, at home and on duty. Thank you for the power you have in my life and for giving me the fuel to get through the trials. Amen.

What, then, shall we say in response to these things?
If God is for us, who can be against us?

ROMANS 8:31

April 8

Unbroken Ranks

Y ou may feel like your life has been too messed up for God to love you or for you to have a relationship with him. In fact, you may even feel like the difficult times are God's way of punishing you for the bad things you have done. But there is nothing you have done or can do that can change the love God has for you. After all, he loved us so much that he sent his only Son for us. How cheap would it make that love look if it were to change based on our performance?

There is nothing in this life, neither seen nor unseen, that can separate us from the love of God. The love he has for us is unchanging and unaffected by anything we could possibly do. Today, know that while you may mess up, sin, or make a mistake, he still loves you, and nothing can change that. What a marvelous reminder of the true power of an authentic holy love.

Heavenly Father, thank you for the inseparable, unchanging love you have for me. Remind me of your unchanging love when I mess up, and rebuke condemnation and guilt when it rises up in me. Amen.

I am convinced that neither death nor life, neither angels nor demons, neither the present nor the future, nor any powers, neither height nor depth, nor anything else in all creation, will be able to separate us from the love of God that is in Christ Jesus our Lord.

ROMANS 8:38–39

April 9

The Burden of Self-Pity

We should never buy into the thought that any life is less valuable to God. At the end of the day, you represent the single hope that Jesus Christ stands for. Yes, you are a living reminder of the hope that all people are created equal. If we will work, commit ourselves, and never quit, then we become the greatest, if we will only serve.

The issue is that few are willing to serve. Many are willing to receive, but few want to actually give. The Creator of all that exists knows *you* and loves *you,* and your life matters to him. In fact, *every* life matters to him. When we are tempted to buy into the fear this world is trying to sell, remember he knows all and sees all. If God does not allow the sparrow to starve, then he will not allow you to suffer for long. He created you to love, to be loved, and to change the world around you.

> *Heavenly Father, if I am ever tempted to believe my life doesn't matter because of my past or what someone else says, remind me of how you feel about me. Help me to show those I encounter the love you've shown me. Amen.*

Are not two sparrows sold for a penny? Yet not one of them will fall to the ground outside your Father's care. And even the very hairs of your head are all numbered. So don't be afraid; you are worth more than many sparrows.

MATTHEW 10:29–31

Chains of Anger

Being in the military, you will likely witness those who cannot control their anger. Whether it is the frustrations on the battlefield or stressors of their daily duties, many cannot control anger because it has them enslaved. Anger is another poison that ruins the blessings in our lives by placing us in bondage. As men and women who are empowered and given authority, many of us walk around in bondage to our own emotions. While others are set free, we remain imprisoned inside our own selves.

The consequences of our uncontrolled anger can be far reaching, expensive, and extremely painful. It can cost us everything we have. When we respond in anger, it is not possible to respond in love because love and anger do not mix. Anger does not produce the righteousness God wants from us. Ask God to root out any existence of anger in you today, which can be the result of unforgiveness, bitterness, or other unresolved issues. Let God handle the problems, vindicate you, and give you his peace.

> *Heavenly Father, I surrender any negative emotions, including anger, to you. I want you to be pleased and glorified with my life and the work I do as a warrior. Help me in my weaknesses. Amen.*

*Human anger does not produce
the righteousness that God desires.*

JAMES 1:20

April 11

Careful at the Corners

If you go to the bookstore, you will find several different books about success—from business success and financial success to marriage success and fitness success. There's something about success for everyone. But many of these will show you how to cut corners on the path to success, which only robs you, the lone participant, in the long run. God has a tremendous reward in store for those who remain committed and consistent in their pursuit of him. Proverbs 2:7 says, "He holds success in store for the upright, he is a shield to those whose walk is blameless."

While we do have an eternal reward awaiting us, there are also consequences here on earth for our actions. They may not happen immediately, but they will happen. Taking shortcuts reduces your experience along the way, cheats you of potential blessings, and prevents you from walking securely before God. Be consistent in your pursuit and be committed to integrity, and the rewards will come.

Heavenly Father, thank you for making my crooked paths straight and laying before me the divine direction you have for my life. Show me the way, and I will follow in it. Amen.

Whoever walks in integrity walks securely,
but whoever takes crooked paths will be found out.
Proverbs 10:9

April 12

Mere Mortals

You wouldn't be in the military long if you allowed fear to control your decision-making. This is not to suggest that there are no times we should have legitimate fear. It is a natural human emotion, but we must control it. As we place our trust and hope in God, we know our life in him is eternal, and our purpose here is to lead others into a relationship with Christ.

Jesus tells us that he came to give us abundant life. We cannot have that kind of life when we live in constant fear. Negative emotions left unaddressed can lead to physical sickness and other ailments. Don't stop with conquering fear in your life but help those who are serving with you. Help them to find the strength to get over the mountain and find freedom. We are mere mortals, but in Christ we have eternal life. Prepare now for what will last forever.

Heavenly Father, there is nothing anyone can do to my soul to take away my relationship with you. The only power fear has in my life is the power I give it, so today, I take that power away from fear. I trust you and place my faith in you alone. Amen.

When I am afraid, I put my trust in you.
In God, whose word I praise—
in God I trust and am not afraid.
What can mere mortals do to me?

PSALM 56:3–4

April 13

All for Peace

Some are assigned to guard a base entrance, closed areas, or other valuable assets. You don't assign warriors to risk their well-being or even their lives for something without value. More so, God has assigned his peace to guard your heart and minds, yes, even in the midst of great evil. You must give his peace access to your heart and mind to experience the full effect. You're the one with the authority over what you allow in your thoughts and affections, so allow his peace to guard your heart and mind. This is the effective and practical purpose of the transcending peace of God.

When we try to bottle up all the hardships we deal with over the years, it will eventually show. Having the peace of God is not merely a state of mind but an inner tranquility in the midst of the storm. It's better than any drug we could take. If you are dealing with the pain of past experiences or trauma, then I encourage you to find practical help—talk to your pastor or a chaplain or find a counselor you can be honest with. There is help available. You do not have to carry this burden alone. God's peace is real and is available to all who will accept and receive it.

Heavenly Father, I open my mind and heart and thank you for the comforting, healing, and renewing peace of your Holy Spirit given to me. Guard my heart and mind. Amen.

The peace of God, which transcends all understanding, will guard your hearts and your minds in Christ Jesus.

PHILIPPIANS 4:7

April 14

Turn Around

When you find yourself on a dead-end street, you can either turn around, or you can stop when you reach the end of the street and stay there. With the latter, you will eventually starve and die. While that may not sound like a future you find promising, it is exactly how many of us live. We let negative emotions weigh us down, carry senseless burdens, and worry about things we have no business worrying about when we should focus on living, our families, and our task and purpose.

We find a lot of references to the "fear of the Lord" in the Bible, but we also find a lot of commands from Jesus to not fear. These are not contradictory statements. The fear of God will cause us to obey his commands, while the fear of this world will cause us to sin and lead us to death. The fear of this world leads to a dead-end street, but the fear of God is the opportunity for us to turn around and head in the right direction. Commit to living from the fountain of life found in the fear of God. Leave the dead-end street and never return.

> *Heavenly Father, reveal to me the benefit and understanding of having a fear of you. I know my fear of this world has skewed my perspective of fear, but I ask you to change it. Amen.*

The fear of the LORD is a fountain of life,
turning a person from the snares of death.

PROVERBS 14:27

April 15

Honor God with Your Authority

Living like we are defeated does not honor God. This is because he created us in his likeness, and his Son, Jesus, empowered us to overcome this world. As warriors, we should live each day victoriously, honoring those we serve and those who are responsible for our lives as leaders. The problem is that most times people only respect those they can benefit from. But in the end, we are supposed to respect everyone.

That sounds like it may cause others to view us as weak or vulnerable, but actually it strengthens us. Respect is something that seems to have died with the greatest generation that has ever lived, and a generation who demands entitlement has taken its place. It's difficult to lead in an environment where people have no respect for authority and feel they are owed everything. But when we honor God with our actions, respect others even when we disagree, and love people regardless, he will bless our lives like we cannot imagine, and we will have great peace as a result.

Heavenly Father, thank you for the unity and peace that comes from respecting others. Thank you for the blessing I receive when I respect others even when they don't respect me. Help my actions to reflect your love to a society who may not love me in return. Amen.

Show proper respect to everyone,
love the family of believers,
fear God, honor the emperor.

1 PETER 2:17

Message and Messenger

A mind properly conditioned for dealing with traumatic situations before they arise will be adequately prepared for the battles that come. If you trust in God, have a heart that is steadfast in his Word and do not lean on your own understanding. Then the sound of bad news will not shake you. The faithfulness of God is reliable, his Word is true, and his promises are always good. How we respond in the moment of adversity will determine the level of our peace and blessing.

If we panic, don't trust God, and fail to lean on him, then we will find ourselves trying to fix the problems with our own solutions, which only leads to more severe issues. We must be even-tempered, have control of our emotions, and have faith that what God says is true and that he will guide our steps. There will be tough days, there will be bad news, and yes, we will see terrible things, but at the end of the day, we will not be shaken because we are founded on the Word and filled with the peace of God.

Heavenly Father, thank you for the foundation I have in your Word, the peace and strength to sustain me through difficult times, and the wisdom to guide me through life's storms. Amen.

They will have no fear of bad news;
their hearts are steadfast, trusting in the LORD.

PSALM 112:7

Take Care of Your Heart

At the beginning of our careers, we start out with sharp haircuts, crisp uniforms, and our very best physically and mentally. As the years roll on, however, the stress piles up. We begin to neglect our bodies, our minds, and our spirits, and soon we are staring down the gauntlet of medical issues, depression, anxiety, sleep apnea, obesity, and joint problems. If we aren't intentional from the beginning, then our health problems will snowball before we have a chance to take control of them.

Maybe your emotions have gotten the best of you, and you have allowed stress to dominate your lifestyle, which can lead to heart disease, high blood pressure, anxiety, and other related health problems. Do yourself and those who love you a favor: go visit your doctor. Ask your doctor to perform a complete physical, check your heart, and advise you on your diet. Start making changes by walking, exercising, and weightlifting. Not only will this help your body become healthier, but it will also help you address and cope with the stressors of the job.

Heavenly Father, give me the drive and self-discipline to begin taking care of my physical body. Help me to remove pride and take the necessary steps to get healthy again. Amen.

Do you not know that your bodies are temples of the Holy Spirit, who is in you, whom you have received from God? You are not your own; you were bought at a price. Therefore honor God with your bodies.

1 CORINTHIANS 6:19–20

Enemies Subdued

What joy it is when God takes pleasure in the way we live. This is not a fantasy available only to a few, but it is possible for each of us through a relationship with Christ. For some, their lives have been tumultuous from the beginning and through no fault of their own. But through the power of total commitment and surrender to the will and purpose of God, we can find peace, joy, and fullness of life through his plan. And as Proverbs 16:7 says, even our enemies will make peace with us.

What kind of life does the Lord take pleasure in? He takes pleasure in the life of a person who is obedient to the commands he has given, especially the greatest command to love God and love others. When we live and operate based on the foundation of that single commandment, everything else will fall into place because it is a godly and holy love, one that is selfless and pure. Know that as you pursue your relationship with the Father, he takes joy in you. He loves you! And as you remain consistent in obedience, he will cause your enemies to make peace with you.

Heavenly Father, thank you for showing me the path to a life that is pleasing to you. Thank you for causing my enemies to make peace with me as a result. Amen.

When the LORD takes pleasure in anyone's way,
he causes their enemies to make peace with them.
PROVERBS 16:7

April 19

Secret Paths Revealed

Early in your career, you probably learned the basic lesson and the critical skill of land navigation. In reality, if you're lost, you may not know it until it is too late. In training, you may have someone who will firmly correct your ways, but it is a lesson you will remember. Land navigation must be second nature in combat. Remember landmarks, specific points of reference, and always know how to refocus if you get off course. What a wonderful reassurance we have knowing God will teach us his ways, his paths, which are significantly better than our own.

We have many options in life, but too often we narrow our perspective to one or two options. We get tunnel vision. It's human nature. Ask God to teach you his secret paths, his ways, and the most efficient direction for your life. These passageways may cause you to avoid danger, or they may bring you to a place where you interrupt an attack on someone else, a place where you can intercede or pray for someone else. Seek God's direction for your life because when you are on his path, your emotions are easier to manage, and life is better.

Heavenly Father, thank you for giving me the ways and paths you have for my life. Reveal them to me so I can walk in them. Amen.

Show me your ways, Lord,
teach me your paths.
PSALM 25:4

Perfected Power

Taking an oath, swearing to uphold the Constitution and abide by the ethics and values of a military code of conduct were all requirements before you obtained the privilege to serve. If all you did was take an oath but never received authority, what good would your service be? Maybe you would have been better suited in a nonprofit or civic organization. At one level or another, power and authority are required to function in the military. It takes a special person to be able to handle that type of power.

When Jesus walked this earth, he not only saw humankind in the physical form, but he saw their eternal being as well. He knew them from the beginning to the end, and he knew everything about everyone. So when Jesus said that "nothing will harm you," he did not mean that if a rattlesnake bites you, it would not harm you. That is foolish. If a rattlesnake bites you, you need to seek medical attention. Rather, the words of Jesus are directed to our spirit man, the part of us no person can touch as long as we are in relationship with the Father.

> *Heavenly Father, thank you for the total power for complete victory in life over every foe, over every enemy, and for complete protection in this physical body and in my mind and spirit. Amen.*

Son of man, do not be afraid of them nor be afraid of their words, though briers and thorns are with you and you dwell among scorpions.

EZEKIEL 2:6 NKJV

Seize the Day

We have limited time and limited energy on this earth. Most of us have limited resources to sustain us, but the intangibles we have inside that make us who we are, like love, faith, hope, and passion, are not limited. When we focus on making the most out of every opportunity, we will get the most out of life. Depending on our own natural strengths, resources, and abilities will only get us so far, but when we adhere to the wisdom we get from God's Word and use what we learn from experience, we can make the most of every opportunity.

There is nothing wrong with planning, whether for the short term or long term. This is wisdom in practice. Having a plan, being flexible, and relying on the power of the Holy Spirit enables us to take a potentially negative situation and turn it into a positive one. Today, even in the midst of evil, make the most of every opportunity, using the wisdom, knowledge, skills, and abilities you possess. God has equipped you and empowered you to make this day great.

Heavenly Father, help me make the most of every opportunity you give me today. Even during great evil and in the face of great danger, help me to reflect your love and mercy. Amen.

*[Make] the most of every opportunity,
because the days are evil.*

EPHESIANS 5:16

April 22

Foiled Plots

Mitigating threats by removing target opportunities or interrupting plans to commit an act of terror is essential in the war on terrorism. When you are proactive in pursuing evil, you have no time to focus on fear or the effects of terror. Your focus is on protecting those you serve, and yet you know you are not alone in your endeavors. Eliminating the acts of violence and terror requires you to focus on the task at hand, not wring your hands in worry and fear.

When fear baits you, remember whose team you are on. You are on the winning team, on the team with the victory already written in the books. There's nothing to fear, for your God is great and mighty. He is using you to foil the evil, violent, and deadly attacks that hateful people are trying to carry out against innocent, everyday, hardworking Americans. Do not allow those who would seek to destroy you to terrify you. Instead, strap up, be courageous, trust God, and do your job well.

Heavenly Father, open my spiritual eyes to see the true power you have given me and open my physical eyes so I can see past the surface and identify the plans of the enemy. Use me to save your people from harm. Amen.

Do not be terrified by them, for the LORD your God, who is among you, is a great and awesome God.

DEUTERONOMY 7:21

April 23

Not My Mission

Most of your assignments are dynamic in nature, meaning it's not always black and white. You may have to do things not directly associated with your "job description." We can't approach these situations with a "that's not my mission" mentality. Rather, we must approach them with a "whatever it takes" mentality to get the job done and get it done right. Wherever you go, your legacy will follow. Will your legacy be "not my mission" or "whatever it takes"? God doesn't give up on us when we do something stupid. No, he remains faithful. For that, we should all be thankful.

Isn't it good to know our God isn't like some of the gods in the Old Testament who provided protection only in their local territories? He says he will go with us wherever we go. God promises that he will never abandon us in difficult places or in places where others may not go. He will be by our side, regardless of where we are. Not only that, but as we trust his commands and lean on his wisdom, he will direct our steps and take us into the fulfillment of the promises he has for us. All his plans for us will come to pass as we follow his path.

Heavenly Father, thank you for never leaving my side, no matter how dark, how dangerous, how treacherous, or how stressful life may be. I know you are always by my side. Amen.

"I am with you and will watch over you wherever you go, and I will bring you back to this land. I will not leave you until I have done what I have promised you."

GENESIS 28:15

Achievable Victories

Throughout your service, you will face situations that seem impossible through your own abilities and strengths. Maybe it is a personal battle or an operation you have trained for your whole life, but when the time comes, you know with your own strength alone you cannot make it through. We can walk around and repeat senseless affirmations and phrases, but until we learn to pair our strength with the power of God, we will never reach our peak in life, and we will never see our full potential.

Moses knew Israel would fail if it depended on its own strength to face its enemies in battle. He took to them the message found in Deuteronomy 3:22 to encourage their faith that God would give them the victory and to strengthen their resolve to lean on the power of God through all battles. Today, no matter what battles you may be facing in your life or service, know that God sees right where you are. Do not lean on your own power and ability to survive because your heavenly Father wants you to do more than *just* survive. He wants you to be victorious.

> *Heavenly Father, thank you for courage, for victory, and for unmatched strength for life's battles. I submit to you my strengths and weaknesses and ask you to give me your power to face life's challenges. Amen.*

Do not be afraid of them;
the LORD your God himself will fight for you.

DEUTERONOMY 3:22

April 25

Born to Win

"You're just an average man, nothing special. In fact, why don't you go kill yourself?" I will never forget hearing those words enter my mind, but the moment they hit my ears, something else happened inside of me. I had walked around with my head down, looking and living defeated, but inside those words triggered an alarm that awakened a sleeping giant. The challenges we face can seem overwhelming at times, but with the proper mindset, knowing we have the power through Christ to overcome and that he has created us to be victors, we are more than able to succeed.

As you progress through your career, remember the power you have as a child of God through the regular reading of his Word, prayer, and worship. You have not only received the power to overcome this world and your enemies, but 1 John 4:4 says you *have* overcome the world. Don't dwell on what you perceive as your weakness. Instead, focus on the power and strength you have through Christ. Remember that you were born to win, which means those negative emotions have to come under control today.

Heavenly Father, thank you for total victory in my life.
Thank you for your Son, Jesus, who has given me power
to not only be victorious but to overcome this world.
Amen.

You, dear children, are from God and have overcome them,
because the one who is in you is greater than the one
who is in the world.

1 JOHN 4:4

April 26

Tent Dwellers

As we age, our bodies begin to break down, ache, and weaken, and we eventually die. Our body is only temporary. In fact, the Bible refers to it as an "earthly tent." Tents are flimsy. We use tents for various purposes in the field, even as a temporary command post. Anytime a gust of wind blows, if we don't have the tent secure, it will fly off and easily sustain damage.

While replacing tents can get expensive and chasing them down in a windstorm can be frustrating, the "earthly tent" we live in cannot be replaced, but our eternal body cannot be touched or affected by human hands. For now, we are merely tent dwellers, and we should stay in touch with the Father as much as possible to ensure our total victory until we receive our eternal reward. Do not worry what others may say or do to you. Those words or actions may affect your feelings, and you can conquer that, but they cannot touch your eternal reward.

Heavenly Father, thank you for the rewards you have prepared for those who love you. Help this temporary body of mine to last as long as possible so I can have the strength, stamina, and endurance to serve until my mission for your kingdom is accomplished. Amen.

We know that if the earthly tent we live in is destroyed, we have a building from God, an eternal house in heaven, not built by human hands.

2 CORINTHIANS 5:1

Hands-On Operations

There comes a time when verbal attempts of de-escalation are no longer effective. There comes a time when you have to go hands-on to put an end to the situation and make sure everyone is safe. That is just the way it is. You can only talk so much, cajole so much, and make so many deals before you have to put someone in zip ties. Do your job as a professional and do not use excess force, but do not allow hesitation based on political correctness to threaten the safety of you or your teammates.

Hesitation for a second can cost you the fight. Many times, God gives us his power through the wisdom gleaned through our experience, training, and mentorship, but he still does intervene supernaturally. We are expected to use what we have, paired with the power of God, and not make stupid decisions. When the time comes and you have to go hands-on, be swift, fair, just, firm, decisive, and professional. They will not overcome you, for God is with you. You are well trained, and you are prepared for the moment.

Heavenly Father, in the moment I am faced with the decision to do battle, do not allow my emotions to make the decision. Help me to have godly wisdom and discernment to make the right call. Amen.

"They will fight against you but will not overcome you, for I am with you and will rescue you," declares the LORD.

JEREMIAH 1:19

April 28

The Right Source

The truth is that society does not hold losers to high standards, but it does for champions. As champions in Christ, we must adhere to and obey his commands. Luke 6:27–28 gives us strong commands, some of the most difficult words Jesus spoke in the New Testament. When he told us to love our enemies, he was telling us to step outside our comfort zones because, after all, how cheap is a love if we only love those who love us in return?

As warriors, if we only protected those who loved us, our service would be in vain. We must do good for those who hate us too. Overlook the hate, the cursing, and the way others mistreat you today, and bless them, pray for them, and love them. Living up to a high standard may seem impossible, but with the grace of God, new mercies every morning, and the power to sustain us, we have what we need to make it.

> *Heavenly Father, thank you for the power to love those who hate me, for the heart to serve those who mistreat me and those who curse me. Thank you for giving me the heart to serve my nation in a way that reflects your love to those I encounter. Amen.*

To you who are listening I say:
Love your enemies, do good to those who hate you,
bless those who curse you, pray for those who mistreat you.
LUKE 6:27–28

April 29

Remember the Good Times

If the day ever comes when you find yourself feeling hopeless, take the time to remember the days when God sustained you. Remember the days he delivered you and all the miracles, breakthroughs, divine interventions, and all the things for which you should be thankful. So many people can share stories of how God has played an intricate role in their lives, and those testimonies will bolster your faith. Remember the days of old. These times may be treacherous, but the battle is not unfamiliar to the seasoned warriors. They have been here before.

Many generations of warriors have gone before you and have seen extraordinary miracles. If they could speak to you now, they would tell of God's faithfulness. In your time of need, remember the promises he has given you. His Word is never failing, and he will always come through for you just in time. Take time to reflect on where you have come from and be thankful for those who paved the way for your freedom, faith, and profession. How can you live in a way that leaves a legacy for future generations?

Heavenly Father, help me to always remember your goodness, even in times of despair, and to come before you with a thankful heart all my days. Amen.

Remember the days of old;
consider the generations long past.
Ask your father and he will tell you, your elders,
and they will explain to you.

DEUTERONOMY 32:7

April 30

Overcoming Betrayal

Selfishness and greed can cause human beings to behave in evil ways, including betraying their own family and friends. You may have experienced this same deep pain in your life. Maybe you have had to have a hard conversation and confront a family member or friend, and they in turn claim you betrayed them. When you feel betrayed, when someone expresses true hate toward you, it can cause a lasting pain in your heart. Hate can create the roots where other issues can arise. We shouldn't allow the actions of others to affect our attitudes, lives, or emotions. Rather, we should love them as Christ has loved us.

You may be tempted to get revenge, argue, fight, or gossip to overcome the pain of betrayal. But in the end, this does nothing productive and drives you deeper into a pit of despair. When we take power over our emotions and learn to express love to those who need it most (in other words, those who hate us), then we are truly demonstrating the love of Christ. This is the way we overcome the pain of betrayal.

Heavenly Father, no matter what others may say or do to me, may my life, actions, words, and thoughts reflect the love and nature of you and the love you've shown me. Amen.

At that time many will turn away from the faith and will betray and hate each other.

MATTHEW 24:1

May 1

Excellence Is the Standard

Fewer bonds are as special as the ones found in the military. Many have relationships with those in their unit, especially their closest teammates, with which no coworker relationships in other professions can compare. Accountability, trust, and a genuine sense of belonging make up the nucleus of this bond, which inherently becomes the standard of brotherhood required to serve and ultimately deploy together. While the bond among service members is unlike any other, it also serves as the ladder of authority for accountability and the standard of excellence, where one generation demands and expects the next to uphold and maintain a standard. This standard of excellence is unique to this brotherhood.

The true definition of excellence is selflessness, servant-leadership, and accuracy. Being bulletproof is one thing, but being an excellent officer goes beyond what can be performed on the street and what is being performed in the hearts and lives of all you meet. Today, accept the challenge to bear the standard of excellence. Maybe your unit has experienced damage to the trust and accountability in its brotherhood. If you are one who has experienced this, know there are people you can trust with your life. Be the leader. Be the bearer of the standard.

> *Heavenly Father, please open my eyes to the importance and value of proper accountability. Amen.*

As iron sharpens iron,
so one person sharpens another.
PROVERBS 27:17

May 2

Love's Power

From the day you graduate basic training and proudly wear your full uniform, there's one question people always seem to ask: "Why did you decide to serve?" If you ask a hundred service members, you will likely get a hundred different answers, but the two you will hear often are "I wanted to help others" and "I wanted to serve." The root of why we serve is simple: love. Love is the greatest motivating factor behind every warrior. It is the greatest force moving us from home to abroad to stand in the gap between good and evil and defend those who cannot defend themselves.

Love is a powerful force indeed. In this case, it is a force for good. Love is patient, and it is kind. You aren't expected to be babysitters or nursery-school workers, but it is possible to let love be the guiding force behind all you do as a military warrior. Today, in all your efforts, let your center guide be the love of Jesus, loving others as he loved us first. When we do this through our examples, our lives have the power to change others, and one life can change a community, a nation, and the world.

Heavenly Father, when I am at my worst, remind me of the greatest power known to humanity: love. Amen.

Love is patient,
love is kind.
It does not envy,
it does not boast,
it is not proud.

1 CORINTHIANS 13:4

May 3

Bring Your Squad Together

Having a teammate who acts as though he or she is already retired is frustrating. If you are easily angered by your partner's lack of action, it is a poor reflection of your own qualities and integrity, but it is also indicative that you may not be walking in love. If you want to motivate a lazy partner, begin digging in to discover the root cause of his or her behavior. As a teammate, you would rather work it out with others without the need for them to receive official counseling from a supervisor. If that laziness goes beyond not doing their job and encroaches into safety issues, then it might be time to tighten up the ratchet.

It is not right to embarrass or dishonor anyone who wears the uniform with integrity, but there is a right way and a wrong way to handle the responsibility of being a service member. Taking responsibility, no matter the rank or position, means holding each other accountable, applying positive peer pressure, and rallying around those who lag behind. Commit not only to holding others accountable but also to holding yourself accountable. Bring your squad together, make a resolution, make a pact, make it official, and work to honor God.

Heavenly Father, guide me as a leader and grant me wisdom beyond my own capability to lead. Amen.

It does not dishonor others, it is not self-seeking, it is not easily angered, it keeps no record of wrongs.

1 CORINTHIANS 13:5

May 4

Quiet Heroes

Maybe you don't attribute quietness to a hero. Having met some of the most heroic men of our generation, I can tell you some of the most dangerous men are the quietest. They are businesslike and relaxed but extremely well trained. It isn't the person who is constantly bragging about his skills who poses the greatest threat; it is the one who is quietly serving, always striving to improve on the day before. These are the people who are often overlooked for honor because they are silently or quietly serving.

When we seek public rewards for our actions, we rob ourselves of the bountiful blessings of God. A true hero is someone who doesn't need to seek out the attention of others to reinforce his or her value. Mordecai, in the book of Esther, was a great example of a quiet hero. He fought to defend the oppressed people of God and even prevented an assassination of the king. What many did not know at the time was that Haman wanted God's people killed. What would our world look like today had Haman had his way and Mordecai not been a quiet hero?

Heavenly Father, may my service be done in an honorable and humble manner, not seeking for my own glory but to glorify your name. Amen.

"What honor and recognition has Mordecai received for this?" the king asked. "Nothing has been done for him," his attendants answered.

ESTHER 6:3

May 5

A Debt Unpaid

For three days and nights we worked around the clock preparing for an upcoming mission. As we were walking away from our training site on the last day after completion, I heard someone yell, "Get down. Hey! Get down." About the time my chest hit the ground, I heard the whizzing sound of a cable fly by my head. It had popped from a nearby pole and would have critically, if not fatally, injured me. "Hey man, thank you. I appreciate you looking out for me on that one. I owe you one!"

There will be many times when you will help someone and that person will want to show his or her appreciation. Like so many we've served, I'll never forget the actions of those who have helped me and the look in the eyes of those I've helped. We should never abandon our purpose to love people, regardless of what they try to do to harm us. We should conduct our service in a manner that exemplifies love. It is because of this debt to love that we walk out our calling with excellence in military service. Today, serve in such a way that others want the same love that causes you to serve with passion and excellence.

Heavenly Father, help me remember the sacrificial love you have always shown me, and help me reflect that love and sacrifice to others. Amen.

Let no debt remain outstanding,
except the continuing debt to love one another,
for whoever loves others has fulfilled the law.

ROMANS 13:8

May 6

Pushing the Pace

Numerous studies observe a direct correlation between a lack of sleep and suicide. In fact, one recent study revealed a key indicator in suicidal tendencies is the lack of sleep or sleep-related issues.[4] For you as a service member, that means you must take extra care of yourself to ensure you get adequate rest, not because you are subject or more prone to taking your own life but because you need the sharpest skills—mentally, physically, and spiritually—to face the ever-increasing evils of this world.

Military service can bring long hours, days, and even months away from home and our loved ones. It is a small price to pay for freedoms home and abroad, but nonetheless, it's a sacrifice that can take a toll on our hearts and minds and on those of our loved ones. Even in the busiest of times, be sure to find time to connect with the people you love, find time for yourself even if it's just a few moments, and rest your mind, body, and soul. Remember that even Jesus took time to rest.

Heavenly Father, give me strength when I must work long hours and am gone for days and months, and give me the wisdom to know when I have reached my limits. Amen.

May the Lord direct your hearts into God's love and Christ's perseverance.

2 THESSALONIANS 3:5

---

4   Rebecca A. Bernert and Thomas E. Joiner, "Sleep Disturbances and Suicide Risk: A Review of the Literature," *Neuropsychiatric Disease and Treatment*, Dove Medical Press, Dec. 2007, www.ncbi.nlm.nih.gov/pmc/articles/PMC2656315/.

May 7

Pray for the Persecutor

We've all had tasks assigned to us that we would rather delegate to someone with less seniority or rank. Everyone has their favorite duties, but as with any job, we take the good with the bad. Maybe praying for those we see as enemies is one of those assignments that we'd rather pass off to someone else. But we cannot profess to be a follower of Jesus Christ and pray only for those who treat us with love and respect. This means we lead by example, not only doing the work we enjoy and love but also doing the dirty work, which includes praying for our enemies and those who persecute us.

When you pray for someone who persecutes you, you are letting go of the poison of bitterness and the seeds of hatred and anger. When Jesus commanded us to pray for those who persecute us, he was telling us this for our own benefit. Not only do we operate in obedience to the words spoken by Jesus, but we are also pruning ourselves of unfruitful and poisonous elements that will prevent our growth in Christ. It may not be an easy task, but praying for those who hate us, persecute us, and despise us will produce marvelous results.

Heavenly Father, help me to pray for those who persecute me. Give me the heart to love my enemies and reflect you to others. Amen.

I tell you, love your enemies
and pray for those who persecute you.

MATTHEW 5:44

May 8

Be an Example

Throughout your service career, you will no doubt encounter superiors who, for some reason or another, seem to rub you the wrong way or with whom you simply do not agree on various issues. Maybe it's their leadership style or the way they communicate with their subordinates. Whatever the case, you must adhere to all moral and lawful commands. As you become more seasoned in your job, you may find yourself wanting to rebut any scolding or correction, but it is probably for your well-being.

You may even want to challenge the rank policies or procedures. Remember that most of them outrank you for a reason. Your goal should be to set an example to those who answer to you or see you as a role model and to demonstrate your skills and ability to lead to those in leadership, even if you are not bearing the rank of a leader. Take the initiative. If you absolutely cannot go without challenging the brass on something, use tact. Don't challenge them in front of the unit.

> *Heavenly Father, help me to respect my superiors even when I believe they are wrong, because the way I treat them today is sowing seeds for how a subordinate may treat me in the future. Amen.*

Those whom I love I rebuke and discipline.
So be earnest and repent.

REVELATION 3:19

May 9

On Conquering

When the orders drop and you have to do your job with others' lives at stake, whether a gun fight or a time-sensitive task, and the chaos comes to an end, the sense of relief and victory is wonderful. Almost euphoric. There couldn't be another level of victory in this lifetime than when you are in a fight for your life and you survive. But God's Word gives us a higher standard—we are "more than conquerors" through Jesus.

I don't know about you, but I want to see what this "more than conquerors" lifestyle is all about. For me, being identified by the Creator of my soul as more than a conqueror means I walk in perfect peace with him, knowing his way is higher, his plans are better, and that he has me in the palm of his hand.

Maybe it means something different to you. Life has a way of giving us different perspectives on topics, which is okay. I want to challenge you today to ask God to reveal to you what a "more than conqueror" version of you would look like. Ask him to show you, through his Word and prayer, what your life would look like if you went from victim to victor, from conquered to more than a conqueror. It sounds like you are royalty to me.

Heavenly Father, reveal my true identity as it is through the right relationship with you. Help me see me as you see me, as more than a conqueror through your Son, Jesus. Amen.

In all these things we are more than conquerors through him who loved us.

ROMANS 8:37

May 10

Serve Like Jesus

In a world where race, politics, and religion create division, each person wearing a uniform can be a demonstration of unity and teamwork toward a common goal bigger than ourselves. Love is the motivating factor behind our service. Jesus came to suffer as a man so that he could provide salvation for all, just as your duties provide a way for the safety and protection of the innocent. He freely gave his life as payment for the sins of all humanity—it was not required. Being willing to serve in the manner you do on a daily basis has set you in high esteem with our marvelous Creator.

In what ways can we live our lives today to resemble Jesus' life? First, be the reason for the restoration of peace and order in lives where chaos, pain, and recklessness abound. Be the reason others have hope again for a future, which is possible if you are a consistent servant of excellence, operating in love, to serve humanity. Resolve today that you will walk in excellence, that you will commit your duties as though you were working for God, because, in reality, you are.

> *Heavenly Father, I commit my duties to you. I give you my calling, my profession, and every situation that may present itself. I know nothing is too big for you. Help me to serve humankind with the love Jesus did. Amen.*

Walk in the way of love, just as Christ loved us and gave himself up for us as a fragrant offering and sacrifice to God.

EPHESIANS 5:2

May 11

Ultimate Cover

An ambush attack from an unseen enemy is one of the most ambiguous threats to military operations. We must also address the threat of traumatic impacts to those who serve. Invisible enemies are not uncommon to those who do battle, but there is a solution. Ultimate cover. The power of the Holy Spirit brings unspeakable blessings, and as followers of Christ, we have access to his power. It may seem, in many circumstances, the visible and invisible enemy already has your game plan. What this doesn't affect is your protection given by a true source of cover. Through complete surrender to Jesus, a right heart, and walking in the living power of God, we experience his love and demonstrate it to others, even in battle.

The single greatest threat we face is refusing to accept and walk in the love of God, for his love covers a multitude of sins. It is not out of love that others stir up conflict or dig for past mistakes; it is out of hate or bitterness. But a person with a heart of love will strive to make things right. Don't allow the actions of hateful people to affect your pursuit of justice or heart for love-driven service. The ultimate cover is love but not some weak, watered-down love. It's the love demonstrated by Jesus. As you serve and live, the love Christ has for you as a believer covers you fully.

Heavenly Father, renew in me a right heart and help me to serve you with excellence. Amen.

Hatred stirs up conflict,
but love covers over all wrongs.
PROVERBS 10:12

Do the Right Thing

The power of choice is a faculty that places humans far above other creatures. Those who enjoy freedom can exercise that power even when it is not to their advantage. We have a choice most days of what we will wear, eat, and drink. We have the choice to forgive or to harbor resentment. We have the choice to show mercy or judgment toward others. Doing the right thing often comes with a price tag, and that price can be determined by the choices we make. Treating other people with fairness and equality isn't difficult. Being firm, fair, and equitable will take you to heights in your career that many other professionals might envy.

Doing the right thing may be difficult in the moment, and the choices the day presents may cause conflict in your mind and heart. But at the end of the day, when you treat others as you would have them treat you, you are a man or woman of character and integrity. Being above reproach is a tall order for any person, but you were meant for this. God created you for this challenge, and you would not be in your position if you were not fully capable of fulfilling your purpose.

> *Heavenly Father, help me see others as you see them and realize that the way I treat others is like seed for the sower. I will reap what I sow. Amen.*

Do to others as you would have them do to you.

LUKE 6:31

The Reason for Lawlessness

The Uniform Code of Military Justice (UCMJ) is in place as the presiding law of all service members. It is even said to be tougher than civilian criminal laws. However, technicalities are occasionally used to bend and break rules, justify sin, and remove the chains from evil. Some of the most violent people in the world have been set free in the name of due process or because of technicalities. The fact that they broke the law in a violent manner had no bearing in the matter. The reason for lawlessness in so many parts of our world, however, isn't the lack of laws, law enforcement, or good government. The reason for lawlessness is sin.

We cannot continue to justify sin and expect lawlessness to dissipate at any point in our lifetime. As long as sin exists, we will have job security. Some, however, thrive on the idea of anarchy in America. But anarchy is a weapon against order and government, and you are the line to hold the peace and keep order in this world. Never allow the political propaganda to distract you from the mission you have as a warrior and peacemaker.

Heavenly Father, thank you for the freedom to worship you in America, and thank you for the laws, authority, and leaders we have. I ask you for strength as I hold the line between anarchy and order in a world of lawlessness. Amen.

Everyone who sins breaks the law;
in fact, sin is lawlessness.
1 JOHN 3:4

May 14

No Greater Love

Around the world, there are brave men and women in uniform who go to work in the most dangerous and hostile environments on the planet. This is the most visible demonstration of love for humankind in our modern times. For those who pay the ultimate sacrifice, theirs is never forgotten. There is no greater love than the love a person exemplifies by giving his or her life for another human being.

What motivates you in all you do? Is it money? Is it the desire to be successful? This is a calling. Somewhere, someday, you may look back and complain about the path you took that led you to this moment. Will you regret the decision to love? Or will it be the decision to resent others?

I challenge you to not only do an immediate inventory of your heart and soul today but to also do a regular inventory to ensure your motives are pure. Like you have heard many times before, the path down the slippery slope begins with one small, innocent step. Let love be the driving force behind all you do. Even when you must become a violent warrior, let the love you have for those innocent people, your brothers and sisters in battle and those at home, be your motivating guide.

Heavenly Father, help me to never tarnish the pure sacrifice given by those who have given their lives for the freedom and protection of others. Amen.

Greater love has no one than this:
to lay down one's life for one's friends.

JOHN 15:13

May 15

My Brother's Keeper

After you are retired or have resigned from military service, the bond you have with your brothers will remain for a lifetime. The deepest hurt I have ever endured was saying goodbye to those who served by my side. There's something substantial about the friendship between two people who are willing to lay down their lives for each other. Yes, we are our brother's keeper. We should *want* accountability with our teammates, and we should strive to see the revival of the brotherhood within our ranks. That bond is irreplaceable. Be the reason someone believes the brotherhood is still alive, instead of giving them a reason to believe it is fading into the pages of the past.

Regardless of what society throws at you, the conflict caused by disagreements or even generational gaps, remember what sets you apart from any other profession in this world is the love you have for your brother and sister. No other profession has such a strong bond among its members as the United States military. Difficult times and changes in personnel, command, or even methods will come, but the bond of brotherhood is to never be broken. Therefore, keep loving each other, doing your due diligence to protect the line.

Heavenly Father, remind me daily that, regardless of differences, I am my brother's keeper. Amen.

*Keep on loving one another
as brothers and sisters.*
HEBREWS 13:1

May 16

Made Perfect by Love

We have the power to change the lives of complete strangers with Christlike love. Our world will never be more at peace than it was yesterday. Your military service ensures that, regardless of how bad the chaos gets, the innocent have protection. At the end of the day, your service is a tremendous act of love. In the New Testament book of Ephesians, the apostle Paul wrote to those residing in the city of Ephesus in a manner to expand their thinking. His words were not like his other letters. Instead he wrote to edify, to encourage, and to summarize the gospel.

All people in all places will not welcome you. It is important to know the place you are in right now and the work you are doing. While it may seem like an imperfect work for an imperfect people, it is exactly what God wants for the people you serve and, more importantly, probably what you need more than anything. So in all that you do, be humble, gentle, and patient, and deal with each other in love.

Heavenly Father, remind me of where I was when you rescued me. Help me reflect your perfect love to a hurting world. Amen.

Be completely humble and gentle;
be patient, bearing with one another in love.

EPHESIANS 4:2

May 17

Well-Rounded Warrior

Thinking back to basic training, you will likely remember one specific lesson more clearly than the rest. Your training covered about every area of being in the military, from weapons and tactics to customs and courtesies, military history, close order drill, and much more. But one thing that binds all your skills, talents, and abilities together as a servant warrior is love. All those bind together, preparing you as a well-rounded warrior to serve your nation and God's purpose.

When you dwell in unity with other people, especially those who serve with you, you empower morale, preparing you to successfully complete the mission before you ever begin. Divided teams fall before they ever see the battlefield. You will be a well-rounded warrior, not when you complete your initial and annual training but when you conduct your duties in love for God and humanity. It would be easy to become cynical and hard-hearted in the world in which we live. But it is my opinion that when you do, you are robbing yourself of the greatest blessing of all—unity.

Heavenly Father, show me the importance and the power of living out your expressed love as a US service member. Amen.

Over all these virtues put on love,
which binds them all together in perfect unity.
COLOSSIANS 3:14

May 18

Selfless Service

Modern culture suggests that to love oneself is the greatest achievement. This notion may not be directly stated, but most advertising, social media, and other mainstream media productions strongly suggest it. What would your life look like, as the end of it neared, if you had only loved yourself throughout your life? Lonely? That would be the best way to describe it.

While it is counterculture at the very least, loving those who cannot repay you is the most rewarding love. But on the other hand, it is not possible to love others with selfish intentions. Selfless love can only come through a heart full of passion for God and his Word and a mind that has been thoroughly renewed by God's Word. Commit yourself to studying the Bible and praying, and God will instill in you a passion to serve humanity. In turn, you will be serving God's kingdom through the service you provide.

Commit to those you serve with, to protect them, to sharpen each other's skills, and to serve your community with excellence and a selfless love. Let your legacy be that you set the path for those who will follow after you to serve with the love of Jesus Christ and that you served with a selfless love.

Heavenly Father, empower me to love others, on duty and off duty, like you love your children and even those who despise you. Amen.

Be devoted to one another in love.
Honor one another above yourselves.
ROMANS 12:10

May 19

A Righteous Pursuit

The only thing better than the pursuit of HVTs (High Value Targets) is catching them. But the catch is the only reason you pursue to begin with. Proverbs 21:21 gives us an idea of another pursuit we should embark on: pursuing righteousness and love. Finding life, prosperity, and honor as a result of pursuing righteousness and love is a wonderful reward for the hunter. Find your way into the chase today by pursuing what will embolden you to become a more excellent version of yourself.

Finding our passion in life can be a challenge when we pursue it over seeking what God intends for us to find. When we lose sight of the goal we are pursuing, we lose confidence, energy, strength, and desire to continue the pursuit. Keep your eyes on the prize of righteousness and love, pursuing these through relationship with Jesus Christ. If your pursuit has grown cold, today is the perfect chance to get back in the hunt.

Heavenly Father, give me the endurance to pursue until apprehending. Grant my feet surety and protect me as I give chase. Give me a desire to pursue you. Amen.

Whoever pursues righteousness and love finds life, prosperity and honor.

PROVERBS 21:21

May 20

Inseparable Bond

If you are new to the military, then you need to know there will be teammates you will share a bond with, and no other relationship in your life can match this bond. This is like the love of God in our lives. His love for us is readily available, and all we have to do is call on the name of Jesus. Some may scoff at the idea that a bond among teammates can be stronger than a family bond, but I propose the notion that no other family experiences such potentially fatal threats and loss as these men and women do. The result is the inseparable bond of those who have served together.

Many veterans will tell you that the bond is not like it used to be. Find a way to initiate and maintain inseparable bonds with your teammates. Be the first to work to make amends in conflict. Don't hold grudges. After all, we're warriors, and our purpose is to protect humanity from itself.

> *Heavenly Father, remind me in my weakest, most difficult moments that you will never abandon me and nothing can separate me from your love. Amen.*

Who shall separate us from the love of Christ?
Shall trouble or hardship or persecution or famine
or nakedness or danger or sword?

ROMANS 8:35

May 21

Power Food

If you have ever had an extended period of time on an operation or training exercise without eating or you have had to function on limited chow and a caloric deficit, then you know the feeling of hunger and anger. It doesn't take long to learn that you need to have the calories and right nutrients in your body to be most effective in getting the job done. Your strength to serve is limited by the care you give your own body. The fruits of a hungry person are not pleasant, but we should desire the fruits of the Spirit above all.

There are times when we fail to bear the fruits of the Spirit as listed in Galatians 5:22–23. However, unlike the limits on food, drinks, and other necessities in this life, there is no limit to what we can indulge on when it comes to love, peace, and the other fruits of the Spirit. Desire strongly to bear these fruits, and you will live a blessed life.

Heavenly Father, give me a hunger for the fruits of your Spirit. Show me the way to bear these fruits and please you. Amen.

The fruit of the Spirit is love, joy, peace, forbearance, kindness, goodness, faithfulness, gentleness and self-control. Against such things there is no law.

GALATIANS 5:22–23

May 22

Restored to Love

There are systems in place to provide assistance if we are facing personal issues. From alcohol abuse to marital issues to sleeping problems, there is help for you. One of the most tragic things about the type of individuals who choose military life is the feeling that we can and should walk through difficult times alone. Nothing could be further from the truth. We are meant to be in community and are encouraged to restore our brothers and sisters. From a heart of love comes a sincere desire to help our own when they are down. In some cases, due to regulations and policies, there are limited options to help our teammates officially, but we can still ensure he or she is cared for on a personal level.

Don't fall into the trap of gossiping about the lives of struggling teammates. Instead, team up with others to find a way to assist them and lift them up. When we do this, we will likely see a department-wide boost in morale, and after all, what could be more rewarding than having a positive impact on the lives of one of our own family members?

Heavenly Father, bring to my attention any desire I have to gossip about the situation of other warriors and give me the strength and wisdom to serve them when they need my support the most. Amen.

Brothers and sisters, rejoice! Strive for full restoration, encourage one another, be of one mind, live in peace.

2 CORINTHIANS 13:11

May 23

Closer than a Brother

If you have ever walked through a point in life where you needed someone to talk to, someone to listen, support, or encourage you, then you know the value of a friend. One of the greatest things about the military is the bond among its teammates. Many would say that this bond has changed over the years. Some say there's division in the ranks, but let one be attacked or injured and see how divided they are. They go from being friends or friendly foes to brothers born for times of adversity.

If you've never fought for the life of another human being, then it's difficult to understand this type of love. It's more than being just a friend, more than being a coworker or teammate. It's a family. There's a reason God called you to become part of the military. The decision is yours today: Are you going to be known as a coworker or a good friend, or will you be called brother or sister? This is your decision. This is your moment. This is your opportunity to be the uniting thread that is part of strengthening the bond of the US military.

Heavenly Father, help me to be a true brother or sister to those in need today. Amen.

A friend loves at all times,
and a brother is born for a time of adversity.
PROVERBS 17:17

May 24

A Heart of Love

Beyond your military duties, you are a man or woman who has a family, friends, and many other people who love and care about you. There are also people you will disagree with, and you will need to confront them about your differences. The way you handle confrontation will determine your blessing on the other side of the issue. Finding the power to navigate through those issues in love is key to a life of peace. If you love God, you are required to love your brothers and sisters as well.

Commit yourself to intentionally dealing with others out of a heart of love, especially in situations of conflict. Even on duty, from a place of authority, you can operate from a heart of love by dealing as fairly and respectfully as possible with the community you serve. During your life, you will face many challenges if you are operating from a heart of love, but this will reap many rewards for you as you are faithful to the commands of God's Word.

Heavenly Father, give me the courage and power and knowledge to live and operate from a heart of love. Amen.

He has given us this command:
Anyone who loves God must also love their brother and sister.

1 JOHN 4:21

May 25

Environmental Management

We become like those with whom we associate. Over time, if you associate with negative, hateful people, their words and actions will affect you. Likewise, if you associate with successful, kind, and positive people, their lives will affect you. At the end of the day, the words and actions of others influence our thoughts. Our thoughts lead to actions, and by those actions we develop habits. From there, either negative or positive circumstances are a result. Many times, we are affected without even recognizing the changes as they occur in our lives.

Our purpose is to create a positive environment, not allowing our environment to affect our lives. For what price will you give up your peace? Use godly wisdom before you engage in a relationship with someone who will be a toxic influence on your life. There are times when you will be required to partner with people who see life differently than you, which is okay, but buying into their views if they are misaligned with what God has for you, your principles, and your values is a mistake you cannot afford to make. Love is a powerful gift. Use it wisely.

Heavenly Father, give me wisdom as it pertains to the relationships I have in my life, at work, socially, and at home. Help me to express your love and protect my heart. Amen.

Better a small serving of vegetables with love than a fattened calf with hatred.

PROVERBS 15:17

May 26

Forging Leaders

What an encouraging promise to know God is waiting for us to seek him. The precedent of the student seeking the mentor was established by God thousands of years ago when he said that "those who seek me find me" (Proverbs 8:17). Of course, there are a few more caveats to that, but the principle rests easy here. If you want to grow professionally, invest in your career by learning as much as possible, respecting your superiors, and setting a great example for others around you. Your selfless sacrifice and initiative to be proactive and professional will take you further than bickering and backbiting. Demonstrate love and be the example of God's love to those you meet today.

There are no guarantees any of us will live to see another day, week, or year. Therefore, it is imperative we begin immediately investing in eternal values. Just as you would seek the counsel of an experienced staff NCO or officer, so take the time to seek God through his Word. While your duties and missions will see both successes and failures, God's Word never fails, and he remains the same forever.

> *Heavenly Father, thank you for the gift of leadership. I give you my goals and ask you to lead me as I lead others today. Amen.*

I love those who love me,
and those who seek me find me.
PROVERBS 8:17

May 27

Secret Information

Oftentimes as a service member, you have access to information many citizens are not privy to. You may have classified information or critical data on people, places, and current events unfolding at home and abroad. We must protect this information from the public and our enemies and not let our personal opinions or fears impact our duties. On the other hand, you have access to the secrets of God's Word as you seek a relationship with him through study and prayer.

During your life, God gives you a purpose that will glorify him, bring you fulfillment, and provide you with the resources you need. Seeking the wisdom of God through his Word and prayer is the most valuable action you can take on a daily basis. His wisdom and his love cover all our offenses and empower us to fulfill our divine purpose in life.

Heavenly Father, thank you for the love you have for me. Your love covers my faults and empowers me to serve you. Thank you for revealing your holy secrets to me as I pursue you in prayer, worship, and studying your Word. Amen.

Whoever would foster love covers over an offense,
but whoever repeats the matter separates close friends.

PROVERBS 17:9

May 28

Undying Love

If the only people who lived were those who expressed love and lived with total love for God and others, what would this world look like? Considering the widespread evil in our world today, from paper crimes to sex crimes, murder, robbery, and genocide around the world, the pain caused to innocent people tears a little bit of their lives away. Your job is to prevent it when possible for people around the world who can't defend themselves and for those in our nation who love and cherish freedom and security. In all things, your duty is essentially to provide a harbor of love for humankind.

Stopping the spread of wickedness will aid in the spread of love. After all, Jesus told us in Matthew 24:12, "Because of the increase of wickedness, the love of most will grow cold." We are at the crossroads of where and when this Scripture points. The love of most will grow cold because of discouragement and lack of justice for the wicked—it is easy to buy into the lie today. Add another reason to your "why" today. Give hope to people. They need it as much as they need fresh air and clean water.

> *Heavenly Father, help me realize the power I have to give hope to humankind. Help me realize I'm doing good for your kingdom when I fight against evil. Amen.*

Because of the increase of wickedness,
the love of most will grow cold.

MATTHEW 24:12

May 29

Big Guns

I f you're going to take out the enemy, you need real fire power and real muscle. You've heard the phrase, "never take a knife to a gunfight," so why would we approach any other area of life differently? Think about this phrase: two is one, and one is none. If you carry a weapon, you need a backup. Having an ample supply of ammunition, defense weapons, and training is essential for victorious warfare. A firearm without training is more dangerous than it is in the hands of someone with proper training, but a firearm with no ammunition is useless. That's what it's like to live this life in our own efforts and in our own power instead of with Christ.

John 6:63 reads, "the Spirit alone gives eternal life." Reading this book may inspire you, and it may even challenge you. But nothing can change your life like the words of Jesus. That's the real firepower and the real muscle. It's the only ammo we need in this battle of life. Don't rely on your efforts or words alone; look to Jesus. His Spirit gives us strength. Today, be intentional about reading the words of Jesus in the Bible. Meditate on them, and let them take root in your heart. Then go forward in your life and let those words change you, lead you, and direct your path.

> *Heavenly Father, thank you for your Son, Jesus, and for the words found in the Bible. As I read your Word, I ask you today to let it take root in my heart and to change my mind. Amen.*

The Spirit alone gives eternal life.
Human effort accomplishes nothing.
And the very words I have spoken to you are spirit and life.

JOHN 6:63 NLT

May 30

Instruments of Justice

Honorable warriors may not have a problem using force to protect themselves or others, but they don't go looking for people to "rough up." The existence of every member of the armed forces is for the benefit of our nation. No innocent people should ever fear your presence, but they should know if they do wrong, they have reason to be afraid. You are an instrument of service, of justice, and, if needed, of superior violence. You are an extension of the hand of God when it comes to addressing the evil of this world, those who would want to destroy the American way of life.

Many who make threats to our nation have no fear, no conscience, and no moral compass, so they have nothing to lose. Serve your nation in a way that everyone who enjoys these freedoms can continue to do so but that those who threaten our way of life live in overwhelming fear. You have received the authority to fight in the greatest human force in the world, the United States military, but you must do so in a way that is honorable. What you do for your nation is for the good of everyone.

> *Heavenly Father, thank you for the calling on my life to serve as a member of the United States armed forces. I ask for wisdom, discernment, guidance, and an even temperament. Amen.*

If I am an offender, or have committed anything deserving of death, I do not object to dying; but if there is nothing in these things of which these men accuse me, no one can deliver me to them.

ACTS 25:11 NKJV

Uncharted Territory

Our physical appearance may change, but our values, morals, and character should remain unwavering. There's no doubt that from the day you first took your oath to serve, you have outwardly changed. But have you allowed your morals, values, or your character to change? What a testament of faith it would be to stand at our EAS (End of Active Service) or retirement and have others say that we were always people of the highest integrity and that no one could find anyone who said anything bad about us.

God made us in his likeness, and while our physical bodies change, our spirits do not. We may gain weight or lose it, but we should never lose our morals and character. Thankfully, Jesus is never changing. He is the same yesterday, today, and forever. The same Jesus who walked this earth nearly two thousand years ago, who spoke life to Lazarus, who healed the blind and the lame, and rose from the dead has never changed. Our relationship with Jesus Christ should be empowering to us as military service members. Today, commit to walking in his unchanging power and being consistent in your walk with the Father. Today is a new day with new opportunities.

Heavenly Father, thank you for the unchanging power of your Son, Jesus. Thank you for the access to the power through the Holy Spirit. I ask you to fill me with your Holy Spirit today. Amen.

Jesus Christ is the same yesterday and today and forever.

HEBREWS 13:8

June 1

Acquainted with the Adversary

It's difficult to see when there's a person firing bullets at you, but that person is not the enemy. The enemy is the evil one, the devil. However, our services will be rendered useless if we fail to stop the threat, and we must do so to protect our teammates, civilians, and ourselves. Having the proper mindset *before* you get into a combat action will better prepare you to respond to it after the dust settles.

Just as you can locate the trigger of your weapon without looking, you also need to be familiar with your spiritual weapons: the Word, your faith in God, prayer, and a mind focused on winning. Having the mindset of a winner means you are honest about the opponent you face, have a clear strategy, and are just in all dealings. Take time today to sharpen your skills as a warrior, to meditate on the Word of God, and to pray and begin developing the proper mindset of a champion.

Heavenly Father, thank you for giving me a clear mind and bringing to memory every piece of training and every tactic I need in the moment I need it. Amen.

Our struggle is not against flesh and blood, but against the rulers, against the authorities, against the powers of this dark world and against the spiritual forces of evil in the heavenly realms.

EPHESIANS 6:12

June 2

Renew Your Mind

Thoughts fill our minds, even beyond our consciousness, more thoughts than we can comprehend or recognize. We identify with thoughts that are tied to our beliefs, which are the thoughts we entertain, and these eventually become the words we speak and the actions we take, leading to life's circumstances and outcomes. Too often we allow negative thoughts to have control over us, causing us to make negative decisions that lead to poor outcomes.

As we fill our minds with the promises of God and command every thought to come into obedience to Christ, we begin to experience a renewed mindset. There is simply no way to have a winning mindset if we are always filling our thoughts with worry, anxiety, doubt, fear, unbelief, or anger. Today, command to come into obedience to Christ these thoughts that come against what we *know* is the Word of God. Begin this process by renewing your mind through daily reading of his Word and intentionally monitoring your thoughts. In a short time, you will notice a drastic change in your perspective, your energy level, and your overall disposition.

Heavenly Father, as I submit my thoughts to you, renew my mind with positive, holy, powerful thoughts to change my life. Amen.

We demolish arguments and every pretension that sets itself up against the knowledge of God, and we take captive every thought to make it obedient to Christ.

2 CORINTHIANS 10:5

Fair and Just

God has given us so much, but the power to choose is the essential foundation of our freedoms and liberties in this great nation. Who else gave humanity free will? With such a gift comes responsibility. There are times when it seems best to dispense revenge, but at the end of the day, we leave no room for God's wrath. This usually costs us more in the long run. Being fair and just goes beyond everyday dealings. It also means having a solid handle on our emotions.

For some, being fair and just means holding true to their word and treating everyone equally, while for others it means not being a person who uses his or her authority to get revenge. This can be tempting, but it is a dark, hollow, lonely road. There have been people who have walked that path, and it did not end well. When we try to do the work only God has the authority to do, we find ourselves writing checks we don't have the money for. Let God handle the dirty work, be a person of your word, be fair, be just, and treat everyone like your grandma is watching, and you will build great relationships.

Heavenly Father, thank you for reasonable courage, allowing you to take revenge when necessary, and giving me the heart to be just and fair. Amen.

*Do not take revenge, my dear friends,
but leave room for God's wrath, for it is written:
"It is mine to avenge; I will repay," says the Lord.*

ROMANS 12:19

June 4

There Is Help

Every man and woman possesses a mind, body, and spirit. Think about what makes up a service member. The mentality of a warrior, the physical training, the spirit of a relentless defender who never backs down. But isolation destroys the will. If you are going through battle, having someone to fight with you is a great feeling. Having reliable men and women who fight by your side is invaluable. But in spiritual battle and even when we face dark moments in our minds, there is a Comforter, the Holy Spirit.

That's the great reminder from John 14:26. First, he is our Advocate, so he fights for us. He comforts us, but only when we allow him to do so. We are empowered by the Holy Spirit to sustain through our career, never alone, never abandoned. Take peace in knowing you will *always* have backup, and you will *always* have a helper, a Comforter, and an Advocate in the Holy Spirit.

> *Heavenly Father, thank you for the power of your Word, for the gift of your Son, Jesus, and for filling me with your Holy Spirit. Make your power known to me today. Amen.*

The Advocate, the Holy Spirit, whom the Father will send in my name, will teach you all things and will remind you of everything I have said to you.

JOHN 14:26

The Power of His Word

"Listen up. For the rest of your lives, you'll remember these moments. This training, the stress, the bonds created. This is forever." The instructor stood at the front of the group and made the final remarks before the class departed for their next assignment. There is power in words. And those words are rooted in our thoughts, belief patterns, the things we hold dear. But what is more powerful and more meaningful is the power of God's Word. Think back over your life, especially the beginning of your military career. Do you recall the words of others? Think about how that has shaped your perspective of your life and whether it was positive or negative.

As you acknowledge the power of God's Word in your life, you will begin to see areas where you can apply it daily in every situation. Whether we are alone or in a crowd, there is something for every part of our lives in Scripture. The power of God's Word even applies to our role in life as warriors, guiding us in integrity, truth, and power. Today, as you see his Word come alive in your own life, think about how it trains you to become a better person, a better warrior, and a better spouse and parent, thus preparing you for eternity.

Heavenly Father, thank you for giving me understanding of your Word and for showing me the power of it in my life. Amen.

All Scripture is God-breathed and is useful for teaching, rebuking, correcting and training in righteousness, so that the servant of God may be thoroughly equipped for every good work.

2 TIMOTHY 3:16–17

June 6

At Peace

When we are in a constant state of frustration, we suffer, and other people around us, especially those who love us, suffer as well. As we live with unaddressed frustrations, they become like an untreated disease. They never heal on their own, and they lead to terrible conflicts in relationships. As James 4:1 says, "What causes fights and quarrels among you?" As we progress through our career and neglect our own personal care, it is easy to find ourselves living in a constant state of frustration.

Finding a place of peace begins with perspective, knowing most of the things we experience or have frustration about are often beyond our control. If we focus on doing our job, let others focus on doing their jobs, and trust God to be God, we will begin to find a peace that we did not know previously in our lives. Take comfort today in knowing that you do not have to carry every burden with you throughout life. You have a Comforter in the Holy Spirit. As you release these frustrations to him, you will find peace in your own life, and your relationships will improve.

Heavenly Father, thank you that, today and through all of my future, I am at peace with myself, no longer in strife because of you. Amen.

What causes fights and quarrels among you?
Don't they come from your desires that battle within you?

JAMES 4:1

June 7

Your Purpose

Aside from being the shining example of hope for our nation, the given purpose of any warrior is to keep peace in the world, restore hope, and uphold the pillars of humanity. Your purpose is beyond simply fighting an enemy combatant. Sometimes, however, it may seem difficult to see beyond a direct threat to you personally. The reality is that your purpose is significantly broader and deeper than your specific role on the battlefield.

Taking into consideration the intersections of your life, there are many relationships and opportunities along the way to invest in the lives of people. You may be passionate about serving the younger generation or the older generation or maybe somewhere in between. It really doesn't matter if you realize your entire purpose in this life, no matter your profession, is to serve, love, and honor God and lead people to Christ through the way you love and live. Take time today to think about the power of God and how he is working in you to fulfill his good purpose.

Heavenly Father, thank you for working in my life to fulfill your good purpose for your kingdom here on Earth. Amen.

I am the vine; you are the branches.
If you remain in me and I in you, you will bear much fruit;
apart from me you can do nothing.

JOHN 15:5 NIV

June 8

An Example of Goodness

Too often our society abuses boundaries of good and evil in the name of free speech. Who will establish the example for what is good? Where is the precedence of goodness? Men and women like you, serving their entire lives, are examples of goodness in this world. Regardless of what happens in the rest of the world, there are many people who still abide within the boundaries of goodness and righteousness. We know where our free will comes from, and we know that our freedom and liberty come from God also.

For that reason, in all you do, strive to continue being an example of goodness and righteousness. This is achievable through your sincere words, your trustworthy actions, and through your professionalism. At the end of each day, at the end of your career, and ultimately at the end of your life, the example of integrity you leave behind will pave the way for many others to come behind you to uphold the standards of goodness and righteousness for generations to come.

> *Heavenly Father, thank you for giving me the position of being an example of goodness. Help me in all I do to be an example of good, to show integrity, and to honor you. Amen.*

In everything set them an example by doing what is good. In your teaching show integrity, seriousness.

TITUS 2:7

June 9

Sheepdogs

There's something that occurs in the brain of a warrior at the sound of gunfire. Immediately, you face the reality of multiple dangers, potential hazards, the need to consider innocent bystanders, and allow yourself to move toward danger and do what you've been trained to do. Nevertheless, you go forward despite the risks. Above all the emotions, your feet move you toward the gunfire, building a line between the innocent and evil. You are that line.

This is the calling of a sheepdog—to protect the innocent and helpless, the defenseless and weak, to relentlessly pursue and apprehend the wolves of the world. You are the price those who do evil must face. You are the sheepdog, the herder, the protector, the defender. Today, you have a lot to be proud of. You carry the calling and honor of serving in a capacity few have the courage to do. Honor God, honor your leaders, love people, and watch the backs of those who serve with you. Never stop pursuing evil.

Heavenly Father, when my body begins to wear down in pursuit, give me breath. Make my feet firm, more swift than those I pursue, and protect me every step. Amen.

The wicked flee though no one pursues,
but the righteous are as bold as a lion.

PROVERBS 28:1

June 10

You Are a Leader

Providing good leadership is not limited to those you serve with. No, it also extends to those you serve. Leadership is a topic many often confuse with a position of rank, but in reality it is occupying the field where you are and exuding confidence in humility, leading the way by example, and providing guidance to your peers. Being dependable and reliable to your leadership is a great way to show yourself as a leader to others around you.

Leadership begins with *you*. It begins with you linking arms and working in unity for one mission. Over time, you become seasoned and achieve rank, so providing guidance and acting as an advisor is natural to you. As you look around the leadership structure of the military, you will notice the chain of command has many "advisors," in both the officer and enlisted ranks, all the way to the very top. Each of these people provides much-needed leadership, and you are part of that team. Know that you are a leader, no matter where you are in the process. Continue your development and trust God's timing, and you will see the rewards in due season.

Heavenly Father, thank you for the position I have been entrusted with. I ask for your favor and blessing and for guidance as I commit every day to you. Amen.

For lack of guidance a nation falls,
but victory is won through many advisers.

PROVERBS 11:14

Honest and True

One of the quickest ways to ruin your military career is to lie. The news of this will spread quickly among your peers and leadership and could even lead to professional consequences. While this may seem extreme, it is, in fact, a prime example of how painful and destructive dishonesty is. You have likely witnessed the terrible results of these actions, and it caused you to cringe while watching it unfold.

It may seem that the easiest way to get ahead or to get out of a situation is to lie or twist the truth to our favor, but at the end of the day, receiving administrative discipline from our superiors or even losing our careers is better than losing credibility and sowing distrust by lying. Maintaining your integrity and character go a long way in life, and the simplicity of doing the right thing begins with your heart and your relationship with God. Today, commit to continuing your life of honesty and truthfulness, living as a hope to others who have lost hope in humanity because of the lies of many.

Heavenly Father, thank you for words that are true and right, that they come from a heart that is after you and to please and honor you. Amen.

Like a club or a sword or a sharp arrow
is one who gives false testimony against a neighbor.

PROVERBS 25:18

June 12

Alert and of Sound Mind

If you wear a uniform, situational awareness is essential for your survival as a warrior on the battlefield. While you may not go on a patrol intoxicated, you may go distracted, which, as a warrior, is as good as being drunk. Taking the time to ensure your mind is focused and alert and that you feel emotionally balanced before duty means you are prepared for the threats you may face. Having a healthy mindset, balanced vigilance, and sound perspective will set you on the right foot to begin your day.

Whatever your goals, think about your mindset today. Are you too relaxed, or are you hypervigilant? It's possible to find a balance that is healthy, where your performance is at an optimum, you get the most out of your day, and you're the absolute best version of yourself. There are also the threats and dangers of life, but this reality does not mean that we should live foolishly or in a way that robs us of our God-given peace.

> *Heavenly Father, thank you for a constant mindset that is prepared for the threats of this world, a mind that is sober and alert but a spirit at total peace from only a source you give. Amen.*

Be alert and of sober mind.
Your enemy the devil prowls around
like a roaring lion looking for someone to devour.

1 PETER 5:8

June 13

Not a Quitter

We could spend much time talking about the valiant acts of people who have fought back in the line of fire, men and women who, when they faced grave injuries in battle, persevered and took the fight to the enemy. Did they face fear? Absolutely. Did they overcome it? You bet they did. We read stories of warriors who have been blown up, burned, or shot multiple times but who did not give up the fight. This is not something taught but something developed in the spirit of every warrior.

We are called to be warfighters, not only in the natural realm of living but in spiritual combat as well. As believers of God, we are called to bear the fruits of his Spirit. But do not think that this makes you soft. Rather, it emboldens you. It solidifies your mindset and prepares you for battle should that day come. Whatever you face in your life today, plant these thoughts deep in your mind: *I will never give up. I will never quit. I know my God will lift me up, and I will persevere and take the fight to the enemy.* Embed yourself in the presence of God through prayer and study of his Word today.

> *Heavenly Father, thank you for giving me a mindset of steel, a spirit of a true warrior, a heart untouchable to this world, and a will that is never broken. I know that with you, I will never quit the fight. Amen.*

LORD, *see how my enemies persecute me!*
Have mercy and lift me up from the gates of death.

PSALM 9:13

June 14

Overcomer

While it may be hard to believe, everything we see is a result of a war between good and evil, "God's side" and the "devil's side": the ripping apart of societies through the eroding of morals, the vanishing consciousness of humanity, the seemingly overwhelming power of hate, and the apparent defeat of love. Any person has the power to overcome evil if he or she will only oppose it with goodness, but few have the courage to face evil in the manner in which you do.

There may be times when the world is chattering with talk that evil will overcome you or that the plans of the enemy seem too great to defeat. Never allow the presence of the terrible things you deal with to change your mission or who you are as a person. Never let these threats keep you from fighting for good, for righteousness, for love, and for peace and hope. Know that the reality of the situation is that you are victorious in Christ, living and expressing love and opposing evil with good. You are the force that stops the darkness in this world. Keep fighting.

> *Heavenly Father, thank you for your overcoming power, for the empowering love to face evil, and for the courage you give me to do good in the face of evil. Amen.*

Do not be overcome by evil,
but overcome evil with good.

ROMANS 12:21

June 15

Adequately Trained

After hundreds of hours of training, you are prepared to serve your nation in your specific military occupational specialty or "MOS." The standards for each specialty may vary, but the goals of training are the same: to prepare you to play your role in the greatest military force in history, the United States military. As believers in Jesus Christ, our equipping does not end with our professional training, for God equips us to do everything good for his will.

While many wonder what the will of God is for their lives, as a believer your purpose is to use the gifts he has entrusted you with to serve the people of our nation, to be a leader of integrity and character, and to honor those in authority. You are to do this as if you are working for God himself. His Word has equipped you to share the love of Jesus through your life. Know your equipping does not end with the gear on your kit but also with what is in your heart and in your spirit. You have everything you need to fulfill God's plan for your life.

> *Heavenly Father, thank you for fully equipping me to fulfill your plan and will for my life. I ask you to help me be a good steward of all that you have entrusted me with. Amen.*

May the God of peace... equip you with everything good for doing his will, and may he work in us what is pleasing to him, through Jesus Christ, to whom be glory for ever and ever. Amen.

HEBREWS 13:20, 21

June 16

You Are Courageous

I n a training session, a new recruit mishandled instructions and completely fouled up an assignment. His instructors came down hard on him, and the entire class paid the price. "If you want to learn, you must remember the lesson!" barked the drill instructor. In the moment of correction, it may seem like your lesson is merely physical. However, courage does not develop in times of peace but rather in the lessons derived in training, prayer, and a relentless pursuit of excellence.

Sometimes our courage comes from moments of error, moments we could learn from, moments we were able to survive and grow from. It is in these lessons that we become stronger and less likely to be discouraged in the fight. There are so many things that you deal with, and you do not even give a second thought to fear in the moment. Allow your past to become your strength and fuel for your future, not chains that wear you down. You have all you need to prepare you for the fight.

Heavenly Father, thank you for courage, for strength, and for never abandoning me in the fight. Amen.

Do not be in dread or afraid of them.

DEUTERONOMY 1:29 ESV

June 17

Crush the Enemy

Until someone has attacked you personally, pointing rudely and making berating comments at you, it is difficult to understand the level some people will go to in persecuting you or giving you a hard time. The same would apply when we encounter unwelcoming local nationals on a deployment. Let them talk, cuss, or call you names. It is irrelevant. But as you remain professional, you are setting yourself up for blessings in the supernatural and victory in the natural.

Persecution against Christians in America is nothing like it is in other parts of the world today or like it was many years ago. People are dying in other parts of the world for their faith in Christ, and we simply must make a commitment to live for him above our own selfish ways. When others persecute you, bless them. Bless them with your words, in prayer, and through actions and deeds. As you do this, you open the windows of opportunity for God's Word to come to life and blessings to flow. Do not speak evil for evil but bless those who curse you.

Heavenly Father, I ask your blessing over all who have persecuted me, cursed me, or wished harm on me. I declare blessing over their lives, their finances, relationships, families, careers, health, and relationship with you. Amen.

Bless those who persecute you;
bless and do not curse.

ROMANS 12:14

June 18

Honor in Battle

Rivalries are good for creating healthy competition. Sometimes this can turn nasty in the competitive culture of the military. Whether it's a teammate or someone from another unit, it takes little effort to create a rival when first place is at stake. But beyond healthy competition, there can be backbiting, gossiping, slandering, or old-fashioned bullying, and you can face high school-style drama in the adult world.

When your enemy stumbles and falls, it may be tempting to initially celebrate and tell the world how faithful God is to vindicate you. While he is faithful to vindicate, we are called to love our enemies. A heart of love for our enemies does not desire to see them fall or stumble, so we should not rejoice in their fall. There is power, strength, honor, and confidence in the silence of a vindicated person. Don't take matters into your own hands. Be a person of honor and let God handle it. And when he does, don't gloat about it.

Heavenly Father, I give those who have mistreated me, those who have wronged me or harmed me in any way, to you. I speak blessing over them and ask you to take control. Amen.

Do not gloat when your enemy falls;
when they stumble, do not let your heart rejoice.

PROVERBS 24:17

June 19

Wise as a Serpent

The mission may have come in as something you dismissed in your mind as low priority, maybe routine. And while you expected the mundane, instead came a well-planned ambush from the enemy, but you were prepared. Why? You have received training, and you've seen the lives of those who paid the ultimate sacrifice, those who did not make it home after an ambush. Their lives were not lost in vain. You have become wiser, more vigilant, and more aware.

It's no secret that there are people who want to harm you through cowardly means, setting traps or luring you into a setup. But having the proper mindset and maintaining situational awareness further prepares us and enlightens us to the tactics of an emboldened enemy. Times are changing, and tactics of the enemy are evolving, but their motives are the same. As a child of God, placing your trust and hope in God and leaning on him for divine help in dealing with humanity will lead you to victory and salvation in times of trouble.

Heavenly Father, thank you for revealing to me the traps of the enemy, the snares set before me, and the ambushes that await. Amen.

They spread a net for my feet;
I was bowed down in distress.
They dug a pit in my path—
but they have fallen into it themselves.

PSALM 57:6

June 20

Powerful Prayer

Taking time to pray doesn't have to be a boring, ritualistic behavior that you dread. Once you discover the power of prayer, it becomes like spending time with a best friend. It's not something you feel obligated to do out of a performance-based love, but it is a sincere desire to know God on a personal level. We get to know him through studying his Word and through prayer, whether that takes place in the morning or in the evening or takes place through whispering prayers throughout the day.

One thing about the darkness we experience as warriors is that it cannot remain where our light shines. Darkness must flee. It is in darkness that most evil flourishes, but the light of God's Word exposes the darkness for us to see, guiding our path through perilous places. Don't look at spending time reading the Bible as a monotonous task you have to do for God to love you or praying as a requirement so God will not send you to hell. No, he loves you, and nothing can change that. Read and pray out of a desire to draw closer to God and watch how your life begins to change.

Heavenly Father, thank you for your perfect Word. I ask you to show me the way. Help me to understand your Word, apply it, and adopt it in my life. Amen.

Your word is a lamp for my feet,
a light on my path.
PSALM 119:105

You Are Strategic

God does nothing by accident. He is a God of order and strategy. When we receive a command to wait, there is a reason for it. A good rule I not only lived by in combat but also shared with others was "never be in a hurry to get yourself killed." There is a time to aggressively press forward, a time to proceed with caution, and a time to take a tactical pause and wait. Sometimes we try to rush into things to fight when it was never our place to do so, when it was God's battle all along.

We cannot take this Scripture as an excuse to do nothing. However, it is a prime example of how we are to recognize the power of God in our lives and understand that he is strategic and orderly and expects us to be the same. There may be times on the battlefield of combat and life when your best strategy is to wait. It may be rare, but stranger things have happened. In life, give God the freedom to work instead of trying to fix all your own problems. Listen and look today. Is God showing you a place in your life where he wants you to simply be still and let him handle the situation?

Heavenly Father, thank you for helping me and fighting for me. I ask you to show me when I need to be still and let you fight for me. Amen.

The Lord will fight for you;
you need only to be still.
EXODUS 14:14

June 22

Never Stop Pursuing

With every act of service you perform, you are sowing righteousness and planting seeds of love and goodness in a world that is often overrun with hate. If you have been unproductive, both on the job and in life, break up your unplowed ground and begin to plant seeds. Pursuing God means you are planting seeds of righteousness in every area of your life, including your home, marriage, relationships, finances, career, and ministry outreach.

For some, this may mean you begin anew with some changes in your marriage or make some healthy commitments in your finances, health, or fitness. For others, this means having an honest discussion with yourself about where you have been in your career, what you have accomplished, and what you need to do to achieve your goals. Seeking the Lord is not some mystical activity. Rather it is part of our everyday lives. Over time, our pursuit of God will result in a harvest of righteousness, a bounty of goodness and blessings that will overtake us. But it begins today with small steps. Have the courage to take the first step.

Heavenly Father, thank you for giving me the courage to take the necessary steps to begin my pursuit of you, to break up the unplowed ground in my life, and to sow seeds of righteousness. Amen.

Sow righteousness for yourselves,
reap the fruit of unfailing love,
and break up your unplowed ground;
for it is time to seek the LORD,
until he comes
and showers his righteousness on you.

HOSEA 10:12

June 23

The Winning Team

Jesus *is* the Prince of Peace who came to bring peace between humankind and God, but the war between light and darkness has never ceased. It is true that Jesus came to bring salvation to humanity, but he also came to defeat darkness. We know this earth is the devil's playground, and the enemy seeks to kill, steal, and destroy, but darkness cannot remain in the light. As a believer in Jesus, you are on the winning team, and as a warrior, you are in the middle of the fight of good and evil.

Our relationship with Jesus makes our peace perfectly complete, and we have been commissioned to serve his kingdom, to love God, to love people, and to engage in the battle through his Word and Spirit. On a practical note, in your capacity as a military warrior, part of restoring peace is, at times, to do battle on behalf of the innocent or defenseless. Sounds familiar, doesn't it? Walk in the truth of God's Word today, knowing you are on the winning team, fully empowered and fully equipped. The battle is already won.

Heavenly Father, thank you for the power to defeat darkness, to overcome evil, and to restore peace and order. Amen.

Do not suppose that I have come to bring peace to the earth. I did not come to bring peace, but a sword.

MATTHEW 10:34

June 24

Eyes on the Enemy

There is glory and suffering as a warrior. Over the years, you have seen one senseless tragedy after another, a pain that discriminates against no age, no social status, and no race. Tragedy can strike anyone at any time. Yet you stand your watch, relentlessly serving and pursuing those who do evil, which is a never-ending battle. As you gather with other warriors, the conversations at times turn dark, and someone may wonder aloud if the pain you endure and the burdens you bear are all worth it.

And then you remember: Where would this world be without watchmen on the wall? You stand guard, pursuing those wolves that prey on innocent sheep, protecting those who stray from the flock into harm's way. You know, deep in your soul, if people like you were not on the watch, then this world would have gone to hell a long time ago. Pursue evil when it comes and strike down those who harm the innocent. Serve and help those who are helpless. But never relent in your duty as a watchman, for you are part of God's plan, delivering hope to people in need.

Heavenly Father, thank you for this honor to serve your people and your kingdom as a watchman—to protect, to serve, and to pursue and apprehend evil. For this there is no greater honor. Amen.

Listen! Your watchmen lift up their voices;
together they shout for joy.
When the LORD returns to Zion,
they will see it with their own eyes.

ISAIAH 52:8

June 25

Command and Control

Some people live their entire life in disarray, with one bad relationship after another, one terrible financial decision after another, parenting problems, or spending time in and out of prison. When you talk to people like this, some tell you none of it is their fault, and some honestly tell you they made a lot of bad decisions. But along the way, you will have the opportunity to intervene and have tremendous positive influence in the lives of people.

Restoring order isn't something that began with the inception of the military. Order is in the nature of God. He desires it in our lives, in society, in churches, and throughout the world. While 1 Corinthians 14:40 is a portion of Scripture where the apostle Paul was reproving the Corinthians for disorder in the church, everything we do in life should be done in a "fitting and orderly way" so we honor God. Even amidst the chaos, remember the work you are doing is part of God's plan. It is pleasing to him, and restoring order in society is nothing to take lightly.

> *Heavenly Father, thank you for showing me the example of order through your Word and using me to restore order in this world. Help me to maintain order in my own life. Amen.*

Everything should be done in a fitting and orderly way.

1 CORINTHIANS 14:40

June 26

Focused Warrior

We may not immediately correlate the words *focus* and *stress* in the same sentence, but research has repeatedly supported the theory that untreated stress, unhealthy lifestyles, and bad habits lead to chronic fatigue and other issues. As military professionals, we understand and accept that part of the job may involve long periods away from home and family, odd hours, high stress, moments of anxiety, and high risk to our personal safety. However, if we allow stress and fatigue to go unaddressed, either as warriors or citizens, it can lead to much more severe issues.

Developing healthy habits for sleep and nutrition, developing solid relationships with partners on the job and away from work, and having a healthy home life will provide you with better opportunities to avoid stress and fatigue and to address them quickly when they do surface. When stress dominates our lives, we live in a place of constant defeat, making it difficult to focus on doing excellent work in the military. Today, find healthy ways to eliminate the stress and build positive habits in your life. Take time for prayer and reading the Bible, give those things to God, and allow him to provide you peace. As you take these steps, you will begin to see a massive improvement in your overall focus in life.

Heavenly Father, thank you for taking the burden of my stress, giving me rest, and giving me precision and for giving me intense focus on you, on duty, and in life. Amen.

You will seek me and find me
when you seek me with all your heart.
JEREMIAH 29:13

June 27

Power to Persevere

There are some people who perform at their prime under pressure and others who crumble at the slightest hint of it. Most military warriors are those who rise to the challenge anytime the pressure is on, performing at their highest levels. Some say it's adrenaline, and some say it's genetics, but at the end of the day, it comes down to character. How we respond to adversity has more to do with *who* we are than *what* we are.

At some time in your career, you may find yourself like the psalmist in Psalm 57:4, in the midst of lions, dwelling with ravenous beasts, and in a less-than-pleasant situation. In these moments, when the tension is at a fevered pitch, your heart is pounding and your mind racing, remember you are more than a conqueror in Christ. Not only do you have your faith and not only are you prepared mentally and spiritually, but you are also one of the most well-trained professionals in the world. Affirm that you *are* more than a conqueror. Never let those skills go stale and never let your relationship with God grow cold.

> *Heavenly Father, thank you for standing with me in the presence of intense pressure. Thank you for making me more than a conqueror before the battle ever begins. Thank you for victory. Amen.*

I am in the midst of lions;
I am forced to dwell among ravenous beasts—
men whose teeth are spears and arrows,
whose tongues are sharp swords.

PSALM 57:4

June 28

Restoration Mission

I'm sure you will agree that it is a tremendous blessing to serve our nation and, yes, to serve even those around the world who may declare their hate for you. To serve in spite of their hate is a wonderful example of love in action. Your service is an opportunity to reveal the true love of Christ through your actions.

When you help restore a person's life by protecting it and the lives of their family, and when you help them obtain the resources and assistance they need to survive, they begin to see through the propaganda and mischaracterizations of America's military and instead see the hearts of the men and women who serve our nation. Think about the ways God has used your service to restore the lives of broken people—through words or actions—and how he has strategically positioned you, even in the presence of your enemies, as a minister for his glory.

> *Heavenly Father, may all those I serve see a true reflection of your loving kindness through my actions and service today, and may you receive my work as an honorable gift back to you. Amen.*

Those who hate me without reason outnumber the hairs of my head; many are my enemies without cause, those who seek to destroy me. I am forced to restore what I did not steal.

PSALM 69:4

June 29

Outlast the Enemy

Our homes are supposed to be safe places, but every year, millions of Americans are victims of burglary, home invasions, and other crimes that rob them of peace in their own homes. There is not one of you who would not defend your property, your family, or your possessions against an intruder, even fighting to the point of death. After healing a possessed man, Jesus used a parable to get the point across to those who were listening.

When we read Luke 11:21–22, it may sound as though Jesus was encouraging us to guard our homes. While there is certainly *nothing* wrong with that, this was not his point. The reference to the "strong man," as consistent with all major commentaries, is Satan, and the stronger man is Jesus. Therefore, as you have been empowered with the life and mind of Christ, *you* have been made the stronger person to overtake the enemy, to disarm him, to plunder his spoils, and to take rightful possession of what is yours. No longer a victim, no longer a slave, no longer defeated, you are stronger than the enemy.

> *Heavenly Father, thank you for empowering me to defeat the enemy, for filling me with your Spirit, for never leaving me, and for guiding me all my days. Amen.*

When a strong man, fully armed, guards his own house, his possessions are safe.

LUKE 11:21

June 30

Always Undefeated

Military service is not for the faint of heart. It's a life that requires you to be resilient, to be able to take a punch and get back up again and stay in the fight, no matter how bad it hurts. Many people have a lot of unanswered questions and may look to you for answers to those difficult, complex questions that we simply cannot answer at times. At any given moment, for a reason not known to us, someone can begin attacking innocent people, causing mass casualties. Your response is the only hope of survival for those involved.

It does not matter how much eviler this world may become, for you can cling to the promise that you will be victorious in Christ. And while we will all leave this life one day, no one can touch our eternal life with him. You may be surrounded by enemies from every side, but you will not be defeated. Stand firmly on the promises of God's Word, for it is alive and active. As you apply it in your life, you will see the fingerprints of God throughout your world.

Heavenly Father, thank you for the promise of your protection. I ask for you to surround me with your covering and protection and that you would guide me with divine wisdom and discernment. Amen.

We are hard pressed on every side, but not crushed;
perplexed, but not in despair;
persecuted, but not abandoned;
struck down, but not destroyed.

2 CORINTHIANS 4:8–9

July 1

Shelter from the Elements

July in the northern hemisphere brings with it soaring temperatures and scorching heat. It's always nice to find a place in the shade to get out of the sun, cool off, and hopefully enjoy a summer breeze. After a long day in the summer heat doing physical training, field operations, or other outdoor duties, getting somewhere out of the elements brings refreshment to your body, which is important if you have to do it again tomorrow.

Psalm 91:4 has a portion of Scripture that applies here: "Under his wings you will find refuge." This is a Hebrew metaphor referring to the protection God gives from oppressive desert heat. If you have ever experienced heat exhaustion, you know heat can wear you down. With the knowledge you have regarding hydrating your body, taking breaks as you are able, and finding shelter when it is feasible, you will be more than prepared to not only survive the battle against the enemy but the elements of weather as well.

Heavenly Father, thank you for providing relief in the elements of our climate. Thank you for protecting me in dangerous weather situations and for guiding my vehicle and my feet as I travel. Thank you for safety all around me. Amen.

He will cover you with his feathers,
and under his wings you will find refuge;
his faithfulness will be your shield and rampart.

PSALM 91:4

July 2

An Unbeatable Team

The heart of every warrior should be to serve his or her nation, to make it a safer place to live, and to protect those who are defenseless against the violent and evil people who exist around the world. The challenges we face in our world are growing, and this requires a strong faith, strong families, and a resilient commitment to our work as warriors. There are those who would suggest evil will disappear with faith alone, but we know that is not possible. We know it requires the brave work of men and women.

Faith and works cannot exist separate from each other. As warriors, we cannot expect to be effective without having both faith and works in our life, for they are truly an inseparable pair. Today, are you matching your faith with the actions and work you do? Will you accept the challenge to pair your faith with your work and see the power of the inseparable pair working together in your life as a believer in Jesus Christ?

Heavenly Father, thank you for the power of both faith and deeds in my life; as I strive to serve you with excellence, you will receive the glory in all I do. Amen.

Someone will say, "You have faith; I have deeds."
Show me your faith without deeds,
and I will show you my faith by my deeds.

JAMES 2:18

Lift the Weaker Ones

There are some who are not as strong as others and some who may lack the aggressiveness that the other "alpha dogs" think they should have. But, my brothers and sisters, I encourage you not to look down on those who may appear weaker than you. You don't have to earn the title of hero. You *are* a hero in the eyes of most every person you serve. You should never demean those warriors who are weaker—physically, mentally, and possibly spiritually—or treat them as less than you are.

We should not merely tolerate weaker warriors. Instead, we should mentor them, strengthen them, challenge them, and help them reach their goals. Who are we to judge the potential of someone who hasn't received a fair shot at serving with us? Through proper mentorship, they can gain confidence and strength to achieve excellence. That is how we keep the line strong for years to come.

Heavenly Father, help me to encourage younger warriors today and help me to diplomatically handle those who, for their own safety and the safety of others, may need to find another career. Amen.

We who are strong ought to bear with the failings of the weak and not to please ourselves. Each of us should please our neighbors for their good, to build them up.

ROMANS 15:1–2

July 4

Warrior Healer

Today is a national day of celebration of our independence as a country, but many times, remembering the sacrifice required to enjoy freedom is lost amidst the celebrations, cookouts, fireworks, and family gatherings. Today, you may be celebrating independence from a past hurt, a bad memory, or a terrible addiction. Maybe you are not up to celebrating like everyone else and instead are mourning a loss or experience. Let today be a day to honor losses and sacrifice and experience the blessings of the freedoms for which many pay such a high price.

This is the hope we have in salvation through Jesus Christ. His promises are always *yes* and *amen*. It is critical that we embrace the promises of God's Word, especially while we deal with the pain and hurt in our world. You can enjoy freedom, knowing there is a promise of peace, healing, and total victory. Your presence represents this hope to many people you may encounter today. Not only are you a guaranteed recipient of God's promises, but you are also a messenger of his promises. Walk in confidence today, knowing not only that God's promises are for you but also that you are part of his plan to bring healing to our nation.

Heavenly Father, help me remember the importance of walking in your power, expressing your love, and being compassionate to hurting people. Amen.

He will wipe every tear from their eyes.
There will be no more death or mourning or crying or pain,
for the old order of things has passed away.
Revelation 21:4

July 5

Live Selflessly

Some may not agree with the position of Pfc. Desmond T. Doss as portrayed in the 2016 film *Hacksaw Ridge,* but no one can dispute his selfless service. Pfc. Doss was a warrior, a selfless servant driven by pure love to serve his nation and fellow warriors. This type of service is only possible through love-driven action. If you want to immortalize yourself, surrender to Jesus and love others as Jesus has loved you. Even in the most daunting moments of combat, selfless service has a place.

What will you do with this knowledge now? Will you store it away and not act on it? This is the same as merely talking about faith and not putting it to work. The most dangerous act of defiance in the face of God is knowing what to do and not doing it. You know now how to best serve and, most importantly, how to love: selflessly. Let the light of God shine through your life through excellent service.

Heavenly Father, strengthen me in moments of terror and grant me peace to provide humanity with selfless service, following the examples you have provided. Amen.

*If you spend yourselves on behalf of the hungry
and satisfy the needs of the oppressed,
then your light will rise in the darkness,
and your night will become like the noonday.*

ISAIAH 58:10

July 6

A Proper Response

It is easy to respond to verbal insults in a negative way, especially for those who are still maturing, regardless of age. While returning insult for insult may seem to offer a degree of temporary satisfaction, it is often the opposite that happens. Thinking back to much of your training, you may recall basic training instructors in your face, yelling, and trying to provoke you to some negative reaction. Most of the time, your response would either further escalate the situation or de-escalate the situation. The power you have to overlook insults that can pay tremendous dividends for you in the future.

How often were you tempted to respond with some sarcastic response or, even worse, a sharper, more negative response to an insult? Most of the time, that situation would have a negative ending without your prudent response to those insults and harassment. What is the proper response to an insult? In most cases, it is silence. Ignore it. In fact, if the world would give less attention to stupidity, we would see less strife in it. When we show a hot temper and respond in an immature manner to the provocation of someone, it shows our areas of weakness, which we all have. Today, be challenged to give no credence to the insults hurled your way by those who bear no value in your life. Rather, respond with prudence.

Heavenly Father, thank you for the wisdom to respond to insults properly and with prudence. Amen.

Fools show their annoyance at once,
but the prudent overlook an insult.
PROVERBS 12:16

July 7

Warriors for Justice and Equality

Justice, equality, and civil rights are subjects of great debate in our society. As warriors, we fight to protect each of these precious pillars of our nation in defense of freedom. We've seen the destruction caused by riots and violence, which have cost the lives and livelihoods of innocent people. One thing we never see, however, is a protest for the lives of fallen military warriors who paid the ultimate price for that freedom.

It may be tempting to get discouraged by those who take to social media to insult our country and culture. It may be frustrating to see the same people you serve also protest the values that you stand for yet never raise their voices to defend the men and women like you who make the ultimate sacrifice. This is part of the heart of a hero. But with each other and God, we can do our work and do it well.

Heavenly Father, if I become discouraged in the midst of a troubled society, help me to remember my purpose and goal. Help me to keep my focus on you and on serving my nation as I serve you. Amen.

By oppression and judgment he was taken away.
Yet who of his generation protested?
For he was cut off from the land of the living;
for the transgression of my people he was punished.

ISAIAH 53:8

July 8

The Greatest Heroes

The chain of command in the United States armed forces exists for a reason: to keep order, to establish a hierarchy, and to maintain a flow of information throughout the organization. However, some of the greatest leaders I ever had the pleasure of serving with were "in the trenches" with the rest of the team. They weren't abandoning their post as supervisors, and they weren't trying to fraternize with the squad. Rather, they were serving.

Take the example of Jesus in relation to his disciples. He did not command them to go and do anything he had not done himself or anything greater than he had done. Leadership is developed in the trenches, nowhere else. Servanthood forges leaders. The greatest servants often make the greatest leaders. Lt. Col. Dave Grossman and co-author Adam Davis said in their book *On Spiritual Combat: 30 Missions for Victorious Warfare,* "If you want to be a leader, bring a towel." This refers to the act of washing feet, as Jesus did before his arrest in the garden. So, do you want to be a leader? Or are you comfortable as a follower? Leaders are not developed in rank but in servanthood. Follow the pattern of Jesus if you want to be a great leader.

Heavenly Father, thank you for giving me the heart to serve your people. Remind me that the level of serving I do determines the level of greatness I achieve. Amen.

Sitting down, Jesus called the Twelve and said,
"Anyone who wants to be first must be the very last,
and the servant of all."

MARK 9:35

July 9

One Unit. One Team. One Mission.

Nothing destroys a command like low morale, but sometimes we have to work through it and overcome it. There are many factors that affect the morale of a command, but one thing we can do is ensure that we focus on being unified at the micro level, from the unit or platoon level to the squad level, all the way up. If we will focus on unity and being of one mission, then the issue of low morale will have less effect on our overall performance.

This mission begins with one person—you. It begins with the decision to be of like mind with others, to work in peace, to compromise with your teammates as best you can, and to work toward one common goal, blocking out the negative influences. When we focus on the same love mentioned in Philippians 2:2, we will see a different atmosphere in our departments. This all begins with us and the person to our left or right, with a decision to stop the excuses and make the change.

Heavenly Father, I resolve to work in unity with my teammates, for one common purpose and one common goal, and remove the dissension and bickering, to eliminate evil, and to bring peace and order to our world. Amen.

Make my joy complete by being like-minded, having the same love, being one in spirit and of one mind.

PHILIPPIANS 2:2

July 10

Expectation of Perfection

Every person who wears the uniform, no matter the rank, experience level, job, or command in which they serve, has an expectation of perfection. This has come as a result of the dehumanization of service members through various media outlets and through the public's perception of us based on movies, video games, and songs. We are all going to make mistakes, and yes, we are all going to sin. But the blood shed by Jesus makes us blameless before God. When we live a life in pursuit of him, every part of our lives lines up in righteousness.

To experience success in our military service, we must have proper motivation in our hearts each and every day. Our character must be impeccable, and our walk must be blameless. Living above reproach means we should live our lives in a way so that no one should be able to question our character or integrity. Know you can trust the path God has for you, and while you lean on his promises, he will release success in your life and shield you all your days.

Heavenly Father, help my life be above reproach for those who see it, and may those who see me also see you. Amen.

He holds success in store for the upright,
he is a shield to those whose walk is blameless.

PROVERBS 2:7

July 11

Granting Mercy, Giving Grace

A quick temper can cause more trouble for you than just about any other issue. It can lead to professional setbacks, have legal ramifications, and divide you from teammates, friends, and even family. There's a time to move swiftly, but your temper should not guide that decision. When we seek understanding and wisdom, know who we are dealing with in our duties and who we are in God's eyes, and have confidence in our training and faith in our eternal God, we display great patience instead of foolish behavior.

On the shooting range, you've likely heard the phrase "slow is smooth, smooth is fast." If you are quick to respond to a situation with a poorly thought-out plan, chances are you will have to deal with more issues as a result of your temper and the way you handle the situation. There are times when we have to let go of the words and actions of others and times when addressing those in the moment would cause more trouble than they are worth. Be someone who constantly seeks the wisdom only God can give. Be generous with granting mercy when possible. Give grace often because there will be times when you will need it as well.

Heavenly Father, thank you for wisdom, patience, new mercies, and grace. Help me in my response to provocation and guide my words in moments when my emotions could get the best of me. Amen.

A person's wisdom yields patience;
it is to one's glory to overlook an offense.

PROVERBS 19:11

July 12

Clear Identity

You wear a uniform so you can clearly represent the United State military. And while most of your life will be out of uniform, when you do wear it, you should feel a great sense of pride. But our identity is not rooted in our work or our service. No, our identity is in Christ. When we lose our identity in the mix of what we do for a job, we risk losing our families, friends, eventually our careers, and our true purpose in life.

We cannot expect to experience change in our lives if we never spend time reading the Bible or praying, for this is where we find and establish our identity in Christ. Then we can walk in the perfect will of God and experience resounding success throughout our careers. Today, commit yourself to a time each day for reading the Bible, praying, and finding your identity in Christ, who *he* says you are in his Word. He will reveal to you his perfect and pleasing will.

Heavenly Father, in a world of corruption and evil, allow my identity to separate me from the crowd. Renew my mind and transform my thinking as I commit to studying your Word and spending time in prayer. Amen.

We all, with unveiled face, beholding as in a mirror the glory of the Lord, are being transformed into the same image from glory to glory, just as by the Spirit of the Lord.

2 CORINTHIANS 3:18 NKJV

July 13

The Blessing of Legacy

There's a great deal of satisfaction when you can protect people who can't protect themselves and help them become productive members of society. It takes a special person to care about others this much, especially people who cannot repay you. But it is proof that the work you do has the potential to be enduring and meaningful. When we have the favor of God in our lives and in the work we do, the lives we interact with will change for the better.

There is no doubt you are equipped to do a great job in whatever capacity you serve in the military, and America is grateful for your service. But when we live our lives independent of faith and the power of God, we lack the necessary fuel to have a lasting impact. Today, commit your pursuit to God, in your personal life, family, career, future goals, and dreams, and as you live in reverent fear of him, his wisdom and favor will rest on you. Then your work will be lasting and meaningful.

Heavenly Father, thank you for your favor on my life, the favor that establishes the work I do and causes the services I provide to have lasting results. Amen.

May the favor of the Lord our God rest on us;
establish the work of our hands for us—
yes, establish the work of our hands.

PSALM 90:17

July 14

Their Only Hope

Will you answer the call when it's your time to hold the line? No matter how dangerous the situation, no matter how risky the circumstances, you are the hope of a hopeless and help-less people. You may be the QRF (Quick Reaction Force) for a unit of warriors you've never met or for a local village of strangers being harmed by a group of hostile terrorist thugs. Whoever it is, you are the hope for those who have no one else to help them. Your responsibility is to simply go when the call comes.

Your power is one that not only can stop evil but also can pro-vide relief to victims and connect them with powerful resources to help them get their lives back on track. Never take your role as a warrior for granted and don't become so hardened that you don't believe the voice of the hurting person who needs assistance. Listen for the cries for help. Maybe those cries are audible, maybe they are not, and maybe the issues are emotional and run deep. Active listening skills can provide you with another powerful resource to make you an asset to those who are hopeless. Today, you may be the answer to their prayer.

Heavenly Father, use me, my service, and my commitment to my nation and this world to help your people in need. I am here. Send me. Amen.

For he will deliver the needy who cry out,
the afflicted who have no one to help.

PSALM 72:12

A Powerful Advocate

At the time of his crucifixion, while hanging on the cross, nailed, bruised, and beaten, Jesus cried out to God, "My God, my God, why have you forsaken me?" Have you ever felt betrayed or forsaken by someone close to you? Even God? This life can be darker than words can express at times, but God does not forsake us. He is our refuge and strength, our stronghold in times of trouble. When we look to God for our help and hope, a deep trust in him rises to the surface of our hearts. He is reliable and faithful in all things.

There should never be a time when vulnerable or hurting people cannot come to you for help and receive it. If you cannot help them, find someone who can. When we advocate for those who cannot speak for themselves, we are reflecting the nature of our heavenly Father, who has always been a refuge for the oppressed. Today, commit your service to advocating for those who cannot speak for themselves, whether they are children, the handicapped, or the elderly. In doing so, you will be demonstrating to them the nature and love of God.

Heavenly Father, help my service reflect who you are and help those I encounter see your love in my actions. Amen.

The Lord is a refuge for the oppressed,
a stronghold in times of trouble.

PSALM 9:9

Warriors Need Assistance

Maybe the memories of your service haven't faded over time, and maybe you need to be reminded of your purpose in the here and now. Warriors need assistance occasionally. There's nothing wrong with that. When one warrior calls for assistance, his brothers and sisters drop what they are doing and immediately respond. We must respond to these requests with prudence and care but swiftly. When we call for help, there is someone who will come to our aid. There will be times when we find ourselves in situations that are overwhelming, but even in those moments we have access to the peace that nobody else in this world can possibly fathom.

Today, know you can call for help—on the radio, on the phone, and in your prayers. If you are battling something privately, there is help. It is not a sign of weakness to seek assistance. You will be better for it in the long run. Even King David, as warrior, king, and shepherd, knew how it felt to need help. As great a warrior as David was, he needed the help of a loving God in tumultuous times. God is no respecter of persons, and he will respond to you too. Call on him and respond to another warrior in need today.

Heavenly Father, I know through all I do for you, there will be times I am overwhelmed. In those moments, remind me that you have taken the burden and given me peace and that you are my help in my time of need. Amen.

Do not be far from me,
for trouble is near and there is no one to help.

PSALM 22:11

A Hero's Honor

We could sit around and complain about all that is wrong in life, in our command, or in our country, but at the end of the day, the only thing that matters is action. Complaining resolves nothing. When we match our faith in God with action and are determined to finish well, we will not be disgraced. Instead, we will receive a hero's honor. We may receive many rewards during our time in the military—medals and letters of commendation—but nothing compares to the rewards we have waiting for us in eternity.

Ignore the discouragement that surrounds you. If you have complaining voices around you, block them out and set your mind and heart to be determined to finish each call, each day, and each shift with excellence for the glory of God. The heart of a hero is not merely to serve but to serve and finish well. Today, I challenge you to dig deep and overcome the negative influences in the world that could easily distract you. Set your sights on the goal and finish strong.

Heavenly Father, thank you for helping me in all I do and for helping me finish strong. Thank you for the determination and willpower to be excellent in service for your glory. Amen.

Because the Sovereign LORD helps me,
I will not be disgraced.
Therefore have I set my face like flint,
and I know I will not be put to shame.

ISAIAH 50:7

July 18

Just in Time

If we are not totally dependent on God, we will falter because we lean on our own understanding. Israel experienced God's divine deliverance on numerous occasions in the Old Testament. While these stories are dated, we can rest knowing that the same God who rescued the Israelites then has not changed, and he is able and willing to rescue us now in our time of distress. When we attempt to live within our own power, strength, and understanding, we find ourselves in difficult situations that we may have avoided if we had called for the help of almighty God.

Even good people face adversity, and we should be prepared to respond to their needs when called upon. Most people do not have the training and experience in dealing with stressful, violent situations. But you do. You know how to address these circumstances and remain in peace while doing it. Fight off the temptation to do it all in your own strength. It is not possible. Lean on the supernatural power of the Holy Spirit and God's Word and watch what he does through your life as you serve your nation.

Heavenly Father, thank you for placing me in the right place at the right time, for putting me in position to serve those in need and in distress. Strengthen me to serve as a warrior in the battles of this world. Amen.

They cried out to the LORD in their trouble,
and he delivered them from their distress.

PSALM 107:6

July 19

The Hope of a Nation

It may seem that righteousness and justice no longer have a place in America. From within, we are destroying ourselves. There is division over every issue at every corner. We cannot seem to agree on anything. Sometimes, it seems like we have lost all hope, and there is no way to be saved. But there is always salvation and hope. Habakkuk is a prophet who makes a complaint to the Lord, and in response the Lord gives him a clear vision of what is to come.

Your service is part of a greater role in protecting the life of this great nation. Through diligent service, you keep the enemies at bay and flush out evil from the lives of the innocent. You play a role in the hope of our nation. What God is doing in America is not over. He will restore righteousness and justice. He will reestablish peace and order in our communities and our nation. Continue to shine as a lighthouse of hope to those who may have no hope.

Heavenly Father, thank you for the hope we have in you and in you alone. I ask for your mercy on my life and on my country. Move in my heart and life and across this great nation in a mighty way once again! Amen.

Look at the nations and watch—
and be utterly amazed.
For I am going to do something in your days
that you would not believe,
even if you were told.

HABAKKUK 1:5

July 20

Victory Celebration

There is an appropriate time to enjoy the fruits of your labor, to celebrate your victories, and to rest. David knew the meaning of celebrating, especially when God delivered him from the hand of so many enemies and repeatedly gave him victory. Likewise, it is necessary for each of us to take time to reflect on the success we experience, the victories we have, and our safety in the face of danger. David was a singer and a dancer—he was demonstrative in his worship and celebration.

Doing life alone is not the way it was meant to be, and when we have people to celebrate with and people to go through difficult times with, it makes the journey a little bit sweeter. Today, take time to celebrate your victories. Celebrate with your family, friends, and your teammates. Take time to bond with those with whom you serve because there is nothing that can replace the power of unity, and a good celebration can help reinforce that bond.

Heavenly Father, thank you for victory. Even though I may not have the victory at this moment, I know I am victorious because of you. Because of that, I celebrate! Amen.

David sang to the LORD the words of this song when the LORD delivered him from the hand of all his enemies and from the hand of Saul.

2 SAMUEL 22:1

July 21

The Storm's Commander

While we know God is with us in all we do, he expects us to use our faith. You use your faith every day, for to do a job with such great risk is a great demonstration of faith. But what happens when we find ourselves in the middle of a hopeless situation? Just like the disciples, we are empowered and expected to use faith to speak to the storm and tell it to be still.

After Jesus rebuked the wind and the waves, he asked his disciples, "Where is your faith?" We all have a measure of faith. Use your faith, exercise it, stretch it, and grow it. Faith is like a muscle or your weapons skills: the more you use it, the stronger it gets. Put it to the test. Match your faith in God with your biblically based actions and watch your life change. Know that Jesus is no longer sleeping, but he expects us to use the faith we have been given.

> *Heavenly Father, forgive me for not using my faith and demonstrating it as I should. Today, I will be a good steward of the gift of faith you gave me. I will honor you, both in the times of peace and in the storm.*
> *Amen.*

The disciples went and woke him, saying,
"Master, Master, we're going to drown!"
He got up and rebuked the wind and the raging waters;
the storm subsided, and all was calm.
"Where is your faith?" he asked his disciples.

LUKE 8:24–25

July 22

Often Outnumbered, Never Outsmarted

In combat, you may find yourself highly outnumbered. The adversary may have more weapons or more soldiers, but he will never have a greater spirit and heart than American warriors. In fact, you may be outnumbered more often than not, but never let them outsmart you or let their threats cause your faith to sway. Do not stand and let them see your fear and do not let those who are against you see you if you bleed.

The prophet in 2 Kings 6:16 recognized he was not alone. He knew his help came from a host of heavenly armies, which is why he said, "Don't be afraid." He knew there were more on his side than there were on the side fighting against him. There may come a day when you are in dire need of help, when you are highly outnumbered and help is a long way away. If that day comes, know that God will and does intervene to help his own. We may be often outnumbered, but we are never outsmarted.

Heavenly Father, thank you for the power of common sense, faith, and wisdom. Thank you for divine protection over me wherever I go and no matter how many are against me. Amen.

"Don't be afraid," the prophet answered.
"Those who are with us are more than
those who are with them."

2 KINGS 6:16

July 23

Make It Count

It may be difficult to see how a believer in Jesus Christ who is persecuted for his or her righteousness could be blessed, but God's Word will never return to him void. Many of you who serve our nation live in a way that honors God and glorifies his name, and because of that, you face various persecutions. You were once required to prove yourself to those you serve with, and as such, you must remain strong and steadfast through persecutions that may come to you because of your love for God.

Those persecutions will not decrease in this present age. In fact, they will only become more intense, and we should remain faithful to the Father to demonstrate our love and heart for his kingdom. We remain strong and steadfast by keeping our focus on the love God has for us and on the eternal reward, not on this present life. We must remember that this life, while it may seem permanent, is but a vapor, and we must prepare for eternity. In doing so, our hearts will align with the Father's heart, and we will focus on loving others in a way that reflects His nature.

> *Heavenly Father, grant me the strength and firmness to stand strong through persecution, to honor and glorify your name, whether I am on or off duty, until my last breath. Amen.*

Blessed are those who are persecuted because of righteousness, for theirs is the kingdom of heaven.

MATTHEW 5:10

July 24

Restore Righteousness

There are only two paths in life: the path of evil and the path of good. You answered the call to hold the line between evil and good so that evil doesn't overtake righteousness, so that those who are enslaved by their own sin do not enslave others. When you take enemy combatants captive, you are essentially seizing them and taking their immediate freedoms because of their evil deeds to humanity. They became a slave to sin and have to pay the consequences for it.

You can also choose to bow to sin, succumb to the pressures of life, give in, and become like those who wear the chains around them. You can be a slave to sin. But this way leads to death. Or if you become a slave to love, bound because God loved you first, then you have a desire to be obedient to the words of Jesus and to love others, which leads to righteousness and life. This is the way of his kingdom, and thus you serve to restore righteousness in this world.

Heavenly Father, thank you for empowering me to address the lives of those who seek to bring evil into this world. May all I do glorify your name. Amen.

Don't you know that when you offer yourselves to someone as obedient slaves, you are slaves of the one you obey—whether you are slaves to sin, which leads to death, or to obedience, which leads to righteousness?

ROMANS 6:16

Poisoned by Pride

Pride and arrogance are traits few people like to be around. Pride is a trait where people place themselves above everyone else, and arrogance immediately divides personal connections. When we allow pride to poison the heart with which we serve, it can taint the fruit of our labor and ruin the entire harvest. Pride and arrogance often lead to evil behavior and perverse speech, becoming a cycle that reinforces itself over time. Pride will ruin a person and often bring with it terrible embarrassment.

It may be difficult to work with someone who is arrogant or prideful or who cannot talk without cursing. But we should not hate the person. Today, ask God to search your heart, to root out any seed of pride so that you may honor him in your work. You have come too far and done too much for his kingdom in our nation to have it ruined by pride.

> *Heavenly Father, search my heart, search me, reveal any existence of evil pride in me and show me. If you find any there, reveal it and remove it so I can become closer to you and bring glory and honor to your name. Amen.*

To fear the LORD is to hate evil;
I hate pride and arrogance,
evil behavior and perverse speech.

PROVERBS 8:13

July 26

Decision Time

If you have been in the military for any length of time, you know there are people who try to lure you into useless arguments that will simply drain your energy, waste your time, and generate a complaint. There are times when a healthy debate is called for, but in general, we should avoid arguing with people who cannot do so in a logical, rational manner. We should not delve into senseless controversies that bear little to no benefit either, for these things often bring no glory to the kingdom of God.

Think about these things from the aspect of profit and loss. What profit does a senseless debate have or investing your time and energy into a foolish controversy? It may generate some, but in the long run, it will bankrupt your personal stock. Your personal reputation will be little to nothing if all you want to do is argue with everyone. It is necessary to walk away from certain conversations, and sometimes this is hard to do. In all we do, we should seek to live in a way that is useful and profitable to the kingdom of heaven.

Heavenly Father, give me wisdom and the wherewithal to walk away from those conversations I may be lured into that will not bring you glory. Help me stay focused on the task at hand. Amen.

Avoid foolish controversies and genealogies and arguments and quarrels about the law, because these are unprofitable and useless.

TITUS 3:9

July 27

Those Who Need You Most

When you have witnessed the works of God with your own eyes and experienced the movement of his mighty hand in your life, it is extremely difficult to contain your praise for him. It is natural to have a feeling that wants to exclaim his praises and share the news with others. Your assignment may be lacking in glamour, but you may be right where you need to be to rescue the poor and connect them to the resources they need to receive life-changing help.

It is important to understand the power of *where* you are always, not necessarily because of the threats but because of the opportunities the location presents. Today may be the time when you get to invest in the life of someone who is ready to change. Never give up hope. Relentlessly pursue and apprehend those who jeopardize the safety of the working, innocent, and needy, for this is the calling on your life, the reason for which you were born. When you do this with excellence, you provide rescue and reprieve to the victims and cause them to say, "Who is like our Lord?"

Heavenly Father, may my actions today cause others to rejoice in your great name. May my service be done with excellence to bring you glory! Amen.

My whole being will exclaim, "Who is like you, LORD?
You rescue the poor from those too strong for them,
the poor and needy from those who rob them."

PSALM 35:10

July 28

Cherry-Picking Commands

When we try to use God's Word like a vending machine, picking and choosing what we want to apply to our lives, we put ourselves in positions of defeat. It's like a police officer writing tickets for speeding, not wearing a seatbelt, and having no insurance, and then driving home while violating all those laws. We cannot, in good conscience, hold others to a standard we cannot abide by.

Jesus was not commanding us to observe all the laws, live in perfection, or die in sin. He was telling us that we should not cherry-pick from the commandments. We couldn't teach the laws in public one way and violate them in private and still expect to receive a blessing from God. That is the epitome of hypocrisy. May your life be a living example of God's Word and commandments. Be careful not to do like the Pharisees. Strive for excellence in all you do, not in the name of legalism but in the name of holiness.

> *Heavenly Father, thank you for the words of your Son, Jesus. Give me knowledge and understanding of your Word as I read and study and help me to carry it with me as I go about my day. Amen.*

Anyone who sets aside one of the least of these commands and teaches others accordingly will be called least in the kingdom of heaven, but whoever practices and teaches these commands will be called great in the kingdom of heaven.

MATTHEW 5:19

July 29

Acts of Valor

One of the first things we learn from our military ethics is not to use our rank or authority for our own advantage. While it may sound like this is something we would never do, one act of pride can lead to a series of consequences that can quickly unravel any good we might have accomplished. We should be mindful, especially with current technology, that we are always at risk of being monitored, but we should be serving with the utmost integrity and character no matter who is watching us.

Selfishness or arrogance should never tarnish our service, and instead, valor, selflessness, and honor should decorate it. Regardless of how powerful or skilled we are, we should never fall into the trap of taking advantage of the position we hold. Today, remain humble, with quiet confidence, always seeking to improve and help those around you to become better at what they do. When we focus on practical measures for being the best at what God has called us to be, he will bless us with greater responsibility along our journey. Pursue acts of valor and righteousness, honor and selflessness, and avoid tarnishing the uniform you so proudly wear.

Heavenly Father, may my service as a warrior bring you honor. May it never be about bringing me personal gain but about benefitting those I serve. Amen.

In your relationships with one another,
have the same mindset as Christ Jesus:
Who, being in very nature God,
did not consider equality with God
something to be used to his own advantage.

PHILIPPIANS 2:5–6

July 30

Spirit Life in Service

We can view our military careers with the mindset that it is a career we can enjoy by serving and helping others and making a difference, or we can see it as a curse. Either way, our perspective will set the tone for our attitude toward our work. But I am telling you, we were called to be free, not to indulge in the flesh or in sin but to serve.

When we grasp the power behind Galatians 5:13, it will change our view of our roles in the military. We will see our position as a life led by the Spirit, where we can serve humankind humbly in love because we are free. What other profession allows us to begin and end each day with the chance to be someone's hero? It may not be flashy, and you may not even realize it when it happens, but years from now, when someone comes up to you and thanks you for what you did, you will realize that your service was not in vain. That, my friends, is the power of a life led by the Spirit.

Heavenly Father, lead my life by your Holy Spirit. May I not take this freedom for granted and indulge in the things of this world but instead serve your purpose. Amen.

You, my brothers and sisters, were called to be free. But do not use your freedom to indulge the flesh; rather, serve one another humbly in love.

GALATIANS 5:13

July 31

Gospel-Wielding Heroes

God uses us to reveal his mysteries to others. He uses everyday, common men and women doing everyday work, which he turns into extraordinary results. We are servants, first of Christ and then to our nation, who are entrusted with the mysteries of his Word, to love people, care for others, serve honorably, and pursue evil. This is not a task to take lightly. You have the heart of a hero, the potential to leave a legacy to our nation.

What greater legacy could any person ask to leave than one of service to God and others? When we as warriors commit our lives, first personally and individually then professionally, to the purpose God has given us, we will see his direction. Through training, mentorship, discipleship, and experience, we will become excellent in service, bringing honor to our leadership and to Christ. Remember that you are on the road to leaving a legacy, so rise and serve with excellence and integrity for the next generation, for your children, and for other people who know you.

Heavenly Father, thank you for giving me a heart to serve and the attributes of a hero. Thank you for searching my heart continually, for leading me by your Spirit, and directing my steps today and every day. Amen.

This, then, is how you ought to regard us: as servants of Christ and as those entrusted with the mysteries God has revealed.

1 CORINTHIANS 4:1

August 1

All Things Made New

A new month brings with it hope, excitement, optimism, and new goals. While it is not possible to predict what this month will bring, it is possible to be intentional in your walk with God and keep your heart in tune with what he is saying through his Word. Maybe this time last year wasn't one you care to remember, and maybe you made your share of mistakes. A new month brings with it fresh opportunities for a clean slate, a new beginning, and a time to create new habits. As a follower of Jesus Christ, you have received every resource to pursue your God-given destiny.

As you begin to establish new patterns of behavior, you will see the goals you set become realities, and new goals will generate after that. The previous month's disappointments will soon fade away, and you will forget it. Today, sit down and set some small, achievable goals in order to create early momentum. Establish realistic goals for every area of your life and watch your outlook on life begin to change.

Heavenly Father, I give you my future. I lay down my past, whether good or bad, and I ask you to take my plans and make them yours. Amen.

He has given us his very great and precious promises, so that through them you may participate in the divine nature, having escaped corruption in the world caused by evil desires.

2 PETER 1:4

August 2

Prepare for Success

Gearing up for a mission requires more than maintaining your weapon, gear, and equipment; it involves significant mental, physical, and spiritual preparation too. It means spending time training on the range, going over endless scenarios, and having a plan for your family if things go bad. This type of mindset and devotion requires sacrifice and commitment, but at the end of the day, you'll be mentally sharper and physically more prepared. Preparation and training are the cure for the onset of complacency, which can take you out faster than anything on the battlefield.

Random equipment inspections and evaluations of TTP (Techniques, Tactics, and Procedures) are a crucial part of every unit's combat readiness. Being "combat ready" means you are prepared at any time to answer the call of service to your nation. Thankfully, we do not have to find our righteousness in our own lives or in our own behavior or performance. We cannot do enough to make it right, but Jesus did. Our righteousness is in him alone, and he makes our paths clear and straight. Today, go in confidence in total preparation, knowing you are well-prepared to face whatever may come your way because of the way made by your Savior.

Heavenly Father, I thank you for the freedom to spend time with you, to know you, and share your love. I know I am prepared, and I can lean on your Word and Holy Spirit. Amen.

Righteousness goes before him
and prepares the way for his steps.
PSALM 85:13

August 3

Safety in Boundaries

Whatever your assignment on duty, being diligent and intentional with your actions is critical to survival. The gift of boundaries and limits exists not as a means of punishment or slavery but to keep each of us free and safe. For some, knowing their personal limits gives them an excuse to overcome them, and in certain situations, that is fine. But when it comes to being reasonable, being prudent, and involving other personnel or the public, we should change our thinking.

While Proverbs 21:5 may not refer to military life and work specifically, we can still apply its principles to our work and lives. Limits and boundaries exist to give us freedom and to empower us. When we learn the true power of obedience to God's Word—his boundaries and limits—we begin to see a tremendous change in our lives. Think about it like this: if we fire our weapon hastily without good sight alignment and picture, we will, at times, miss our target. Being hesitant isn't the answer either. We have to strike the perfect balance. Finding the sweet spot will bring tremendous freedom in your career.

Heavenly Father, I ask for your wisdom and discretion today. Bring to mind the training and instruction I have received and help me remain vigilant and disciplined. Amen.

The plans of the diligent lead to profit as surely as haste leads to poverty.

PROVERBS 21:5

August 4

Poise in Adversity

Life has enough challenges of its own, but with the added stressors of military life, it can seem overwhelming to even the strongest of warriors. Think back to your boot days when you were first learning the skills you needed to be an asset to your unit. Often, consequences like push-ups, an occasional working party, and maybe some yelling from your local NCO (Non-Commissioned Officer) followed mistakes you or others made during those days. Those moments were preparing you to be the very best warfighter when the day comes to do your job, the day when it counts.

Regardless of the amount of training we receive, we will make mistakes during our career. Our mental capacity to overcome the pressure and make sound decisions determines how we learn to respond to adversity. If we cannot respond in a mature manner to the slightest adversity, then our margin of error will be low. Don't focus on stumbling or mistakes today; rather, focus on being excellent through the process of each step you take. Everything you learned was for a reason. Be intentional in all you do, in your thoughts, words, and deeds.

Heavenly Father, grant me the power to not only face but to also overcome adversity today and every day. Thank you in advance for guiding my steps. Amen.

We all stumble in many ways.
Anyone who is never at fault in what they say is perfect,
able to keep their whole body in check.

JAMES 3:2

August 5

Preventive Maintenance

Anything in our life requires maintenance if we want it to last for an extended period of time. Our relationships, health, vehicles, and weapons all require us to perform preventive care so we can get the most from them. We often neglect our bodies to tend to our families, thus failing to seek preventive care from our family physicians, which often leads to more serious health issues later in life. If we had addressed these sooner, appropriate treatment could likely have been a viable solution.

What level of trust would you have in battle if you never maintained your weapon or your skills? The same concept applies to every other area of life. Taking care of our bodies is a requirement if we want a long and prosperous career in military service. This means we must maintain excellent fitness standards, be gallant in relationships, and be good stewards of all we possess. Today, be a good steward of God's gifts by taking the proper steps for the preventive care of your body, relationships, and even material possessions.

Heavenly Father, stir my heart to pursue you in fitness, relationships, career, finances, and spirit. Show me the importance of being a good steward of all you have given me. Amen.

*No one ever hated their own body,
but they feed and care for their body,
just as Christ does the church.*

EPHESIANS 5:29

August 6

Heart of a Servant

The presence of a well-equipped US service member on the battlefield can be an intimidating show of force. In many cases, our presence alone can deter hostile activity and bring comfort to the innocent. Regardless of your job specialty, as a military warrior, you took an oath and have a responsibility to protect those who cannot protect themselves. It is part of our ethos to defend the innocent in the harshest of environments and circumstances.

Holding the line against evil requires proactive strategies and staying ahead of hostile activity to ensure peace and order. There is a reason why those who violate what is right fear justice. This is not a fear of physical harm, unless justified, but of facing the consequences of their actions. Today, serve with honor. Protect with dignity and courage. You have been fully equipped, completely prepared, and wholly trained to face what this world has for you. Do not be afraid but be of good courage.

Heavenly Father, use me as a servant for those who do good and as your agent for those who do wrong. May I be just and fair in all I do today and forever. Amen.

For the one in authority is God's servant for your good. But if you do wrong, be afraid, for rulers do not bear the sword for no reason. They are God's servants, agents of wrath to bring punishment on the wrongdoer.

ROMANS 13:4

August 7

Firing Range to Fighting Mat

Over time, thousands of rounds of ammunition will fire through your weapons so that you can become and remain a proficient, skilled marksman. Range time is enjoyable, but its purpose is to prepare us should we need to use lethal force. We must stay up-to-date on many areas of training, including firearms, ground fighting, and tactics. The same skills you need to be victorious in a ground fight—using your hands and feet—are not the same skills needed to be a highly accurate sniper or accurate with any of your other weapons.

There is significance in the phrases "hands for war, fingers for battle" in Psalm 144:1. Preparing our "hands for war" means preparing for hand-to-hand combat, which is a ground-fighting strategy, and "fingers for battle" means being excellent with weapons. You are not just going to war prepared, but you are also going locked and loaded, ready to walk away victorious. That is the message God has given us through his Word, a message of redemption, mercy, grace, love, and empowerment. Our power does not come from our weapons; it comes through pursuing the ways of God according to his Word.

Heavenly Father, please stir in my heart a hunger for you. Grant me wisdom to know I can only succeed in battle with you as my Lord. Amen.

Praise be to the Lord my Rock,
who trains my hands for war,
my fingers for battle.
PSALM 144:1

August 8

Pressure to Compromise

We often find ourselves in a situation of potential compromise when we face a decision between violating our moral, religious, or ethical standards or even our personal convictions. The fact is that bad decisions made in a moment of compromise have directly affected us all or someone we know. The root of every action is a result of what is in a person's heart. Compromise with sin begins with one small step that seems harmless at the time. It all begins at the heart of a person, when he or she justifies an action that is wrong.

In these moments, we often face temptations based on perceived needs or desires. In these times, we choose to make the wrong decisions when we trust in our own ability rather than trusting in God, or we trust in our timing more than in God's timing. In a world where the pressure to compromise is constant, resolve today to stand firm on the principles of God's Word, to honor him with your actions, to trust him to supply your needs, and to strive to keep your conscience clear before both God and others.

Heavenly Father, please guide my steps today. Give me discernment and strength. Grant me willpower to overcome the temptation to compromise when it is not good for me. Amen.

I strive always to keep my conscience clear before God and man.

ACTS 24:16

August 9

The Enemy of Temptation

Preparing for training or deployments means preparing for threats. Through peers and leadership, we learn the necessary skills to navigate difficult and challenging situations, many that others have faced before us. While it is not always easy or convenient to prepare, it does require tremendous mental toughness, self-discipline, and self-control. Regular training, repetition, and becoming so fluent in our skills that they become part of our natural behavior means we will be precision ready when the time comes to use those skills.

In the same manner, we should commit to preparing our hearts and minds for the day of temptation through spending time in prayer and the regular reading and studying of God's Word. This is not a means of measuring performance or another box to check off so we can get into heaven, but it is to equip us for those moments when we are tested and tempted to the max. Today, commit your desires to God and commit to spending regular time in prayer and studying God's Word so you will be prepared in the moment you need it most.

Heavenly Father, lead me not into temptation. Grant me strength and grace. Prepare my heart to be victorious over evil and resist temptation. Amen.

No temptation has overtaken you except what is common to mankind. And God is faithful; he will not let you be tempted beyond what you can bear. But when you are tempted, he will also provide a way out so that you can endure it.

1 CORINTHIANS 10:13

August 10

Peace in Chaos

If everything around you seems to be falling apart, remember that God is in control. Maybe you ask yourself, *Why would God allow this to happen?* God doesn't cause bad things to happen, but he is with you through it. We live in a fallen world full of death, pain, sickness, and misery, but there is a promise: Jesus can (and will) speak to the storms in your life. One word from God can change the direction your ship is heading.

Make him the Lord of your life. Ask him to speak to your storms, and he will. God has not promised us a life of ease, but he has promised a great Comforter and a peace that surpasses all understanding. Remember who is aboard your vessel. God's not asleep, and he is fully aware of what is going on in your life. All you are required to do is speak to the storm and tell it to be still. God will either calm the storm or give you peace through it all.

Heavenly Father, thank you for the strength and resolve to head into the storms of life with you aboard my vessel. Secure me through these storms and grant to me peace that surpasses all human understanding. Amen.

As they sailed, he fell asleep.
A squall came down on the lake,
so that the boat was being swamped,
and they were in great danger.
LUKE 8:23

August 11

Procedure of Authority

A basic principle of authority is that we must first submit to a higher authority. Everyone—from the bottom to the top of the military ranking structure—has someone to submit to. As believers in Christ, we understand the importance of honoring those in authority, and we know what it means to respect those in leadership positions. As military service members, we have a duty to respect our superiors, fulfill our oath of service, and honor God within whatever capacity of authority that we operate.

From time to time, leaders may treat you unfairly. This can lead to a jaded perspective of those in your chain of command. However, you cannot use the excuse of cynicism to rebel against leaders who are responsible for your life. Find a way to be at peace with those you serve, regardless of their position. Today, remember that you reap the seeds you sow. In other words, by submitting to authority now, you will appreciate the submission of those for whom you are responsible when you hold a position of higher authority later. Therefore, seek to honor God in all you do regardless of who is in charge or how they may treat you.

> *Heavenly Father, give me humility to submit to those who are responsible for my life while on duty. As I honor those in authority over me, glorify your name. Amen.*

Let everyone be subject to the governing authorities, for there is no authority except that which God has established. The authorities that exist have been established by God.

ROMANS 13:1

August 12

Clearing Corners

What lurks around dark corners may be irrelevant or potentially dangerous. It can make or break you, so be prepared for the worst. The problem with corners is that we lack sight of what's beyond them. Finding the courage to go into the darkest, most violent places is what sets the best apart from those who do nothing more than talk about what they would do. Cover the corners. Clear the room.

Some who read this may wonder how God can lead us, or maybe they want practical examples of how God leads us. First, he has provided each one of us with access to the best training. Second, he gives us discernment, wisdom, and insight if we ask him. Third, there is supernatural protection. God speaks with a still, small voice. His leading is subtle most of the time, and if he leads the little ones, he will lead each man and woman in uniform. You may find yourself on unfamiliar paths, but he will guide you.

Heavenly Father, guide my steps, and in the dark and unfamiliar places, I ask for your divine protection, discernment, and wisdom. Amen.

I will lead the blind by ways they have not known,
along unfamiliar paths I will guide them;
I will turn the darkness into light before them
and make the rough places smooth.
These are the things I will do;
I will not forsake them.

ISAIAH 42:16

August 13

A Presidential Invitation

As Americans, it is difficult to understand the significance of the invitation of a king. Our form of government is different, but imagine if the president of the United States invited you to dinner. While all those who ridiculed you watch with envy and in amazement, you receive the favor of the most powerful person in the nation. In those moments, you could forge favor and life-changing relationships. But the uniqueness of this is that *we* did not prepare the table; God the King did.

In Psalm 23:5, David was referring to an enemy who watched on as David dined with the King of Glory, often a momentous occasion that took place as part of a covenant relationship. Our preparation for duty is not just training. It is also accepting the King's invitation to the table he has prepared, to dine with him while our baffled enemies watch. Today, know you can sit at the table with the King of kings and dine on the Bread of Life while you serve your country. You are in a covenant relationship with the Father, and this world can do nothing to break that.

Heavenly Father, thank you for the invitation to the banquet you have prepared for me. I humbly accept your invitation to your table in the presence of my enemies! Amen.

You prepare a table before me in the presence of my enemies.
You anoint my head with oil; my cup overflows.

PSALM 23:5

August 14

A Mission of Discovery

Gathering accurate battlefield intelligence is essential in targeting the enemy, reducing collateral damage, and accomplishing the mission. For thousands of years, researchers and scientists have searched for evidence that supports the existence of Jesus and his resurrection in addition to other biblical miracles. Others have sought these same ancient artifacts to disprove his existence. We know the truth because we believe in the Truth.

Among the countless powerful statements Jesus said is one found in John 14:11: "At least believe on the evidence of the works themselves." Essentially, Jesus was saying, "If you don't believe what I am saying, at least believe that the miracles you have witnessed are evidence of the existence of the Father." Evidence of the Truth is all around you, and you can find answers to anything you have questions about in his Word, in our hearts, and all around us.

Heavenly Father, help me to see, not only with my physical eyes but with my heart, the truth, the evidence of who you are. Empower and activate my faith for service to you. Amen.

Believe me when I say that I am in the Father and the Father is in me; or at least believe on the evidence of the works themselves.

JOHN 14:11

August 15

Never Back Down

We all want an easy life, a life without conflict, trouble, or resistance. That is, unfortunately, not a reality. Every day we live, we have to make choices—choices of good and evil, healthy or unhealthy, ethical or unethical. You may come across opportunities to save a life and change someone's destiny or be the consequence for another person's actions. Today, you may be tempted to take a small step down a slippery slope of immorality, unethical behaviors, and conduct unbecoming of an officer. You have the choice.

You possess the single greatest power that separates human beings from any other form of life on our planet: the gift of free will and choice. You have the power to make the decision to deny your own desires and pursue the things God has for you in life. Whether in combat or on the battlefield of life, you may be presented with options to cheat yourself, give in to temptation, or quit on life. Deny those and pursue the greater and significantly better things God has in store for you.

Heavenly Father, when I am tempted today, give me courage and strength to make the right decision. Give me courage to do the hard things in order to please you. Amen.

Whoever wants to be my disciple must deny themselves and take up their cross daily and follow me.

LUKE 9:23

August 16

Relentless Pursuit

If we are to experience peace in this world, we must first have men and women who are willing to fight to defend and restore order when necessary. Pursuing peace means we are required to pursue the evil lurking in our world. You must steady your trembling knees, take a deep breath, and stand in the gap between good and evil. The innocent of the world who cannot defend themselves depend on it. There will be times we are called not just to stand against evil but also to pursue and eliminate it.

Who will pursue the evil in our world in order to restore peace? At times, we must embrace violence to restore order. To restore order, suppress evil, and seek peace, we cannot turn a blind eye to atrocity. Be relentless in your pursuit of those who seek to do harm to those in your community. Train like you will not get another opportunity to train. Pursue the evil in your world like nobody else exists to do it.

Heavenly Father, grant me courage to pursue the vilest criminals. Give me boldness to chase, wisdom to know when to retreat, and, most of all, grace through it all. Amen.

Turn from evil and do good;
seek peace and pursue it.

PSALM 34:14

August 17

Divine Direction

The ability to navigate the battlefield is an essential skill for a warrior. It's a skill that's taught in basic training from day one and increasingly reinforced depending on your job and experience throughout your service. On the battlefield if you don't know where you are, you can't get where you're going, can't locate the enemy, and can't call for support. Navigation is not only critical to the success of the mission, but it's also key to the safety and survival of your teammates and you.

When we depend on our natural ability to get somewhere, we can become easily distracted. With guidance, we are less likely to become distracted, but it sometimes takes a little extra time. Maybe you are not where you want to be in life today. Maybe things haven't quite worked out the way you wanted them to. Know that you are not at the end of your rope. This is not the end for you, and you will find a blessed future if you seek the direction found in God's Word. He will guide you.

Heavenly Father, guide my steps and give me direction. Provide me with supernatural discernment and wisdom. Amen.

Direct my footsteps according to your word;
let no sin rule over me.

PSALM 119:133

August 18

The Armor of God

The modern-day battlefield requires warriors to utilize the best equipment available. Kevlar, body armor, and a good SAPI plate can be the difference between life and death. While body armor reduces the likelihood of a fatal injury from a gunshot or explosion, it is not guaranteed to prevent serious injury or death. There are points of weakness and limitations in our physical armor, and even the strongest armor in existence has areas of vulnerability. We need to use our body armor in conjunction with our training, skills, and knowledge of the incident. Only then can it provide us with the most support and protection possible.

Just like our physical armor requires more than the armor itself, we are to gird ourselves with the armor of God: the helmet of salvation, the shield of faith, and the belt of truth. Prepare for battle by studying God's Word today. This will strengthen your faith, encourage your spirit, and prepare you for the attacks that may come your way. God is not seeking your perfection or performance. He desires a relationship with you, and you will not be disappointed.

> *Heavenly Father, thank you for giving me the training, knowledge, and wisdom to know how to effectively use the armor you provide and the armor I wear on duty. Amen.*

Put on the full armor of God,
so that when the day of evil comes,
you may be able to stand your ground,
and after you have done everything, to stand.
EPHESIANS 6:13

August 19

Shield of Victory

Threats on the modern-day battlefield are ever increasing. Early in the Iraq and Afghan wars, deployed troops rode in soft-skin Humvees without protection much less a hardened gun turret. Fast forward to today, and we have state-of-the-art equipment and armored vehicles with gun turrets and shields protecting us from IEDs and elevated sniper fire. Without the shield, the risks of injury or death are higher. But with the shield, the likelihood of not only survival but also victory exponentially increases.

God's strength is immeasurable. His timetable is not the same as ours. But we can depend on his strength, support, wisdom, and protection in times of crisis. He has given us his shield of victory. The writer of Ephesians tells us the shield represents faith, which we can increase by properly exercising our knowledge of God's Word. The only combatant to the arrows of the enemy, also known as his lies, is the truth of God spoken in faith. When others count you out, God has your name in the win column. You are more than a conqueror, but don't neglect to train with the shield. Invest your time in the truth of God's Word today.

Heavenly Father, I know asking for an increased level of faith is a dangerous prayer. But I know you love me. Help me to grow my faith in you. Amen.

You have given me your shield of victory.
Your right hand supports me;
your help has made me great.

PSALM 18:35 NLT

August 20

A Noble Legacy

Many who join the military aspire to reaching the coveted job of a sniper. In the book of Judges, seven hundred select troops were precision skilled. They were selected because their skills were superior to all the rest. What do you want to be known for thousands of years from now? Maybe future generations will remember you for your generosity, or maybe they will know you for your service to others. If you want to leave a legacy, you need to be excellent at what you do, but to be excellent, you must first be committed.

What is your target? If you hit 50 percent of what you aim for on the range, you would not be allowed to remain on duty until you became proficient with your firearm. The two important thoughts to take away from today are to be courageous enough to go after big goals and big dreams and to have the guts to set a stake in the ground and decide what your legacy will be. If you go for it, be known for winning. Be excellent, be humble, and be consistent.

Heavenly Father, guide my hands, my mind, and my heart. Give me wisdom on when to take the shot and when to holster. Amen.

Among all these soldiers there were seven hundred select troops who were left-handed, each of whom could sling a stone at a hair and not miss.

JUDGES 20:16

August 21

Correct Your Mindset

We can learn from mistakes, failure, pain, and loss. We receive wisdom to prepare for these types of experiences, just as we learn to prepare for violent attacks. If we aren't careful, one mistake can turn into more if we let it get to us. It's best to not let these types of things get us down. For some, pride is an issue that keeps them from overcoming a simple mistake, but it should only strengthen their resolve to continue to improve, to press forward, and to strive to honor God in all they do. Quitting is not an option.

Having this type of mindset is necessary to be successful while serving. It would be foolish to step out on a patrol with a weak mindset, thinking no one wanted to bring you or your teammates harm. Evil exists. The enemy wants to destroy you and your family. You know your own weaknesses. With proper perspective, you can live in a place of love that is motivated by power and not fear. Let God take the things you see as mistakes and failures of the past and use them to propel you into your divine destiny.

Heavenly Father, give me eyes to see the threats of the enemy toward me, my family, my brothers and sisters, and those around me. Amen.

Even if you should suffer for what is right, you are blessed. "Do not fear their threats; do not be frightened."

1 PETER 3:14

August 22

A Sound Strategy

Everyone may not know your thoughts, but eventually, if you dwell on them long enough, they will lead to behavior and action. Then the public may know the circumstances of your behavior. According to the National Science Foundation, our brains produce over fifty thousand thoughts per day. That is, on average, around thirty-five thoughts per *minute,* and that is if we count the hours we sleep. Naturally, all our thoughts are not going to be positive, wholesome, or just.

We experience a renewing of our mind through reading, meditating on, and studying the Scriptures found in the Holy Bible. Watch your thoughts. Identify the negative and unhealthy thoughts, and begin to act to remove those from your thought patterns. The thoughts of a righteous person are just, but the thoughts of a wicked person are full of lies. What we think about will eventually become part of our discussion, and what we talk about will eventually become part of our behavior. What will you dwell on today?

Heavenly Father, please help me to keep watch over my thoughts and let them remain pure and holy. Give me strength to conquer my thoughts and let them be pleasing to you. Amen.

The plans of the righteous are just,
but the advice of the wicked is deceitful.
PROVERBS 12:5

August 23

Protect Your Focus

It wasn't too long ago that I was driving and began looking at something to the right, and without noticing, I gradually began to swerve toward the right shoulder of the roadway before I corrected my mistake. Many of us have found ourselves in this dangerous situation. Our destiny becomes the place where we keep our focus. If we focus on the wrong things, we will arrive at the wrong destination. Obviously, our intention while out on a patrol is always to have roaming eyes, but there are times when we must protect our eyes from threats, temptations, or other issues.

When Jesus instructed us to seek his kingdom first, there was a reason behind it, and it has nothing to do with performance-based love or legalism. He wanted us to know the way he *intended* life to be lived, not the way the enemy has perverted it. So where is your focus? If we are not intentional about what we focus on, then we will focus on the wrong things, leading us to make bad decisions and have negative outcomes. When we keep our eyes on Jesus, however, his undying love will affect us.

Heavenly Father, keep my eyes on you amidst all the distraction in this life. Help me keep my focus on you. Amen.

I keep my eyes always on the LORD.
With him at my right hand, I will not be shaken.

PSALM 16:8

August 24

Battle Ready

Warriors spend every moment preparing for battle. It isn't merely the skillset that makes a warrior; it's his or her response to evil. You might have heard the phrase "fight or flight," which explains our bodies' response to stress or perceived danger. It's a survival mechanism. Some of us choose to engage the evil while others flee.[5] According to Harvard Medical School, this same response can be triggered beyond the context of combat, such as a traffic jam, a deadline at work, or family stressors. We must prepare ourselves not only for the encounter with the enemy but also the response of our bodies.

The enemy never rests. He is always strategizing how he will kill, steal, and destroy. But we are not given a spirit of fear; we were created for such a time as this. When battle is at hand, we must be the terror that the enemy fears, which requires us to possess courage and self-control. Master yourself through surrender to God. Learn to lean on him and remember that he has given us power over fear, stress, and worry. If we're preoccupied with negative feelings, then our minds are divided, and our focus is diminished. Prepare to engage. Be the terror the enemy fears.

Heavenly Father, give me courage and self-control. Grant me power to conquer those who seek to destroy me and cause harm to those in my community. Amen.

Rulers hold no terror for those who do right, but for those who do wrong. Do you want to be free from fear of the one in authority? Then do what is right and you will be commended.

ROMANS 13:3

---

5 "Understanding the Stress Response." *Harvard Health Publishing,* Harvard Medical School, Mar. 2011, www.health.harvard.edu/staying-healthy/understanding-the-stress-response.

August 25

Set Apart for Purpose

While we live in this world, we do not have to become like this world. While the rest of the world is trying to handle problems on their own, we depend on the strength and power of Christ and his peace to sustain us. There is significant power when we receive this revelation—it means total healing for the individual. Jesus really does change everything.

The pattern of this world is simple: hate, evil, greed, and pretty much the opposite of everything the Word of God says is good. We must be conscious of our thoughts, be of sound mind, and meditate on the words and promises found in Scripture. When we do this, our lives will change, and we will be prepared to serve from the inside out. There is nothing in this world that the love of Jesus cannot change, and when we begin to think like him, we speak and live according to his will. Then we are fully empowered to be victorious.

Heavenly Father, thank you for this day, a day to surrender my will, my thoughts, and my ways to yours. Do not let me fall into the pattern of this world but let me honor you and please you in all I do. Amen.

*Do not conform to the pattern of this world,
but be transformed by the renewing of your mind.
Then you will be able to test and approve what God's will is—
his good, pleasing and perfect will.*

ROMANS 12:2

August 26

The *It* Factor

The process of becoming a proud member of the US military is not an easy task. If you don't know, only less than half of one percent of the US population serves in the military. After you volunteer, you must qualify by making it past the MEPS (Military Entrance Processing Station) process, then you have to make it past basic training and your specific job training, followed by getting accepted by your peers at your first unit. But there is something that seasoned service members look for in new boots beyond a person who knows the basics. They are looking for someone with something special about them: the *it* factor. Nobody can really put a finger on what *it* is, but it produces some of the finest warriors on the battlefield.

If we only focus on developing skills, knowledge, and fitness, then our careers will be lackluster. Our walk with Christ is the same way. If we think we can know the Word of God and do nothing with it and live without his power in our lives, then we will quickly become weary in battle. We possess the *it* factor only when we are in Christ, as he is the vine, and we are the branch. He is our true source, and he is available to you today.

> *Heavenly Father, may my life produce the fruits of your Spirit all the days of my life. Amen.*

Remain in me, and I will remain in you.
For a branch cannot produce fruit if it is severed from the vine,
and you cannot be fruitful unless you remain in me.

JOHN 15:4 NLT

August 27

The Unsullied Servant

Some have said that the three main things that can cost you your career in the military most quickly are relationships, finances, and substance abuse. When any of these three areas are issues outside of work, they cause problems at work. Most service members will never violate the UCMJ (Uniform Code of Military Justice), but many have been tested. The question is what happens when *you* are tested? It's more than a matter of self-will or self-control. It's also a matter of walking in integrity at all times, not only for your sake but also to honor God.

Sharp uniforms and boots, meticulously maintained gear and weapons, and impeccable grooming won't mean much if we aren't people of integrity. Temptation can come in many forms, and if we are not in constant pursuit of a relationship with Jesus, we can take a step down that infamous slippery slope. In fact, if we have the mindset of *I'd* never *do that*, then we inevitably become the next to do whatever *that* is. Be intentional about integrity. Be intentional about the decisions you make, even if you believe nobody's watching.

Heavenly Father, in my moments of weakness, give me strength. In my moments of temptation, give me a clear way out and the willpower to take that way. Help me to remain a person of integrity throughout my entire career. Amen.

Better is the poor who walks in his integrity than one who is perverse in his lips, and is a fool.

PROVERBS 19:1 NKJV

August 28

Primed for Success

Too often we overcomplicate the process of success. Asking God for success is usually the last thing we think about when facing a challenge. Instead, we may ask God to give us direction or to make life and decisions easier for us. Why not ask for total victory and a strategy for that victory? There will be many challenges in life and many obstacles to overcome, but today, don't pray *for* victory. Place your flag of victory in the ground, knowing you are already victorious before you face those challenges.

Here are a few thoughts to carry with you as you start or end your day. First, success comes with us choosing to acknowledge Christ as our only Rock, our only Refuge and Hope. Second, Psalm 118:25 says, "LORD, save us! LORD, grant us success!" There is significant power in unity. When we collectively gather to cry out for the power of God and for him to grant us success and victory, we can be sure he will hear our cry. Spend time dwelling on what it means to call on God individually and corporately, reflecting on the power found in both gatherings.

> *Heavenly Father, I thank you for hearing my cry for assistance, my call for victory, and I know you will grant me success in whatever I face for your glory. Amen.*

LORD, save us! LORD, grant us success!
PSALM 118:25

August 29

Reject Evil

Consider how you would respond if you saw your teammate engaging in a compromising situation. Suppose someone saw you in a position that might leave you accused of something you'd never do, and the circumstances made you seem guilty. Those who know you best might believe your innocence, but sometimes the accusation itself can damage your reputation. Avoiding the appearance of evil doesn't mean you live on eggshells, but it does mean that you use wisdom and the resources at your disposal. Find a way to protect yourself before you find yourself caught in a compromising situation.

You will have countless opportunities to engage in immoral and unethical behavior, and people will take your words and actions out of context to paint you as the villain. Avoid even the appearance of evil. Be intentional with your decisions and know that you are under the microscope 24/7. Today, be aware of your surroundings and the traps of the enemy. Rejecting every kind of evil means rejecting enticing opportunities.

Heavenly Father, give me eyes to see temptation and the traps of the enemy. Help me not be blindsided or have spiritual tunnel vision. Amen.

Reject every kind of evil.

1 THESSALONIANS 5:22

August 30

Duty Stations

At the end of the day, your number-one goal is to go home safe. Doing your job with excellence does not always mean everyone will be satisfied with your services. When you report for duty, go in with the goal to be the best in your unit. You are not in a competition to berate others but to sharpen each other to be excellent in all you do. Look out for your teammates and their well-being, both on and off duty. Hold each other accountable and make sure you are all using proper and safe tactics.

Encourage your teammates. Guard your heart against cynicism and unhealthy, negative emotions. Be cautious against substance abuse, and if you are married and have a family, do not neglect them for your coworkers. Both are important, but the family you have at home is your primary responsibility. Seek to be a blessing and strive to have a positive influence, regardless of what life throws at you. When you do these, when it's time to end your day or, one day, your service, you can say you fulfilled your duty to your country and to God and did it all in good conscience.

Heavenly Father, guide my steps today. Protect not only my physical body but also my emotions, my heart, and my mind. Give me success in all I do for you. Amen.

Paul looked straight at the Sanhedrin and said, "My brothers, I have fulfilled my duty to God in all good conscience to this day."

ACTS 23:1

August 31

After Action Review

Many units conduct AAR (After Action Reports) after a major event in combat. This process allows those involved to focus on immediate issues that they identify and addressed to be better prepared for future operations. A term that is becoming more common in readiness is *resiliency*. Understanding any potential mental, physical, or spiritual issues that may already be present or knowing how to respond to an issue in practical terms is crucial to the healing process.

As believers in Christ, our peace comes from a higher source. Furthermore, as service members, we know the burdens of life that often seem too heavy to bear. The promises of God's Word for the righteous, meaning those who are followers of Christ, mean he will sustain them, that no burden will cause them to be shaken from their faith as long as their faith is in God. No matter what you have faced or will face today, know that the burdens you take on can be cast on the Lord, and he will sustain you. You will not be shaken. Place your faith in him completely and watch your strength increase.

Heavenly Father, thank you for sustaining power, the unction to cast my cares on you when I want to carry them myself, and the firm foundation of faith in you so I will never be shaken. Amen.

Cast your cares on the LORD and he will sustain you;
he will never let the righteous be shaken.

PSALM 55:22

September 1

Imitation

Many us choose to serve because of the example of a service member we looked up to in our youth. The uniform, the confidence, the willingness to serve something bigger than themselves displayed something special, and we wanted to have it for ourselves as these heroes led the way for us. Following the steps of righteous leaders is something we should *all* do by imitating their faith, finding their godly habits, and mirroring what they do. We all have a tendency to imitate bad behavior as children; it's natural. But as adults, we should imitate greatness.

As believers in Jesus Christ, the highest prize is running the race and receiving our reward in eternity. But as we serve our heavenly Father, our nation, and our neighbors here on Earth, we should strive to imitate the greatest people to ever wear a uniform. Maybe they had some areas of weakness, or maybe they were great warriors whose family lives were in shambles. No human warrior is perfect. However, by focusing on their Christ-like qualities, you are on a journey to becoming a well-rounded warrior, prepared for victory and expecting nothing less than excellence.

> *Heavenly Father, I set my eyes on you. Give me good examples to follow but never let me forget the example set before me by your Son, Jesus. I want to imitate greatness, which begins by pursuing you. Amen.*

Remember your leaders, who spoke the word of God to you. Consider the outcome of their way of life and imitate their faith.

HEBREWS 13:7

September 2

A Clean Conscience

Going to sleep with a clean conscience has more value than any shameful deed to shortcut success or cut a corner on the job. Maybe you read that and think, *That sounds cheesy.* But the weight of guilt can bury you. If you allow it, guilt will take its toll on your mind, body, and soul. It all begins with one decision—a small, simple, innocent decision. Maybe the decision was to cheat for a promotion, which sounds really bad, but in the big scheme of things, it didn't seem all that bad at the time.

What's the value of a clean conscience? Does your past have some scars on it? That's a good sign you were living. If you made some bad decisions over the years, the good news is that there's still time to make things right, to clear your conscience, and to do the right thing. It's never too late to repent and turn your life around.

Heavenly Father, like many others, I have a scarred past. I ask you to forgive me, give me wisdom on how to move forward regarding my mistakes, and give me grace and mercy daily. Thank you for loving me and forgiving me. Help me live above reproach to bring glory to your name. Amen.

We reject all shameful deeds and underhanded methods.
We don't try to trick anyone or distort the word of God.
We tell the truth before God, and all who are honest know this.

2 CORINTHIANS 4:2 NLT

September 3

The Power of Words

It's easy to speak harshly off the cuff in a moment of anger or when emotions get the best of you. But we know this seldom leads to fruitful and positive outcomes. When you raised your right hand and took the oath of lifelong service, you also accepted the fact that you would seek to live a life above reproach and of utmost integrity. This applies to how you speak to others, family, friends, superiors, subordinates, and, yes, even adversaries. Think about the implications of your words as they can far outlive the moment of emotion-driven response.

This is why it is so important that we love God and others with a pure heart and exemplify gracious speech, even in the face of hatred. Not only will we experience resounding success throughout our lives, but we will also develop meaningful relationships with people and find favor in the eyes of our leaders. Today, if you are tempted to speak words that are less than gracious to another, take a moment and think about how that might affect your eternal investments.

Heavenly Father, my tongue is hard to tame. I am asking you to help me keep my mouth shut when I need to the most. When I speak, let my words be few and let them matter. Amen.

Whoever loves a pure heart and gracious speech will have the king as a friend.

PROVERBS 22:11 NLT

September 4

A Military Standard

Every profession has a professional industry standard for doing business. Like many other professions, the military also adheres to certain standards. SOPs (Standard Operating Procedures) set the guidelines by which you carry out your duties, perform on the battlefield, and even address administrative functions. Likewise, you can be sure your conscience is clear and clean when you operate according to the procedures of God's Word. Treat others fairly and equitably, be firm, and do not become discouraged in your service. Speak with concrete truthfulness and love those who serve with you.

The industry standard is not some fairy-dust love. Rather, it is a love that smells of gunpowder, sweat, and dusty gear. This industry standard doesn't look like the books tell you, and many of today's warriors may have fallen away from the tight-knit brotherhood of old, but that bond is still the standard. Jesus set the standard when he gave his life for us. The least we can do is hold each other accountable, strive to sharpen one another's skills, love our families, and serve our communities with nothing less than excellence.

Heavenly Father, thank you for the standard set before me today. Give me the spirit of excellence in all that I do and let all I pursue honor your name. Amen.

With Christ as my witness, I speak with utter truthfulness. My conscience and the Holy Spirit confirm it.

ROMANS 9:1 NLT

September 5

Lasting Integrity

The number of traps that can claim your career, good reputation, character, or even your family are astounding. Maybe I sound like a broken record, but it is necessary to remember that one bad decision can change your entire life. Consequences can last a lifetime. Whether that sounds fair or not, it is still true. My hope for you is that you will cling to righteousness and integrity and that you will always err on the side of being upright and flee from any potential immoral, unethical, or criminal decisions.

One decision can change the life of your family. Just one decision can change your career status. One decision can lead to a domino effect of terrible results that will take you to a place you never dreamed you could be—physically, emotionally, and mentally. Let others call you a holy roller or Bible thumper or boring. Let them call you whatever, but you must be the one left standing at the end of the day with your character, integrity, and reputation still intact. After all, we serve our nation as we are serving God, and we should do it in the spirit of excellence.

> *Heavenly Father, do not lead me into temptation but deliver me from evil. Protect me from the snares of the enemy. As I place my hope in you, may integrity and uprightness protect me. Amen.*

May integrity and uprightness protect me,
because my hope, LORD, is in you.
PSALM 25:21

September 6

Intangible Powers

We are trained and completely equipped to perform our duties specific to our military occupational specialty in about any situation that could present itself. We can experience the vilest evil this world has to offer, but we also see the fruits of our labor at times. The intangible powers we possess do not begin and end with our ROEs (Rules of Engagement). Rather, they begin with our character, integrity, and ability to persevere through adversity.

Each of you reading this has the same access to the Holy Spirit as revealed to us in the New Testament. Jesus said he was leaving us a Comforter who would empower us to face these times in which we live. You have access to the resources you need to be a successful service member, regardless of your capacity. You also have access to the resources needed to be successful as a follower of Jesus Christ. Tap into the intangibles today and experience a new level of strength like you have never experienced before.

Heavenly Father, I know the gift of your Holy Spirit is something I need, and I receive it through relationship with you, through accepting your Son, Jesus. Fill me now with your precious Holy Spirit and empower me to be victorious in life. Amen.

I know that you are pleased with me,
for my enemy does not triumph over me.
Because of my integrity you uphold me
and set me in your presence forever.

PSALM 41:11–12

September 7

Never Compromise

You may lack rank and position and have little authority, but with time in service and experience, the opportunity will present itself for you to climb the ranks. If, while you are laying the foundation for your career, you establish a pattern of compromise, what precedent does that set for you as a leader? The light will always reveal what happens in the dark. This means that what you do in private, whether good or bad, will be revealed to the world at some point. You cannot easily repair your integrity. Protect it and do not compromise.

Lying as a military service member can create a multitude of issues amongst your teammates and leadership. Your credibility may be ruined. No one will trust you. Never compromise your integrity for any reason, even if it means you are going to face uncomfortable confrontation. Deal with the issues that may compromise your integrity early on. If you have made some mistakes, confront them. Ask God for wisdom, read and discover what his Word says, and seek godly counsel. Today is a new day, brothers and sisters. Strive for excellence in all you do, for God's glory and to honor the shield.

Heavenly Father, let my words, my actions, and my thoughts bring you honor and glory today. Let my service be done in excellence and do not let me bring dishonor to my service, my nation, or to your great name. Amen.

The LORD detests lying lips,
but he delights in people who are trustworthy.
PROVERBS 12:22

September 8

Whom Do You Serve?

The challenges you face in today's society are numerous and are significantly different than they were two decades ago. Mainly because of the presence of social media, the availability of live streaming through smartphones, and the various social media platforms, any given situation can be blown out of proportion before those involved can give a valid response. While these challenges can cause you frustration and stress, it is important to remember a few key points.

First, you are serving the innocent, pursuing evil, and protecting those who are defenseless. They need you, and they depend on you. But most importantly, you are serving God. In everything you do, act as if your watch commander is God himself. You may have the best leadership in the country working in your command, but there will be things you disagree with at times. When you remember *whom* you serve and *why* you serve, discouraging times will tend to depart from you much more quickly. Set your sights on the things God has for you and pursue his path relentlessly.

Heavenly Father, remind me today, as I prepare for duty, that I am serving you, working for you, and serving as a warrior for my nation and to bring you glory. Amen.

Whatever you do, work at it with all your heart, as working for the Lord, not for human masters.

COLOSSIANS 3:23

September 9

Watch Your Feet

Times may come when you see evil people prospering while you seem to struggle to get by. You see bad people with enough money to pay off your mortgage while you work tirelessly to make each month's payment on time. Or maybe you know someone who cheats the system, cuts corners, and is a complete fraud who got that promotion over you. It may seem unfair, and it can be discouraging if you think about it from that perspective. But would you rather be known as corrupt and rich or be blameless and poor? These aren't necessarily your choices, but if it came down to it, which would you choose?

Be the person who sticks to your guns, never compromising character, integrity, or sacrificing reputation for a few bucks. Your future, at this moment, is unsullied, and all you have to do is the right thing and avoid any stupid decisions. Remembering the reasons why you began this journey is key to making the right decisions when in such positions. Don't give it all up in one moment of bad judgment or over a short temper. Your future is bright, and you can accomplish great things. Don't let the ways of the perverse corrupt your path.

Heavenly Father, thank you for making my path straight, providing me with light in a dark world, and equipping me to accomplish my purpose in life. Amen.

Better the poor whose walk is blameless than the rich whose ways are perverse.

PROVERBS 28:6

September 10

Truth Benders

There are not many things that hurt as deeply as someone we love and trust betraying us. Being a person of integrity, learning to forgive, and letting God be your vindicator will set you light-years ahead of many people you encounter. The past several days have dealt a lot with integrity, and it may seem a bit redundant or even elementary here. But this is the day you realize that your integrity is a weapon in your tool kit against those who would seek to bring you harm.

When you live in such a way that you can keep a clear conscience, are a person of integrity, and live and work with a spirit of excellence, you refuse to give the enemy a foothold in your life, and you refuse the enemy an opportunity to gain ammunition to use against you. While it may seem like it is basic or foolish to keep hounding on the importance of walking the line, it is for our own good and for God's glory and so that we do not dishonor the uniform we wear.

> *Heavenly Father, I submit to you my life, my plans, and my desires. Help me live in such a way that I keep a clear conscience, making good decisions and maintaining integrity and being upright before you. Amen.*

[Keep] a clear conscience, so that those who speak maliciously against your good behavior in Christ may be ashamed of their slander.

1 PETER 3:16

September 11

United We Stand

Americans will forever remember September 11, 2001. For a moment, our nation became one. People united across political, cultural, racial, and religious divides. We were truly the United States of America. But somewhere along the way, we faltered and forgot. Maybe apathy took over. I'm not sure if we just forgot how it felt that day, how our guts sank in our stomachs when we saw those planes fly into the Twin Towers, but if we are to survive as a nation, we must come back together again.

We've lost confidence in each other. Dare we ever lose confidence in the one who is to our left, our right, in front, or to our rear in battle. We're being brought to our knees by division, for the only way to destroy the heart of America is to rip her apart from the inside out. But there's hope. Can we keep our emotions in check in the face of total devastation? If total war breaks out, will we remain confident, not in our abilities but in God's sovereignty and power? Do not be shaken by the roars of the enemy. You are not alone in this battle.

Heavenly Father, thank you for unity, for victory, and for helping me to serve in a way that not only honors you but also honors the sacrifices made by so many who have given their lives. Amen.

Though an army besiege me,
my heart will not fear;
though war break out against me,
even then I will be confident.
Psalm 27:3

September 12

Seeds of Thought

Thoughts are an intricate part of the process of becoming who God created us to be. Pursuing a life of service and doing what is right does not begin with action. Rather, it begins with a thought. As you did not magically become a member of the world's greatest military in history without careful consideration, planned action, and countless sacrifices, so, too, is the process for making other life changes. Results do not appear out of thin air without first taking the time to think them through, planning a course of action, and weighing the consequences. We do not lose weight without putting in the work, and marriages do not improve without proper maintenance. But efforts begin somewhere deeper.

Our efforts originate with our beliefs and thoughts. What we dwell on will eventually affect our actions and habits. Poor choices are often the fruits of negative, impure, and unholy thoughts. Through a consistent habit of reading the Bible, prayer, and healthy relationships, we can begin to develop a pattern of thinking that will lead to a life of fruitful results that honor God.

Heavenly Father, thank you for the gift of my mind. Thank you that I have the capacity to think and choose. Help me renew my mind through studying your Word, seeking you, and pursuing healthy relationships. Help me to evict negative and unhealthy thoughts. Amen.

Brothers and sisters, whatever is true, whatever is noble, whatever is right, whatever is pure, whatever is lovely, whatever is admirable—if anything is excellent or praiseworthy—think about such things.

PHILIPPIANS 4:8

September 13

Pursue Justice

The qualities you possess are intangible, and many of them already existed before you took your oath to serve our nation. For some, the training requirements only sharpened those qualities, such as self-control, discipline, inner strength, and an even temper. In your career, one of the most influential resources you have access to is your words. The way you use your words begins with inner strength, self-control, and discipline.

From training to deployments or time in your favorite spot at home, your pursuits in life will require self-discipline and strength. This includes strength from your physical body and from within as well as strength from God and from his Word. Today is an opportunity for you to shift your focus to your inner strength, to be intentional with your words and actions, and to commit to a lifestyle that is self-controlled, upright, holy, and honoring to God.

Heavenly Father, thank you for the gifts you have placed inside me. Draw the best of those gifts out of me so I can serve you and your people with excellence and integrity. Amen.

He must be hospitable, one who loves what is good, who is self-controlled, upright, holy and disciplined.

TITUS 1:8

September 14

Maximum Sentence

It seems like a lot of people who violate the law do so because they lack a good conscience. God rooted a conscience deep in the souls of all people, but many of the issues we struggle with in our nation are a result of broken families, absent parents, and the lack of structure in the home. If we want to instill morals, we first have to impart the will for a person to do right and good from the earliest years. But affecting the will of another person is a perilous task.

Boundaries exist to protect the health and well-being of society. Those who violate the law face consequences, some harsher than others. Your mission is to stand guard, to hold the line against the parts of the world that are lawless and where evil is rampant. Your integrity matters well beyond here and now. Hold strong to your principles, walk in love, but give those who seek to do harm a reason to fear the consequences of their evil decisions.

Heavenly Father, equip me in mind, body, and spirit to serve my community, even those who despise what I stand for. Help my life remain unsullied so that I live above reproach, never bringing dishonor to the uniform, the flag, or, most importantly, to your name. Amen.

It is necessary to submit to the authorities,
not only because of possible punishment
but also as a matter of conscience.

ROMANS 13:5

September 15

Immovable Force

Your training and experience are two ways God keeps you safe while you're engaged in your duties. But even before that, you received the fundamental pieces of knowledge to earn your position and prepare for your specific job. Those experiences are rooted deep in your mind. But we lose our power and authority when we lack integrity and credibility, both of which we can find through following the principles in God's Word.

God's promises for you are many, and he never fails, even when those promises don't always come through like you expected. With a solid foundation in faith, family, training, and brotherhood, you will be an immovable force. Seek to be rooted in the Word of God through consistent study, prayer, and fellowship. Then he establishes our path and ordains our steps, directing us according to his will. There are times when it is tempting to go our own way and let God catch up, but we lose our security in him when we do so. Commit your ways, your words, and your actions to him, and he will secure your steps.

Heavenly Father, establish my feet in the ways of your Word. Let my walk be blameless before you because of your Son. Help me to become an immovable force as I remain in you and you in me. Amen.

The one whose walk is blameless,
who does what is righteous,
who speaks the truth from their heart…
Whoever does these things will never be shaken.

PSALM 15:2, 5

September 16

The Evidence of Success

Faith is believing without seeing, and for many, this is a tough concept. In fact, many warriors want proof before believing, but this is not faith. Jesus told us the kingdom of God is not the same as this world. The principles of God require us to have faith, and faith requires wisdom. The keys to well-being lie in the hands of wisdom. When we seek the wisdom found in God's Word, we find his favor and the foundation for a life of integrity. Any other foundation is short-lived and will lead to destruction and frustration.

In five, ten, or twenty years, when you look back at your life, you should see the evidence of success being the fruits of integrity, wisdom, and well-being. When others speak of you, they will speak of your good name, and you will have significant favor in the eyes of God and others. But this does not come without a cost. You must be willing to lay aside the temptation to analyze the nature of God or to seek the evidence of his existence, and simply believe in him. Pursue his wisdom. Above all the things in life that you will be tempted to pursue, pursue wisdom, and your life as a warrior on and off the battlefield will be abundantly fruitful.

Heavenly Father, thank you for the availability of your wisdom. Above all the things I could seek today, like riches and possessions, I ask for your wisdom, for in it are the keys to integrity and well-being. Amen.

*You will win favor and a good name
in the sight of God and man.*

PROVERBS 3:4

September 17

Not on My Watch

Anytime there is an ongoing military operation, the general public wants to know all the details, but it is not tactically sound to reveal the strategies in use. This is one of the perils of media coverage in combat operations. You don't want the enemy using our media outlets to gain a tactical advantage over those who are actively engaging in warfare. The motives of the enemy and those who would attempt to put a spin on military operations are seldom positive or pure.

But at the end of the day, the motive and goal of your service is love. It's love for your fellow warrior, for your family, for those you protect, and even those who hate you.

Whether you admit it or not, the root of all you do as a military warrior is in being a servant. Your heart is that of a servant who will stop at nothing less than holding the line of peace, order, and justice. The goal of your daily duties, at home or abroad, is to base the leadership and commands you issue on love for others. Serve with excellence, serve with pride, and operate from a place of love.

Heavenly Father, remind me in all circumstances, whether in peace or in battle, that the root of all decisions involving humanity is based in love. To restore order, peace, or in pursuit of justice, I do it all for you. Amen.

The goal of this command is love,
which comes from a pure heart
and a good conscience
and a sincere faith.

1 TIMOTHY 1:5

Act of Honor

Leadership begins with you and the way you respond to your supervisors. This is a call to honor those who are responsible for your actions, safety, and well-being. Great leaders take time to develop, and this development begins the day you take your oath and the first time you put on a uniform. It begins the first time you learn how to take an order and follow through with it, trusting the leadership and direction of your superiors.

This is not a call to bow to dictatorship or immoral behavior. Instead, it is a call to make the job of those who rank higher than you a joy and not a burden. If your superior's job was a burden because of your actions, what benefit would it be to you? Acts of honor mean you may not like the person behind the rank, but you respect the authority that person represents. Make your first duty an act of honor by showing confidence in your leaders today. In turn, you will honor God.

Heavenly Father, thank you for the gift of honor. Show me the power and purpose of honoring leaders and show me the reciprocating gift of honoring leaders on my path of development. Amen.

Have confidence in your leaders and submit to their authority, because they keep watch over you as those who must give an account. Do this so that their work will be a joy, not a burden, for that would be of no benefit to you.

HEBREWS 13:17

September 19

Integrity on Watch

We hear a lot of talk about "doing the right thing," but what exactly does that mean? Doing the right thing means our internal conscience and integrity guide our interactions with others, our submission to leadership and authority, and our compliance with the laws. From a young age, we are influenced by teachings of faith, our beliefs, training, and parenting, and each of these plays a role in how we view what "doing the right thing" looks like.

When we base our thoughts, decisions, and actions on the standard of God's Word, we are safely placing ourselves in a position to do the right thing according to his ways. As we live in obedience to God, we live in a place of integrity and character, bring honor to God and our leaders, and position ourselves for earthly and heavenly rewards. Keep your eyes on the right prize and do not be discouraged in times of difficulty. Do the right thing even when no one is looking, for this is the measure of your character and the standard of your integrity as a service member.

Heavenly Father, thank you for the standard of what is right and just. Guide my feet and my mind, helping me to make the right decisions in your sight and in fairness to your people. Amen.

To do what is right and just
is more acceptable to the LORD than sacrifice.

PROVERBS 21:3

September 20

Truth in Action

Perhaps you learned the hard way the old adage that if it isn't documented, then it didn't happen. As long as you can articulate why you took a certain course of action, you should be okay. The definition of righteousness is "acting in accord with divine or moral law, free from guilt or sin; morally right or justifiable; a righteous decision."[6] While you will slip up along the way, your integrity will guide you. Your righteousness will lead you. The temptations you face or the mistakes you have experienced will not destroy you.

Truth in action is your actions being guided by God's Word, his principles instilled in your life, and the fruits they bear as a result of your consistency in pursuing him. Truth in action is your perseverance through adversity and not allowing the first sign of trouble to sway you. Sin tarnishes each of our lives, but Jesus has made us clean and equipped for faithful service to his kingdom.

Heavenly Father, let your Word be my guide and let your laws be written upon my heart so that my sins will not be seen through your eyes but through the price that Jesus paid. Guide my steps and let the integrity I develop as I pursue you sustain me and guide me all my days. Amen.

The integrity of the upright guides them,
but the unfaithful are destroyed by their duplicity.

PROVERBS 11:3

---

6 "Righteous," *Merriam-Webster.com*, accessed October 25, 2017, https://www.merriam-webster.com/dictionary/righteous.

September 21

Serve the Helpless

It's no secret that being in the military is hard work—sometimes physically, sometimes mentally, and sometimes emotionally. And there are times when it is tough on us in all three aspects. Paul did not lead us to believe that serving others was a task to take lightly or one that would leave us with soft hands. It is tough work, and without the hearts to serve those who cannot help themselves, our world would be a darker place.

Our purpose goes beyond *just* hard work and serving others. Our purpose is to serve as a light to the rest of the world, that we can be both the line between total chaos, evil, and mayhem and a life of peace, order, and lawfulness, all while being people of integrity, love, and purpose. As Jesus told us, "It is more blessed to give than to receive," so we should strive to serve our nation and those around the world who need us with an eager and willing heart.

Heavenly Father, thank you for the call to serve my nation, and thank you for the ability to give. I ask for your favor and blessing on all I do as I pursue you, your purpose, and remain steadfast in integrity before you. Amen.

In everything I did, I showed you that by this kind of hard work we must help the weak, remembering the words the Lord Jesus himself said: "It is more blessed to give than to receive."

ACTS 20:35

September 22

Matters of the Heart

For some people, debating about senseless topics brings them pleasure and gratification. As followers of Christ, we are to avoid foolish debates and doing things that do not advance the purpose of God's kingdom.

There are things that we must decide on our own, whether they are good for us or bad for us. In Romans 14:14, the "unclean" thing referred to was food. We are not, as Christians, prohibited from eating food, but we are exhorted to eat using self-control. There are many issues that the Bible does not plainly list as sin but that are matters of the heart or matters of your own personal convictions. You must decide what those convictions are, based on what the Bible says and on the foundation of a relationship with Jesus Christ, so you can follow through with a clean conscience.

> *Heavenly Father, thank you for giving me personal convictions based on my relationship with you. Give me the strength to stand by those convictions in difficult and trying times. Amen.*

I am convinced, being fully persuaded in the Lord Jesus, that nothing is unclean in itself.
But if anyone regards something as unclean, then for that person it is unclean.

ROMANS 14:14

September 23

The Keys to Freedom

Through bad decisions or unfortunate events, some people may find themselves in the midst of total chaos, pain, or trouble, and as military service members, you may be tasked to restore the lives of these people to the order God originally intended. Like many of you, I have often found myself perplexed at some of the decisions people make. While at times they act under the influence of alcohol or drugs, during bad relationships, or under other circumstances, many people make dumb decisions all on their own. One of the root causes of the downward spiral of our nation's moral status is the lack of fear of God, the lack of a moral conscience, and a lack of integrity. That is where you come into the picture.

When we fear God, when we revere him as the self-existing, holy, true God, we then find the knowledge of God because we enter into fellowship with him. The true keys to freedom lie in having a reverent, holy fear of God, pursuing a relationship with him, and being filled with the knowledge of God—not just the knowledge but the understanding also. Take your keys and help someone else find freedom.

Heavenly Father, show me through your Word the benefits of reverently fearing you before I learn through life lessons so I may find favor in your eyes and the understanding and knowledge of who you are. Amen.

You will understand the fear of the LORD and find the knowledge of God.

PROVERBS 2:5

September 24

Lay It All on the Table

Imagine you are on a QRF (Quick Reaction Force) assigned to swoop in and save Jesus from the enemy. Only when you get there, he refuses the help. That's what John 2:24 sounds like. Jesus knew all the people around him and didn't want any of them to handle him. That may be off theologically, but the notion that he knows everything about us, including our thoughts, intentions, and motives, can be disconcerting. While our outward actions may look good and pure, what are our motives and intentions?

It's time we put all our hidden baggage at the feet of the One who has called us to give him our burdens. God already knows what we need and what we are battling, but he desires a relationship with us and wants us to come to him with thanksgiving. If you feel burdened, know there is someone who cares, who desires for you to bring your issues to him. He knows everything you are carrying, secretly or openly, and is willing to give you peace and strength for the journey.

Heavenly Father, I lay my burdens before you. I know you see and know all that is going on in my life, and you know my heart. I ask you to search me. As I draw near to you, draw near to me. Amen.

Jesus would not entrust himself to them,
for he knew all people.
He did not need any testimony about mankind,
for he knew what was in each person.

JOHN 2:24–25

September 25

The Weight of Serving

There may be times it seems your service is not effective in the big scheme of things. You may feel ineffective and irrelevant. But you are an element in the balance of all things. Your service, along the service of many others, past, present, and future, hold at bay the evil lurking in our world. It is imperative to remember your service to the nation and God is not individualistic. No, it's part of the balance of justice, that which must be measured. Be sure to measure up!

You are part of God's divine plan for the people in your nation. Your service, heart, and integrity are all pieces that God uses to reach the hearts and lives of people across our country. God is the one who bears the weight of justice and the balances of life, not you or me. Do not be discouraged if it seems like the scales are in favor of the evil or the corrupt because soon enough things will be brought to balance by the weight keeper.

Heavenly Father, you control it all. Sometimes I don't understand it, but I trust you nevertheless. Help me to serve as a good and righteous piece of your force for good and for justice. Amen.

Honest scales and balances belong to the LORD;
all the weights in the bag are of his making.

PROVERBS 16:11

September 26

Be Dependable

Sharing equipment and vehicles can be necessary during hi-tempo operations with limited resources. If you ever experienced alternating with a team who was sloppy, leaving trash in the vehicle, not cleaning and properly maintaining equipment, or not filling up the fuel tank, then you know the frustration of dealing with people who are not dependable. But even if they were not reliable when it came to keeping things clean or maintenance, you could always count on them to throw down if you needed them on the battlefield. It's the nature of dependability that we look at, not just the circumstances.

I'd rather have a teammate who was sloppy at times but was dependable to have my back and be the first to jump in a fight if I needed help. A dependable person is a true blessing, and he or she will receive rich blessings in life. If you want to find dependable friends or dependable teammates to back you up, then make sure that is what you exude toward others. Focus on who you want to be tomorrow, be dependable to those who need you, remain faithful to the Father and your community, and watch God honor your commitment.

Heavenly Father, thank you for your rich blessings in my life as I pursue you and as I am dependable to those whom I serve and serve with. Amen.

A faithful person will be richly blessed.

PROVERBS 28:20

September 27

Walk Humbly

Mature people of excellence do not walk around telling others how good they are. Their actions speak for themselves. Boasting about your own skills and accomplishments is one of the quickest ways to alienate yourself from others. If we feel the need to boast about our accomplishments, it is easy to stop the process when we remember our own success is nothing compared to the work Christ has done for us, and we can do nothing good apart from his power.

There is much required of us as service members, but at the end of the day, the essential requirements are that we act justly, love mercy, and walk humbly with God. Our commands and the nation have many expectations of us, but when we align ourselves with the expectations and standards of God's Word and walk in humility, we will find ourselves living in a place of favor and blessing with our colleagues. Strive to encourage those around you, build morale, and help those who serve with you and who may be facing difficult times.

Heavenly Father, in all I do today, with much power or little power, help me to do it in humility, knowing you hold the keys to heaven and earth, life and death, and power and success in your hands. Amen.

He has shown you, O mortal, what is good.
And what does the LORD require of you?
To act justly and to love mercy
and to walk humbly with your God.

MICAH 6:8

September 28

Willful Wrong

Blatantly committing wrong against your code of ethics is expo-nentially worse than an honest mistake, just as it is a sin to know that you should do good and not do it. In some cases, a per-son can knowingly and willfully harm someone by committing a malicious act. However, just as much harm can occur when people turn away from someone who needs help. If you know to do good, then why would you choose not to do it? The answer to this ques-tion is rooted in integrity.

You, as a person of integrity, will undoubtedly never turn your head to a crime or from person in need, and your heart for ser-vice will change the course of the lives of many people. Today, you know what you need to do. You are required to place yourself in the face of danger for those who cannot defend themselves—the innocent who have been preyed upon by the evil of this world. To them, you are an angel sent from heaven. Never turn a blind eye to an opportunity to change someone else's life. In so doing, there you will find significant blessings on the other side of the challenges that await.

Heavenly Father, show me what good I ought to do today and give me the mindfulness, strength, and courage of heart to do it. Amen.

If anyone, then, knows the good they ought to do and doesn't do it, it is sin for them.

JAMES 4:17

September 29

Person of Integrity

It is a certainty that what is done in darkness will eventually be revealed in light. Maybe not in this life but eventually, for all. This is where the dire need for true character and integrity among warriors lies. When you are in a place of adversity and no one is watching, how do you respond? That's what forms character. Integrity is the measure of our response in adversity, even when the outcome has no bearing on our well-being.

The way we respond to adversity will impact the situations we face. Let those who want to complain and fuss have their way, as long as we know we are doing right according to the law, according to the Constitution, and in the eyes of God. We have nothing to be worried about. Cover yourself and make sure you remain a person of integrity so that you have access to the power of integrity when you need it most.

Heavenly Father, thank you for the vindication that comes as I pursue relationship with you and as I remain a person of integrity in my career. Guide my steps and my actions. Amen.

Let the LORD judge the peoples.
Vindicate me, LORD, according to my righteousness,
according to my integrity, O Most High.

PSALM 7:8

September 30

Prepare for Victory

For nearly every situation you face, there is a plan or a strategy for victory. In fact, there are contingency plans and immediate action drills for every possible scenario you face on the battlefield, and much preparation is required on your part. You know it is unreasonable to expect success in any capacity without having clear direction, integrity, and character. But you also need significant planning and the ability to make split-second decisions. Your path to victory may seem like a tricky one, but it is not impossible.

The role of integrity in your daily duties is like the role of your heart in living—without it, you cannot thrive as a warrior. Your righteousness, your integrity, and your reputation may not be spotless. You may have baggage in your life or some skeletons in your closet. But when you turn your focus to pursuing Christ and accepting his sacrifice and payment for your sins, then he will make your path straight in all you do, giving you the direction for victory every day and on every tour of duty.

Heavenly Father, thank you for giving me total clarification and complete confidence in who you are and the direction you are taking me. I submit my life to your leading. Amen.

The righteousness of the blameless makes their paths straight, but the wicked are brought down by their own wickedness.

PROVERBS 11:5

October 1

Superior Strength

We always learn to feed our bodies with proper nutrition so we will have fuel for our day. Adequate exercise, nutrition, and sleep are all part of building and maintaining physical conditioning and strength. But we are mere mortals, believe it or not. These bodies will wear down and give out over time. Often, when we are tired, we depend on resources that are not beneficial for our health—energy drinks and sugary foods, not to mention the exorbitant amounts of caffeine we consume.

When we lean on bad habits, old thinking, and the easy way out, we make small daily decisions that lead to terrible long-term consequences. If you want to be a man or woman with superior strength, first acknowledge your own areas of weakness. Changing nutritional habits takes time, but making small daily lifestyle changes can lead to superior strength in the long term. Depending on the wisdom of God's Word and understanding that strength comes through him will empower each person to live at a higher level of physical energy, mental clarity, and more strength to perform your daily duties.

Heavenly Father, open my eyes to the bad habits that are weighing me down from achieving superior strength and teach me to depend on you. Amen.

I can do all this through him
who gives me strength.
PHILIPPIANS 4:13

October 2

Your Secret Weapon

Your mindset is the key to not only surviving the battlefield but also thriving in the military. Without a doubt, one of your weapons is courage. When deployed on a daily basis, military service members face threats of bodily harm and death and threats of the same for their teammates and local nationals. Maybe you aren't afraid of dying, but would you be afraid of a life-altering injury or maybe the death of your teammates? You will begin to experience mental and emotional fatigue if you remain in a hypervigilant state. Your secret weapon isn't on your kit, in your gear locker, or in your MRAP (Mine Resistant Ambush Protected vehicle). Your secret weapon lies in the courage, strength, and power received through the promises of God.

It is no secret, however, that you face potentially deadly situations every day your feet hit the floor. Being courageous doesn't mean you make unsafe or irrational decisions. It isn't an excuse to be reckless and act without caring for others. Having this strength and courage through a relationship with Jesus means you are an empowered, well-rounded warrior with an arsenal of secret weapons at your disposal. It begins and ends with a life in pursuit of God.

Heavenly Father, go before me in training and operations. You see all and know all, and I need your strength, your courage, and your wisdom to face the circumstances ahead of me. Grant me victory. Amen.

Be strong and courageous. Do not be afraid or terrified because of them, for the LORD your God goes with you; he will never leave you nor forsake you.

DEUTERONOMY 31:6

Mere Muscle

I s it enough to be the strongest in the unit? Contrary to what everyone may think, muscle isn't enough. By our own physical power, we will only be able to train to a certain max, fight to a certain limit, or run for a certain distance before fatigue sets in. Maybe you are in the best physical condition of anyone in your command, but at some point, you will give out in energy. That is why we rest, why we have teammates, and why we have backup.

For thousands of years, God has been providing people with supernatural strength to accomplish his divine purpose and will. Do not depend solely on your own strength to accomplish your mission today. We are all mortals, and we all have limits, both physically and mentally. But by the Spirit of God and his Word, we are unstoppable. Maybe we have limits and rules on this earth, but I assure you that we serve a limitless God. When he says he will strengthen you and help you, you can bank on it.

Heavenly Father, help me operate within my own personal strengths and limits. Give me wisdom to know when I need to ask for help. Amen.

Do not fear, for I am with you; do not be dismayed, for I am your God. I will strengthen you and help you; I will uphold you with my righteous right hand.

ISAIAH 41:10

The Power of Two

There are very few other professions in this world that ask people to go into the types of situations you may face during your service. You are required to be mentally sharp, physically fit, and emotionally sound, ready to respond in a breath to a threat to you, a team member, or a civilian in need. When you are operating in your duties, you rely on information passed along by others, sometimes another unit over a radio providing you with the most accurate information possible.

Knowing someone else is working with you to handle the situation should allow you to experience some degree of peace. Likewise, knowing God goes before you in all you do provides peace. The power of two is significant. Two warriors. Two units. Strength in numbers improves the likelihood of success. Having the peace of mind that you are never alone in your duties will empower you to a place of excellence in your duties. God goes before you, but you are still responsible to prepare for the battle.

Heavenly Father, thank you for the peace in knowing you care enough about me to go before me and protect me. Give me the insight and discernment today on every call. I am listening for you. Amen.

For the LORD your God is the one who goes with you to fight for you against your enemies to give you victory.

DEUTERONOMY 20:4

October 5

Grit of Grace

Some people work better under pressure while others work better when they have significant margins. When your tour of duty is suddenly extended or changed, it can either motivate you or demoralize you. If you want to stand out above the rest, find a way to keep a positive attitude regardless of your external circumstances, especially those you cannot control. If you are a believer in Jesus Christ and a keeper of his Word, then you know the strength you receive is not from yourself or the things going on around you. In fact, your strength comes from him alone.

When Jesus said, "My grace is all you need," he meant that in life, to get through difficult situations, all we need is the willingness to accept and receive his grace and allow it to work in our lives. Think about what that means for you today. Even if all you have is the grace of God, you've got more than a skeleton crew because you have access to the greatest source of power in creation.

Heavenly Father, I need your strength today. I need your grace and your power to cover my weaknesses. Thank you that your power is now free to work through me. Amen.

Each time he said, "My grace is all you need. My power works best in weakness." So now I am glad to boast about my weaknesses, so that the power of Christ can work through me.

2 CORINTHIANS 12:9 NLT

October 6

Share My Burdens

What a comforting thought it is to know that Jesus not only paid the price for our sins, but he also invites us to bring our burdens to him. A good teammate will jump a call for you so that you can take a break or handle other military matters. If you are facing an impossible task or maybe you are working on a project by yourself today, know there is someone who says, "Hey, let me grab that for you. Let me help you with that one."

In fact, maybe anxieties, thoughts, worries, or other issues no one else knows about burden you. Jesus knows. Right now, he is asking you if you will allow him to help you. Don't be a task hog! Learn to accept the assistance of others. Learn to accept the competent assistance of a holy God. Today, walk in the comfort of knowing that God cares about you. Go to work knowing he loves you, that he wants the best for you, and, even if your current circumstances don't reflect it, that he created you to live a victorious life. But we cannot do it alone. We must have the assistance of the teammate any of us could request—almighty God.

Heavenly Father, when I feel I am facing this world alone, remind me that you are ever present and right beside me. Amen.

Jesus said, "Come to me,
all of you who are weary and carry heavy burdens,
and I will give you rest."
MATTHEW 11:28 NLT

October 7

Reserve Power

You're trained to give one more ounce of effort, go one more mile, give more than anyone else, to impose your will against the enemy. It means you will be required to learn to tap into the reserve power you have physically, mentally, and spiritually. Our bodies are allotted so much strength, even through extensive training, and at some point, fatigue kicks in. But thanks to God for the beautiful gift of adrenaline and a second wind!

Just as each person has a given amount of strength, so each person has a measure of faith. Your faith grows based on how you use it. While faith is not expendable, our physical strength is. Our physical strength will grow weak, and as we age, we will naturally become weaker and more fragile. Understanding we are not equipped to fight alone and learning to battle within our own circle is critical to achieving victory and staying healthy. You may not be as young as you once were, which means you may have to depend on the assistance of others to get through difficult battles.

Heavenly Father, give me wisdom to know when I am operating outside my own limitations, both physically and mentally. Grant me strength to endure difficult situations and wisdom to know when to call for help. Amen.

The LORD is my strength and my defense;
he has become my salvation.

EXODUS 15:2

October 8

Heart of a Champion

You will encounter people who require accolades for their services for everything they do. Their motivation and intentions may be pure, but their desire for public recognition poisons the potential for any future return on their service. The honor of a champion servant is in the heart. One of the most effective maintenance tasks we can perform is asking God to search our hearts for impure motives and hidden sins and to make us clean in his sight. The heart of a champion is not self-seeking, but it is selfless in service.

The heart of a champion is relentlessly pursuing his or her Creator, seeking ways to serve that reflect the Father in a positive light. You are a representative of God's kingdom here on earth. Your life should reflect the heart of a champion, one who is strong and places your hope in God alone. In the midst of a world of selfishness and greed, be the one who shines through with the heart of a persistent, consistent, and relentless champion. Be a warrior of excellence, reflecting the Father to the world and bringing glory to his name.

Heavenly Father, if there is any part of me that is weary, weak, or ready to quit, give me strength and fresh life. Search my heart and reveal any impure motives or hidden sins and make me clean before you. Amen.

Be strong and take heart,
all you who hope in the LORD.

PSALM 31:24

October 9

Not by Might

There's a common phrase used when military members work in a policing capacity and arrest or capture a bad guy: "Stop resisting." It's a command we are trained to give, along with a catalog of other commands, procedures, and steps to stay safe and out of a JAG review. Our efforts alone may take us a long way in life because, after all, we were gifted by God. But when we try to resist his ultimate plan for our lives and do it all alone, we lose the power available to us through relationship with Christ.

Maybe today you hear the still, small voice of God whispering to you, "Stop resisting." His plans are better than yours. I've tested it out in my own life. When we try to live on self-sustaining power, our own efforts, and our own plans, we live in a place of constant struggle. Sounds familiar, right? The power of surrender is tremendous, and we cannot adequately define it here in this devotional. Surrender your plans, your abilities, and your dreams to the One to whom they belong. At the end of the day, you will be glad you did.

Heavenly Father, I surrender my talents to you. I give you all I have, all I am, and all I ever will be. I want you to be the Lord of my life and have total control. I submit to you. Amen.

Finally, my brethren, be strong in the Lord and in the power of His might.

EPHESIANS 6:10 NKJV

October 10

Facing Foreign Foes

If people tell you they have no fear in life, they are saying one of two things: one, they do not know themselves well enough to properly identify the emotion of fear, or two, they are lying. Our response to fear, not the presence of fear alone, can be a sign of weakness. God has given you the power to face any enemy that may present itself to you. But to be properly prepared to address fear, you must do a few things.

First, what channel does fear move through in your life? Does it move through the filter of anger, hate, or your own plans and ideas? Or do you move fear through the filter of God's Word? When we live our lives according to his Word and filter fear through what his authority states, there is no reason to fear, and there is nothing mere people can do to us. Because, after all, we are eternal beings living in temporary vessels. It's more about mindset than it is about equipment, so make sure you have a healthy thought process going into battle today.

Heavenly Father, knowing you are for me, want the best for me, and go before me in battle gives me peace and strength because I know that victory is mine. Grant me power to face and defeat fear in my life. Amen.

The LORD is for me, so I will have no fear.
What can mere people do to me?

PSALM 118:6 NLT

October 11

Focus on Fundamentals

It is easy to get so focused on the desire to become more skilled and proficient that we forget about keeping brushed up on the basics. There is no benefit to building a nice mansion on a faulty foundation. The basics provide the solid foundation we need. But they also need regular refreshing and inspection. In your pursuit of Christ, don't become so focused on what you can "get" from God that you forget about seeking a relationship with him.

One fundamental practice is continually searching God's Word for truths to apply in our lives. Even on days you don't feel like praying, whisper a prayer. On days you don't feel like reading the Bible, read just a verse. Keep your feet moving forward today while staying focused on the fundamentals of the faith. The temptation to slack off and quit will get stronger the longer you go without spending time in prayer and reading the Bible. And when you do avoid these practices, you will not be prepared to face the enemy on the day you encounter him. Be prepared always and don't neglect the fundamentals.

> *Heavenly Father, the basics of my salvation are faith and believing in you and the work you completed at the cross. Thank you, God, for your love and mercy. Keep my steps consistent and firm, my hands steady, and my eyes focused on you. Amen.*

Search for the LORD and for his strength;
continually seek him.

1 CHRONICLES 16:11 NLT

October 12

Repeat Offenders

Many businesses and professions depend on repeat business to grow, sustain, and even keep the doors open at times. The business of the military should not be one that desires bad guys to rise up but one that stands as a ready deterrent that prevents them from doing so. We don't want repeat customers to keep us "in business." In fact, maybe you have experienced frustration or even discouragement from seeing new conflicts flare up just as another ends or a new terrorist leader arising just after the old one was taken out. Jesus gave us a specific promise relating to this issue.

If the King of kings said in John 16:33, "Here on earth you will have many trials and sorrows" (NLT), what more could you expect? His follow-up to that dark reminder was, "But take heart, because I have overcome the world." Your repeat offenders may be causing you to experience some discouragement, or maybe you are carrying the weight of a crumbling marriage to work with you. Either way, your Father in heaven cares for you. His mercy is new every single day, and he isn't about to abandon you.

Heavenly Father, I want to thank you that, because you have overcome the world, I am empowered to overcome this world also. Thank you that I have peace in you regardless of the circumstances around me. Amen.

I have told you all this so that you may have peace in me.
Here on earth you will have many trials and sorrows.
But take heart, because I have overcome the world.

JOHN 16:33 NLT

October 13

Unrelenting Effort

Discouragement, frustration, family pressure, finances, health, and relationships are just a few areas that can destroy your attitude and destroy your military career if you let them. Your tireless efforts serving our nation do not go unnoticed. There are many people, regardless of what you may see on the news and hear about in the media, who support you, love you, and care for you. America is a grateful nation. In fact, more people support you than oppose you.

At times, it may seem like you are fighting a losing battle. It may seem like you are using a small needle to plug a hole in a dam, which will inevitably break while you stand on the other side. Do not lose faith and do not be discouraged in the good service you are doing today. Somewhere in the world there is a man, a woman, or a child who, because of you, will experience the best day of their life on what could have been their absolute worst day. Your harvest of blessings has not passed you by. God has not forgotten you. He knows your name and will reward you in a handsome manner if you will persevere.

Heavenly Father, give me strength that only comes from you to serve when it is difficult. Help my unbelief, my attitude, and my outlook. Amen.

Let's not get tired of doing what is good.
At just the right time we will reap
a harvest of blessing if we don't give up.
GALATIANS 6:9 NLT

October 14

Maintaining Resolve

Picture yourself standing on the unpaved street in the middle of two saloons. The only things moving other than your beating heart are the dry tumbleweeds blowing in the light breeze. The heat is radiating off the ground. Across the way stands another man, holding a gun, with a crazy look in his eyes. You know the look. You've seen the look before, maybe in thoughts or dreams, or maybe face-to-face. If all warriors allowed intimidation tactics to work, who would hold the peace? Who would respond to aid the innocent?

During your life, there may come a time when someone threatens you or your family. Maintaining poise and a sense of resolve in the face of individuals like this is critical to your victory. If you crumble under their intimidation, they win. However, if you remain firm and courageous, it is not only a slap in their face, but it is also a demonstration of faith in what God said he would do on your behalf.

Heavenly Father, instill in me courage, unseen to any other, and wisdom to know when it is time to move out of the way. Intervene on my behalf, protect me, guide me, and direct my steps. Amen.

Don't be intimidated in any way by your enemies. This will be a sign to them that they are going to be destroyed, but that you are going to be saved, even by God himself.

PHILIPPIANS 1:28 NLT

October 15

Strategy for Victory

Before you take over any operation, you are most likely briefed with a left seat, right seat turnover by whoever you are relieving. During the briefing, you receive important information regarding enemy threats and activity, outstanding operations to conduct, or other details that will be addressed during the tour. Most, if not all, of these will require additional planning and strategy before you engage. Seldom will there be a time when the strategy does not require you to lean on your teammates and for them to lean on you for support.

Our source of strength as individuals is limited, and our impact as one will be minimal. But as a team or unit, well trained, with a good plan, there's nothing that can stop you. Today, may you realize that the single greatest source of strength comes from a solid relationship in Jesus Christ. Humans may fail you, but God will not. God is faithful, and he never changes. He will guard you and prepare you on the day you encounter evil.

Heavenly Father, show me the power of unity. Reveal to me the secrets of my strength found in relationship with you and help me to be a godly leader in all I do. Amen.

The Lord is faithful;
he will strengthen you
and guard you from the evil one.
2 THESSALONIANS 3:3 NLT

October 16

Ultimate Backup

The day has come, and you have been consistently training in the gym and on the range, not only preparing your body but also your mind. Today could be the day you get the call that changes your life forever. What is the game changer that gets you through it? For you, it may be extra ammo or the extra training you invested in ground fighting or maybe the extra time spent running. But if you don't believe in yourself and have faith in all the training you invested in, what good is it?

The number-one resource you have at your disposal is faith. When the days get morbidly dark and all you can smell is the gunpowder leftover from your worst nightmare, God's peace will never leave your side. Your best backup officer cannot be with you around the clock. The good news is this: you have access to the peacemaker, anytime, anywhere, and under any circumstances. Faith in God is the game changer that will help you through your darkest hour.

Heavenly Father, there will be times when I won't feel your presence, but I know there will be times I need to absolutely know you are listening. Strengthen my heart so that, in my hour of need, the enemy will not be victorious. Amen.

The Lord stood with me and gave me strength so that I might preach the Good News in its entirety for all the Gentiles to hear. And he rescued me from certain death.

2 TIMOTHY 4:17 NLT

October 17

Beyond the Weight Room

If you could look back over your time of service, I am sure there are things you would do differently. Maybe you would have focused on better nutrition, getting more sleep, or spending more time with your family. Whatever the case, there may be something you would like to change. For some of you, many days you have time to train, either in the gym, at the trail, or on the range. While there is nothing wrong with training in the weight room or on the running trail, we should establish goals beyond the tangible.

One thing none of us would regret acquiring is common sense. Proverbs 8 is a unique chapter in the Bible where wisdom is "speaking" to the reader. In fact, wisdom says, in Proverbs 8:14, "Common sense and success belong to me" (NLT). Today, ask God for wisdom. Obtaining wisdom is a wonderful goal, but asking God for it is the way to obtain it because he will direct your steps. You will enjoy a substantial and fruitful career and life, seeing many rewards, if you live in the wisdom of God.

Heavenly Father, there are many things I need today.
Of all the things I need, I ask for your divine wisdom in
all I do. Amen.

Common sense and success belong to me.
Insight and strength are mine.
PROVERBS 8:14 NLT

October 18

In the Hot Zone

One of the most important lessons you will learn early in your career is the difference between cover and concealment. If you stand behind a pine tree, you will not find favorable results if you are the target of enemy gunfire. We sometimes believe that just because we don't see God, he doesn't see our actions or thoughts. Don't be fooled. He sees and knows all we do. It is a wonderful thing to serve a loving, merciful heavenly Father. The bullets may fly in life, but if you don't have adequate cover, you are in for some big trouble.

Nearly two thousand years ago, Jesus provided ultimate cover for the bullet of sin, that one thing that could bring us eternal death if we left this life without a relationship with Jesus. He didn't put a bandage over it. No, he provided total coverage. If you have ever been in a gunfight, then you know the comfort true cover brings. Your fortress stands ready for you today. He is ready to act on your behalf, but he desires one thing from you: relationship. Having God as your fortress when adversity comes will give you peace and remind you that he has your back.

Heavenly Father, thank you for the gift of salvation, the ultimate source of cover for me in the line of fire. Thank you for strength and protection. Amen.

You are my strength, I watch for you;
you, God, are my fortress.

PSALM 59:9

October 19

No Place for Cowards

Some people have said that a team is only as strong as its weakest member. When we refer to the weakest link in terms of skill set, physical strength, or ability to perform, most are on a high-performing scale. Even on these specialty teams, the "weakest" member is not weak in terms as most would define. What defines a weak person? Maybe you say *mindset*. Maybe you think of *skills* or *physical ability*. It is none of these. A coward is a weak person. It is these men and women who break down the power of a team to operate as one unit.

The courageous men and women who go into harm's way carrying out their duties to the United States are the strength of our nation. They are the true definition of strength and power, but we must each ensure those who are not as strong, whether physically or mentally, come up to par. We win battles before we even fight. Now is the time to win the battle. These times need courageous warriors, and there is no room for cowards. Be strong. Stand firm. Be on your guard.

Heavenly Father, my courage is a tool as a hammer is to a carpenter. Grant me the skills of a master tradesman in courage so that I may serve my community with excellence. Amen.

Be on your guard;
stand firm in the faith;
be courageous; be strong.
1 CORINTHIANS 16:13

October 20

Care Package

Few warriors on deployment will argue that receiving a care package from the States can change the entire outlook on the day. It doesn't matter if it's sent by family, friends, or the caring support of a local community. Local churches send cards from the congregation, snacks, and plenty of wet wipes. Some of the best care packages to receive are from schools with heartfelt reminders from kids of how much they appreciate your service and fighting for their freedom. Sacrifices made during the holidays never go unnoticed.

This is a great reminder of the powerful impact your selfless military service can have on others. We should strive to reflect God's kind, caring nature and care for those who serve our nation and those we protect around the world. Think of the impact your service has had on the lives of so many. Jesus performed many miracles during his time on earth, but compassion preceded them all. Be a man or woman of compassion today. Show someone that you care because it could make a difference in their life forever.

> *Heavenly Father, thank you for giving me a heart of compassion to care for those who are in need. Thank you for helping me to always maintain a heart tender toward you. Amen.*

The LORD is good, a refuge in times of trouble.
He cares for those who trust in him.

NAHUM 1:7

October 21

Finish Strong

At the start of your service, you were required to take a solemn oath to support and defend the Constitution of the United States against all enemies, foreign and domestic. Your oath would have been empty if you stopped at the point of the promise and never presented a fulfillment to the promise. We should rejoice in knowing that God did not stop at the point of the promise. Rather, he fulfilled the promise through his Son, Jesus. But he did not stop there. God has a good purpose for your life, and he will work in and through you to fulfill it, if you are willing and allow him to do so.

Our willingness to allow God to work in and through our lives often seems like a complicated process when it simply requires total surrender and submission to his plans. Don't stop with just a promise to allow God to do a work in you today and don't stop serving others because things may have gone bad in the past. Allow God's power to work in and through you today and watch his good purpose for your life come to fulfillment.

Heavenly Father, I surrender my heart and life to you, totally and completely. From my family to career, plans, and dreams, I give them all to you. Work in me to fulfill your good purpose for my life. Amen.

For it is God who works in you to will and to act in order to fulfill his good purpose.

PHILIPPIANS 2:13

October 22

Know Your Point Man

With a tap on the shoulder, he signaled to the point man that the team was ready to make entry. It was time to work. The point man is the first in the door, usually the first to encounter the attacks of the enemy. In the Old Testament, before battle, musicians were sent out first. The praise of God went before his people because they knew that their victory rested solely in the hands of God. You may be standing at the door of a dangerous situation today. Know there is real hope in God's Word just for you.

Psalm 28 is a prayer of David seeking deliverance from peril at the hands of malicious, evil, and seemingly God-defying powers. David, even in the midst of attacks and the onslaught of the enemy, declared the faithfulness of God. If we will declare God's faithfulness and protection, he will not fail us. There is a supernatural release when we declare his Word. Today, know your point man. You are not the first person in the door anymore. He goes before you in all you do.

Heavenly Father, thank you for being my shield and strength. I place my trust in you. My heart rejoices in you, and I praise you, for you are good. Amen.

The LORD is my strength and my shield;
my heart trusts in him, and he helps me.
My heart leaps for joy,
and with my song I praise him.

PSALM 28:7

October 23

Discernment on Duty

It is easy to cherry-pick verses to match our own desires. Many have done this, which has created division in the church. Luke 10:19 refers to the power of the enemy—the evil one, not the physical enemy. This can be reinforced with the fact that we battle not against flesh and blood but against principalities and powers, which is exactly what we are up against. Your enemy is not the person standing in front of you, cursing you or threatening you with harm. Your enemy is the one who roams this world, seeking someone to kill, steal from, or destroy. Know your enemy's strengths and weaknesses and all your enemy's habits.

Your enemy may look like a list of bad guys in your AO (Area of Operation), but those men and women are included in the whole package that Jesus paid for on Calvary. Like it or not, he paid the price for all who will accept and receive him. As a servant, it is our highest duty to represent well not only our unit and our nation but to also represent our God well. Be a good ambassador but be wise and know your enemy.

Heavenly Father, thank you for helping me identify the tactics of the enemy and giving discernment on duty. Amen.

I have given you authority to trample on snakes and scorpions and to overcome all the power of the enemy; nothing will harm you.

LUKE 10:19

October 24

Muscle Memory

Every time you train with your weapons or with your hands, you build muscle memory. The more you train, the more natural your skill, and the more proficient you become. There are times, however, when your hands may fail you. In a moment when your adrenaline is rushing through your body, your heart rate is skyrocketing, and there is imminent danger, you may do things without even thinking about them. But it may become difficult to perform at an optimum level if you have not prepared in training and with physical conditioning.

What a great comfort there is in knowing we are not the first to concern ourselves with our limited strength and power. Even the psalmist acknowledged this fact. Do not neglect your training and conditioning but also know there is One who will strengthen you when your body fails you. This is no excuse to neglect training. I am of the philosophy that if we, as mortal men and women, will do our best in training and conditioning, then when we need him, our eternal God will supplement our weaknesses with his strength and grant us victory.

Heavenly Father, I place my life in your hands.
Strengthen my heart and my hands and hold me
steady through every situation. Amen.

My flesh and my heart may fail,
but God is the strength of my heart
and my portion forever.

PSALM 73:26

October 25

No Place to Hide

At some point in life, most of us will be required to face our darkest fears. When David was on the back side of the battlefield, before he faced Goliath, he prepared. He may not have known who or what he was preparing for at the time, but he was preparing nonetheless.

There will come a time when the only ones on the battlefield are you, your "Goliath," and whatever (and whomever) you have by your side. There will be no cover, no place to run, and no place to hide. Maybe it isn't on the deployment. Maybe it is behind closed doors with someone other than your spouse or after you've had too much to drink and get behind the wheel. There will come a time when you must face your giants.

The Lord is eternal, and believers often refer to him as the Rock. While you will be face-to-face with your giant at some point, now is the time to prepare for that battle. Gather your stones, prepare your sling, and suit up with the armor of God. Strengthen your faith in God alone and know your trust in him is not, nor will it ever be, in vain.

Heavenly Father, grant me victory in every battle I face. Do not lead me into temptation today, but give me the strength, willpower, and wisdom to walk away from the lure of the evil one. Amen.

Trust in the LORD forever,
for the LORD, the LORD himself,
is the Rock eternal.

ISAIAH 26:4

October 26

Divine Strength

There may be times when you feel weighed down by the physical or emotional burdens you carry. In fact, fatigue in battle occurs often and is normal. When we experience fatigue, it is a sign our bodies need rest, and it is a reminder that we are human beings. But for those who serve, rest is often not a possibility due to assignments and duty requirements. It is during these times when we rely on the reserve power our bodies are equipped with: adrenaline. But when that runs out, it is important to know it is not the last resort, and we are not running on empty. Our strength to serve must come from a deeper well than our own physical strength.

When we read the Scripture found in Habakkuk, it would be easy to write it off as a fairy tale or even suggest that, while it may have been true then, God doesn't work like that anymore. But I promise you that there are people out there right now who have witnessed God's intervention on the streets. Lean on God for your strength. Listen to what his Word says and heed his guidance. If you do, he will cause you to excel in what you do, whether on deployment or at home.

Heavenly Father, thank you for preparing my heart for victory, for strengthening my feet, and for granting me favor in your eyes and in the eyes of others. Amen.

The Sovereign LORD is my strength;
he makes my feet like the feet of a deer,
He enables me to tread on the heights.

HABAKKUK 3:19

October 27

Dead or Alive

Listening to all the threats and propaganda made by foreign leaders or militant terror groups toward U.S. service members can cause a great deal of stress if you allow it. If David was in distress because people were threatening to stone him, it wouldn't be out of the realm of possibilities for us to feel stressed if people threaten to kill us because of the uniform we wear. It is human nature to respond to threats with fear or anger, but we must find strength to be courageous and overcome those fears.

You are empowered to face your fears by the strength given through the Holy Spirit. When we spend time in prayer, reading the Bible, and keeping our focus on God's promises, it positions us for victory instead of defeat. Do not be fooled, for the enemy wants you, your family, your peace, and your life. He wants you, either dead or alive. It's up to you whether you will bow down and let him take it all or if you will find strength in God, stand, and be victorious.

Heavenly Father, thank you for the work completed by your Son, Jesus, on the cross at Calvary. I ask for your strength to face the threats made against me today. Fill me with your Spirit so I can accomplish your will. Amen.

David was greatly distressed because the men were talking of stoning him; each one was bitter in spirit because of his sons and daughters. But David found strength in the LORD his God.

1 SAMUEL 30:6

October 28

Ask for Help

Psalm 39 is a unique chapter in which David found himself asking God to grant him mercy from his present suffering. Essentially, David hit a dead end. Nothing else was working, and for whatever reason, whether his perception or reality, he believed God was rebuking him for his sins through sickness. Psalm 39:7 is a perfect example of how David felt during his time of trouble: "Lord, what do I look for?" Maybe, like David, you've hit a dead end and things don't seem to be going so well for you anymore. Like David in this particular Psalm, when we don't know what to pray, simply asking for help is plenty.

Waiting on further instructions from God can cause languishing, but do not jump ahead and make your own way. It will not help you in any way to do this. If you find yourself at a dead end, waiting on God, take the time to be still and listen to what God is saying through his Word. Take the time to rest. Then once you have done all you were equipped to do, wait on God, for he will not fail you. Ask him for direction, and he will lead you.

Heavenly Father, I'm not sure where to go from here. Direct my steps. Guide my feet along the path and make my way sturdy and sure. I give my future to you. Amen.

Lord, what do I look for?
My hope is in you.
PSALM 39:7

October 29

Slow Is Smooth

In a culture where waiting is not acceptable, being wise, taking a little extra time along the way, and being sure of your next step can set you apart from the crowd. Waiting for God is not a pleasant experience if you are accustomed to moving at your own pace. But it is in the season of waiting that you gain strength, wisdom, and favor in God's sight. In fact, many times, we can avoid our heartaches and troubles if we would simply be still and wait on what God wants us to do next. He still leads, regardless of what society may say. He still speaks. Simply open his Word and listen.

Being strong in God may seem as far away from being a warrior as you can imagine, but your family will appreciate it. In fact, it is one of the defining factors in your becoming a warrior. To take heart means you are encouraged because of God's Word, his ways, and his promises. Wait on the Lord. Slow is smooth. As a professional military warrior, you know the importance of getting it right the first time. Take a little extra time, get it right, wait on God, listen to him, and, in the long run, you will be glad you did.

Heavenly Father, I submit to waiting on you. I will be encouraged by your promises, your Word, and the strength you provide. Amen.

Wait for the LORD;
be strong and take heart
and wait for the LORD.

PSALM 27:14

October 30

Overcoming Mistakes

There's a time in our lives when mistakes have few consequences. Think about toddlers. The decisions they make are often menial at best. Teenagers make decisions that can affect the rest of their lives. Your decisions can mean death or life. In training, often there is greater margin for mistakes. What do you do in training when you make a bad decision or if you jack something up? You learn from it and keep moving. There may be consequences, but they can help you improve.

When we make mistakes in training, they are easy to overcome, and there is little to be embarrassed about. When we make mistakes in public, however, it can be humiliating. Being held to a high standard of excellence can take its toll on you, but knowing you will inevitably make mistakes means you have the time to develop the character to accept responsibility for them and make things right. When you are weak, it is a prime moment for the strength of Jesus Christ to shine through. And if you trust in him, he will direct your steps, even through the messes.

Heavenly Father, even in my mistakes, may your name be glorified. Give me strength of character to own up to my mistakes, even when it is difficult to do. Amen.

I delight in weaknesses,
in insults, in hardships,
in persecutions, in difficulties.
For when I am weak, then I am strong.

2 CORINTHIANS 12:10

October 31

The Power of Mentoring

During the span of a generation, we can change our world. It takes one generation to change the world for the better, but unfortunately, it also takes one generation to destroy the world. When we take time to invest in the younger generations, the returns and rewards can last for generations to come. Do not underestimate the value of investing in young lives. Our strength is not limited to ourselves as individuals or even as a single unit. Instead, our strength spans an entire community. The true power of mentoring is relationship building, during which there are many obstacles to overcome when investing in the next generation.

Jesus was about building relationships, even when it meant reaching outside the comfort zones of his culture. Earning the trust of those coming behind you may seem like an overwhelming task, but it will help you throughout your life. You are where you are because someone invested in you, so take time to pay that forward to the next generation so they will be equipped and empowered to do the same.

Heavenly Father, our strength comes from you and you alone. Our influence lies in numbers, spanning across our agency and community. Show me the path and value of relationship building. Amen.

Through the praise of children and infants
you have established a stronghold against your enemies,
to silence the foe and the avenger.

PSALM 8:2

November 1

Training Time

There are many reasons why we should invest in keeping our bodies in excellent physical condition. The performance of our duties regardless of our occupational specialty requires a healthy and fit body. But what about the stress of the job? If we take great care of our bodies, we will respond better to stressful situations. We know the importance of taking care of our physical bodies, but how much more important is it to take care of our spiritual person?

Dear friends, make it a priority to take good care of your spiritual being, as it is much more valuable than taking care of your physical body. You should train your spirit by exercising faith, meditating on God's marvelous words, and serving him in love. Our bodies are temporary, and they are the only physical bodies you and I will have. Take good care of yours to be a good steward of the gift God has given you. Training goes beyond qualifying on the range or getting new certifications. Training our skills is great, and staying physically fit is good, but training our spiritual person is what matters most.

Heavenly Father, give me proper perspective on the importance of taking care of my mind, body, and spirit to honor you. Amen.

Physical training is good, but training for godliness is much better, promising benefits in this life and in the life to come.

1 TIMOTHY 4:8 NLT

November 2

Take Care of Yourself

I t is easy to develop negative and destructive habits to face the stress of our daily duties or deployments, from alcoholism, smoking, smokeless tobacco, overeating, not eating enough, and relationship problems...well, you get the drift. If you break the smokeless tobacco habit but replace it with drinking fifteen sodas a day, have you really made any improvements? Or if you quit the tobacco and sodas but worry all the time, where is the improvement?

At the end of the day, it is your choice to take good care of your body. Even if you are not a believer in God's Word, you should have a desire to maintain good health, not only for optimum performance on duty but also for better quality of life and longevity. I challenge you to look beyond the typical habits, look beyond the physical bad habits, and seek the deeper reason why they became habits to begin with. Take care of yourself, not only your physical body but your mental health and spiritual well-being too. As iron sharpens iron, challenge those around you to do the same.

Heavenly Father, guide my hands and feet. Reveal to me the unhealthy habits in my life and give me strength to change them. Help me make taking care of my body a priority. Amen.

Don't you realize that all of you together are the temple of God and that the Spirit of God lives in you?

1 CORINTHIANS 3:16 NLT

November 3

Body Blows

If you have never been in a fight, it is easy to talk about getting up after being hit in the mouth. In fact, it is easy to talk about anything, but actually doing it is another issue. This is one of the reasons why we train diligently, not only to learn the skills but also to become familiar with fighting. We want to know how to respond in an actual fight. Physical punishment can be discussed on a number of levels, whether it is the physical punishment we give our children as parents or the physical punishment our bodies endure in extreme weather conditions as we serve our communities. Or it could mean the physical punishment God sent in the Old Testament.

God doesn't send sickness, but we live in a fallen world. Thankfully, Jesus took the only physical punishment we ever have to pay. The punishment he bore for us paid the price for all our sins. Yes, your instructor or superiors may enforce physical training on you that may seem like punishment at times, but it is to prepare you to face evil in the streets. Body blows aren't always a bad thing. Prepare for battle!

Heavenly Father, thank you for strength to endure,
power to win, and wisdom to know when to retreat.
Amen.

Physical punishment cleanses away evil;
such discipline purifies the heart.
PROVERBS 20:30 NLT

November 4

Trembling Knees

You don't have to admit it, but there are times in your daily duties when fear could get the best of you. Fear can lead to a host of additional issues. The way I see it, we could allow fear to motivate us or debilitate us. Either way, it is our choice how we respond to it. If you have ever been in a situation when your knees shook, your hands trembled, your heart raced, and you felt like you were going to lose your last meal, then you know the importance of strengthened hands and knees.

If you are dealing with issues in your life today, know that while the fear may be present and real, it does not have control over you unless you give it control. Hebrews 12:1–11 begins with a discussion about spiritual discipline and the correlation between physical discipline and discipline from God. Therefore, the writer of Hebrews 12:12 was likely speaking to those whom God had disciplined. Walk in boldness today, even if your past, no matter how recent, was not pleasing to God. Today is a new day. Your future is going to be beautiful.

Heavenly Father, thank you for courage to face the vilest of enemies. Thank you in advance for victory in every battle. Amen.

*Take a new grip with your tired hands
and strengthen your weak knees.*

HEBREWS 12:12 NLT

November 5

Breaking Ties

Medical research has shown the correlation between negative emotions and physical sickness.[7] Maybe you have internalized anger or secret fears or unforgiveness stuffed away deep in your heart. Most of us relate healthy bodies to nutrition and exercise, but it goes deeper than those two categories. Sometimes we have to break ties with our past, whether it is failure to forgive ourselves of past mistakes or to forgive someone else for something he or she may have done to us. Maybe it is time to move on and let the past fade away into history. But if you are to be truly strong in spirit and in body, then you have to address these issues.

There are no easy answers in dealing with the negative emotions we harbor. It is possible, however, to be free from these emotions, which, in many cases, are the single barriers between where we are in life and where we desire to be. Negative emotions are faith inhibitors. I encourage you to strive for a 3 John 2 mentality. Begin breaking the ties between your soul and negative emotions, and the rest of your health and wellness will fall in line.

Heavenly Father, reveal to me any negative emotions I am harboring that you want me to surrender to you. I know you want the best for me. Amen.

Dear friend, I hope all is well with you and that you are as healthy in body as you are strong in spirit.

3 JOHN 2 NLT

---

7   "Anxiety and Physical Illness," *Harvard Health*, November 2008, accessed July 27, 2017, http://www.health.harvard.edu/staying-healthy/anxiety_and_physical_illness.

November 6

In It to Win It

There are similarities between the analogy of a single runner winning a prize in a race against a bunch of people and the "narrow is the way" statement in the New Testament. Many people want the prize at the end of the race, but only a few will achieve it. What are you doing to ensure your completion of the race? Thankfully, we have received everything we need to claim victory in this life. But just like a runner, we have to be mindful of a few things to give ourselves the best chance of success.

First, keep your heart guarded. There are many things vying for your passion but only One who is worthy. Second, be sure to stay in your lane. If you cross over into another lane, you will cause great distraction, pain, and setback for another participant. Finally, pace yourself. If you begin the race by exhausting your limits, then you may not have enough power to finish strong. The Lord calls us to be more than conquerors in this life. Help someone else find victory, and you will enjoy your victory much more.

Heavenly Father, keep watch over my heart and help me keep my heart guarded in this race. Help me to finish better than I started and to gain strength and not grow tired. Amen.

Don't you realize that in a race everyone runs, but only one person gets the prize? So run to win!

1 CORINTHIANS 9:24 NLT

November 7

For the Sake of Honor

There are times when it seems the work you do is endless and that holding the line is an overwhelming, unbearable task. At times, it may even seem like a useless effort. Brothers and sisters, this is a lie. The work you do is not only necessary, but it is also an act of honor to those brave souls who have paid the ultimate sacrifice. Those who gave their lives for others paved the way for you to serve with excellence. Do not allow discouragement to pin you down.

If for no other reason, serve for the sake of honor. Serve for the sake of those people who held the line before us and those who stand on it today as a bulkhead between good and evil. Let us strip off the weight of discouragement that slows us down. Let us remove the weight of worry and serve with vigor and excellence. We have waited for this day and have all prepared for this moment. For the sake of honor, we serve.

Heavenly Father, embed in my spirit the culture of honor and show me the significance of honoring leaders and those who have gone before me. Amen.

Since we are surrounded by such a huge crowd of witnesses to the life of faith, let us strip off every weight that slows us down, especially the sin that so easily trips us up. And let us run with endurance the race God has set before us.

HEBREWS 12:1 NLT

November 8

A Winning Battle Plan

What good are your tools and training if you have no strategy when you need to use them? Your purpose is specific: you are to uphold the Constitution and serve honorably. Being precise with your aim is critical, not only to stopping the threat but also for protecting life. So, warrior, what is your winning battle strategy? You cannot base it solely on physical weapons and strength. It must also rely on a relationship with God.

There are a few things to keep you on target when you are running the race or fighting the good fight. First, remember your goals. Knowing what you are pursuing is good when you are in the trenches. Second, remember your training. Having the knowledge and skills to get the job done is essential to your success. Last, have passion. Passion will be the thing that pushes you those last hundred yards after you have run six miles. Giving you the boost you need to get to victory, passion will take you farther than pursuit alone. Get the job done but have a plan, have the training, and never stop tweaking your skills.

> *Heavenly Father, I ask that you help me be prepared to hold the line between the evil that exists in this world and the innocent who do not know it exists. Give me the fire I need to get through the race and the grit to get through the fight with victory. Amen.*

I do not run like someone running aimlessly;
I do not fight like a boxer beating the air.

1 CORINTHIANS 9:26

November 9

Fit to Fight

Hopefully you never have, but if you have ever engaged in a fight for your life, you probably didn't stop and think about the training you received. It came to you naturally, much like second nature. It was because your instructors deposited into you the knowledge and skills for combat action through classroom instruction and practical exercise. Much like the way your training was deposited in you, so, too, faith is deposited in you through a relationship with Jesus Christ.

You are only fit to fight the good fight of faith through having first received the deposit of faith and keeping the faith and being a good steward of your gifts. You are not only commanded to keep and preserve the faith given to you, but you are also challenged to stretch your faith. Anyone can pick a fight and anyone can start a race, but only those who are equipped, prepared, and properly trained can finish well. That takes a stretch of faith.

Heavenly Father, thank you for the deposit of faith, for the gifts and power to accomplish the mission you have placed me here to do. Thank you for the victory. Amen.

I have fought the good fight,
I have finished the race,
I have kept the faith.

2 TIMOTHY 4:7

November 10

The Toll of Worry

Worry is something we may not think about as a major issue because it has often been with us so long that it is deeply embedded in our thought processes. But when you leave for your duty, you don't want to take pressure from your family life, finances, or other issues to work with you. Not only are you placing yourself at greater risk, but you are also placing those who depend on you at greater risk.

The toll of worry is significant. It is mental and physical, internal and external. It affects us as individuals and those we love, care about, and work with. The toll of worry can be life-changing because it divides our attention and focus. When we are holding the line, worry is not something we should have to deal with. Take inventory of the worries you are harboring. You don't have to discuss them with anyone if you don't want to, but talk to God about them. He's listening, and he's ready to give you peace. Tomorrow will come, but focus on the task at hand for today.

Heavenly Father, I confess my issue with worrying. You do not want me to worry but to have total confidence in you. Today, I place my situations, circumstances, and other worries in your hands. Help me to focus on the work at hand today. Amen.

Do not worry about tomorrow,
for tomorrow will worry about itself.
Each day has enough trouble of its own.
MATTHEW 6:34

November 11

Today Is Your Day

A special operations patrol of six men moved cautiously deep into a Taliban invested AO (Area of Operation) on a reconnaissance mission. The crack of the air and zipping sound of a 7.62 round from an AK-47 assault rifle broke the quiet of the early morning. The fight was on, and within seconds the team was under fire. A Taliban fighter stood from his cover to shoulder fire an RPG (Rocket Propelled Grenade). A 22-year-old sergeant stopped in his tracks, made an about face, stood without flinching in a steady offhand position in a hail of gunfire, and fired a single, deadly round at the enemy, hitting his mark and saving his team. The team went on to suffer zero casualties and killed over a hundred enemy fighters in a five-hour battle.

You might ask yourself, *Where do you find such people?* The answer is in the mirror. You are that warrior in some capacity or another, willing to do your job against all odds, steady in the face of imminent danger of the sake of others. Today is Veterans Day—your day—and we thank you for your service. Let's reflect and give thanks to the One who has sown a warrior spirit into our souls. The apostle Paul ended Romans 11 by letting us know that all things, seen and unseen, were made by, for, and through God.

Heavenly Father, thank you for being my source, my only portion, the only cup I need. Thank you, Father, for meeting all of my needs and putting a warrior spirit within me for today and for the battles ahead. Amen.

The Lord is my rock, my fortress and my deliverer;
my God is my rock, in whom I take refuge,
my shield and the horn of my salvation.

2 SAMUEL 22:2–3

November 12

A Healthy Mindset

Having the right mindset can mean the difference between coming home in one piece and not coming home at all. It is critical to have a healthy mindset, but it is also necessary to know what the root of a negative mindset is. Our natural desires to rebel against the nature of God govern the negative mindset. We can develop a healthy mindset only when we focus on the things God speaks to us through the Bible, through healthy eating and exercise, and through healthy relationships.

We give power to defeat instead of victory and life when we focus on the negative circumstances we see with our eyes. As believers, God calls us to walk by faith, which is a critical part of having a healthy mindset. Be challenged to check your mindset today. Are you focused on the wrong things? Are you dwelling on the past? Are you worried about the future? If you can answer yes to any of these questions, then take your problems to Jesus in prayer. Through studying the Bible and prayer, you can experience a new mindset today.

Heavenly Father, thank you for a clear mind, a mind focused on the tasks at hand, a mind that is governed by the Spirit and not the flesh. I submit my mind to your power and not my own. Amen.

The mind governed by the flesh is death,
but the mind governed by the Spirit is life and peace.

ROMANS 8:6

November 13

The Warrior Spirit

There's a lot of talk about decisions that affect morale by orders, policies, and leadership. We've all heard of the will of those who get burnt out and buy their time to EAS (End Active Service), usually because the spirit of their unit was negatively affected beyond a workable point. As warriors, we do not back down from a challenge, a threat, or a fight—our spirit is not timid or easily broken. The heart and soul of every man and woman in uniform is to serve, which means facing the fiercest of enemies at times. There is no place for a timid spirit in this profession.

We gain power over fear and timidity when we accept Jesus Christ into our lives and receive the Holy Spirit as the Spirit does not give us fear or timidity. He gives us power, love, and a sound mind or self-discipline. So while others struggle with the power to defeat negative thoughts, fear, worry, or lack of self-discipline, as a believer, you have the Spirit within you to face it all.

Heavenly Father, thank you for equipping me with your Spirit, a Spirit of victory, a Spirit to face and overcome adversity, a Spirit to face fear and hate, and to operate in love and self-discipline. Amen.

The Spirit God gave us does not make us timid, but gives us power, love and self-discipline.

2 TIMOTHY 1:7

November 14

The Cycle of Peace

No one likes being on fire watch or, even worse, barracks duty. These may seem like insignificant duties. but they are necessary for keeping the security and peace for those under your watchful eye. For most, knowing they can let their guard down because you are alert brings a tremendous amount of peace, especially if they need sleep so they can focus on their own duties to come. You give more peace than you realize, which is a result of perseverance through the resistance you face from those who are insubordinate to your authority.

When we offer security for our teammates, we give peace to them. Jesus gave us his peace, a peace that would give us power over fear. Today, you may encounter someone who has experienced a breach of peace in his or her life, and you may feel beckoned to restore that peace. As a servant, do your best to ease their troubles, calm their fears, and soothe their pains. But nothing compares to the peace that God gives. Walk in God-given peace today and become a vessel through which it flows to others. Become a healthy part of the cycle of peace.

> *Heavenly Father, thank you for using me to bring peace to your people. Thank you for strength to stand, courage to fight, and words to speak in difficult moments. Amen.*

Peace I leave with you; my peace I give you.
I do not give to you as the world gives.
Do not let your hearts be troubled and do not be afraid.

JOHN 14:27

November 15

Worrier or Warrior?

When you think of a service member who is fit for duty, you probably imagine a person who is strong, confident, stable, and consistent. It is difficult to balance being a worrier and a warrior. The truth is that most of the things we worry about will never occur. When we are anxious or worry about problems at work or at home, we often craft scenarios in our minds that cause terrible health issues and distract us from being effective in our duties.

So today, if you are guilty of worrying or being anxious, like most everyone else who has ever breathed air, then resolve to surrender those bad habits to your Master. We are bound by love to serve him, and it is because of that love he wants us to cast our anxieties and cares on him. Take regular inventory of your thoughts and check your "worrier/warrior" status often to make sure you are on the right side of the fence. Begin today and every day with the best preparation, which is a clear mind and a full heart. Resolve to give up the worry and anxiety today.

Heavenly Father, thank you that you care for me enough to take my worries, anxieties, and cares. I surrender them to you; I give them to you. I no longer want them in my life. Thank you for peace. Amen.

Cast all your anxiety on him because he cares for you.

1 PETER 5:7

November 16

The Thankful Servant

Perspective can change a lot. If we were thankful for all we had, would we have time to constantly desire more? If many of us took this approach, society would see a shift in the right direction. As it is now, however, many issues we deal with are because of selfishness, greed, ungratefulness, and hate. A thankful attitude shifts our minds off the negative and places our perspective on the good, on what we have, and on our accomplishments.

It is difficult to be a thankful service member who is fit for duty *and* a person who is battling discontentment or self-centered anxieties. In many cases, we have turned our focus inward and taken it off the mission, the people we serve, and those we serve with. Shifting our focus to a thankful lifestyle forces the removal of inward centeredness and replaces it with a healthy focus on God, others, and mission. Ask God to help you with shifting your focus and lifestyle to that of thankfulness and watch the useless worry and weighty anxiety begin to dissipate from your life.

Heavenly Father, you did not design me to carry anxiety or worry. I give it to you. Please give me a heart of thankfulness and show me the true gift and power of having a heart for thankfulness as a US service member. Amen.

Do not be anxious about anything,
but in every situation, by prayer and petition,
with thanksgiving, present your requests to God.
PHILIPPIANS 4:6

November 17

A God of Order and Peace

The scene of combat is usually chaotic. The first order of business is to eliminate the threat if it still exists, then to render aid to the victims, to gather info on those in battle with you, and to plan the next steps. When you step on the battlefield, the atmosphere immediately begins to change, and if the threat remains, notice is served that the violence is ending. Your function as a member of the US military not only brings order to chaotic situations, but it also brings peace in a moment of violence.

An evil world, full of violent, hate-filled humans determined to destroy innocent lives, calls for men and women who are driven by love and willing to meet the violent evil with superior, righteous violence. God is a God of order and peace. But sometimes, the achievement of peace comes through the victorious efforts of superior righteous men and women. Your words, demeanor, and calm presence are all measures God uses during moments when the enemy intends to destroy the lives of innocent people. Don't take the work you do for granted. Today, as you serve your nation, remember the God you serve is not a God of disorder but a God of peace, and you are his instrument to bring peace to his people.

Heavenly Father, thank you for giving me the skills and power to restore order and bring peace in this world. Direct my words and my steps; guide my hands as I serve you. Amen.

God is not a God of disorder but of peace—
as in all the congregations of the Lord's people.

1 CORINTHIANS 14:33

November 18

Never Out of the Fight

If you haven't yet, there may come a day when you physically engage someone who is stronger and meaner than you, someone who refuses to go down, someone who is determined to win at all cost. It doesn't take long to find yourself on the wrong side of the fight. If that day comes, remember your training and what you are fighting for. It may seem like hours waiting on backup in a one-minute, all-out fight for your life, but that minute could mean the difference between life and death.

Just because you are in distress and pressed down, your face against the dirt and the bad guy having a momentary edge, doesn't mean you are out of the fight. You are never out of the fight. There's another grunt left. There's another swing, another kick, another move. There's a warrior inside you waiting to rise at the right moment to get up off the ground. This is your moment to rise. Maybe you have faced spiritual oppression, but today is a new day. You are never out of the fight unless you quit, and that is not an option.

Heavenly Father, give me another flicker of fight. Give me one more arrow with more accuracy. Give me more wisdom and discernment than those who seek to destroy me. Give me strength to face whatever may come today. Amen.

The LORD works righteousness and justice for all the oppressed.

PSALM 103:6

November 19

Your Peacekeeper

There are many hours of ongoing training beyond basic training. We are required to stay fresh on TTPs (Tactics, Techniques, and Procedures), occupational skills, and PMEs (Professional Military Education). One area of training is in firearms. This training is unique in that, if we do not train often, our skills will deteriorate over time. Practice is required. If you go to the range today and try to talk on your phone, not only is the range master probably going to dropkick you, but you will also not be accurate if you fire a round. It is because your mind is not on the target.

When our minds are steadfast or when we lean on God with our whole being, we live in a place of peace. But Isaiah 26:3 doesn't stop with saying we will have "peace." He says we would have "perfect peace" if we keep our minds steadfast on God and trust in him. This means we are not trusting in our strength alone, worrying about our problems or the issues that may come tomorrow, but we lean on the promises of God. He will not fail. If he promises perfect peace, then he will give it, even in the face of adversity.

Heavenly Father, I choose to lean on you. I need you and cannot do life without you. I place my focus on knowing you, loving you, and demonstrating my trust in you. Amen.

You will keep in perfect peace those whose minds are steadfast, because they trust in you.

ISAIAH 26:3

I've Got Your Back

When you check into a new unit, the first thing you usually think about is who you will be working with. You want to meet your new teammates and be able to quickly say to one another, "I've got your back." We say it to reassure each other that we are not alone and that we are on the same team. There are times, however, when it may seem like no one else has our backs. Considering the number of dangers we face, it is good to know there are others who look out for our well-being. There's a reason you strap on body armor. But it's interesting to note that the armor of God doesn't mention a cover for our backs.

Thankfully, over two thousand years ago, Jesus provided the spiritual covering for our backs when he bore our sins on the cross. That was the ultimate "I've got your back." Jesus took "I've got your back" to the max. There's no greater love than the love he demonstrated for us, and it should be an example of how we protect each other on and off duty.

Heavenly Father, thank you for covering my areas of weakness that are exposed for the enemy. Thank you for protecting me and providing an example of covering others. Amen.

*"He himself bore our sins" in his body on the cross,
so that we might die to sins and live for righteousness;
"by his wounds you have been healed."*

1 PETER 2:24

Medicine for the Heart

If you ever deploy to a war zone or natural disaster site, it isn't hard for you to develop a cynical attitude because of what you witness. You see some of the most terrible sides of humanity, which can take a toll on anyone. You can let all the negative emotions layer up over the years before they fester into a mess and leave you wondering what happened, or you can make changes now. One of those changes occurs in your heart. Proverbs 17:22 refers to a "cheerful heart," but what makes a heart cheerful?

For one, it is good to pace yourself and realize that you cannot save the world in a day. Knowing your limits allows you clear borders to operate within. Learning to number your days is a tremendous way to gain a cheerful heart because you learn the perceived or real problems in life are not as bad as you originally thought, and you soon realize they have little to no eternal significance. When our center focus is Christ, we do not place our hope in this world or on anything in this world, which significantly changes the status of our heart and should encourage each believer in Jesus.

Heavenly Father, I thank you for giving me a cheerful heart! Even in turmoil, adversity, chaos, and pain, thank you that my heart is focused on you and not on this world. Amen.

A cheerful heart is good medicine,
but a crushed spirit dries up the bones.
PROVERBS 17:22

November 22

Fully Equipped, Completely Supplied

There's no such thing as having too much ammunition. There's also no such thing as having too many guns, but all those add weight to your load—and lots of it. It takes much more than guns and ammo to survive combat action. You have to have skills, tactics, wit, grit, a dependable team, and the support of a military force behind you. You are required to be fully equipped at all times and one hundred percent supplied with everything you need to get the job done.

In most units, obtaining supplies and equipment first requires making a request. In Philippians 4:19, Paul was speaking a blessing over a church that had recently given sacrificially to help meet an urgent need of his. His blessing was reflective of the nature of God, meaning that "according to the riches of his glory in Christ Jesus," God is the source of all we need, both tangible and intangible. If you doubt your skills, abilities, or knowledge or wonder if you're fully equipped for the mission, remember whom you serve. He will not fail you if you entrust your needs to him.

Heavenly Father, thank you for equipping me and supplying me with all the needs I had for the mission. Thank you for giving me all I need in life. Amen.

My God will meet all your needs according to the riches of his glory in Christ Jesus.

PHILIPPIANS 4:19

November 23

The Unwise Leader

It is possible for you to encounter some questionable leadership decisions over the span of your career. In fact, it may have already occurred. The challenge with gaining rank and experience is balancing confidence with wisdom and not crossing the border into arrogance and haughtiness. Those are dangerous places to live and walk in, and the results are rarely positive. When our perceptions of ourselves are unhealthy to any extreme, it alienates us from family, friends, and coworkers. And if we see ourselves as something we may truly not be, then we position ourselves for serious pain, disappointment, and potential disaster.

While the daunting task of submitting to poor leadership is less than appealing, as subordinates we are required and commanded to respect those in authority and to make their jobs easier. Today, take inventory of your own perception of yourself. If it is at any extreme and unhealthy, then realize the fear of God is the beginning of making the necessary changes. Don't get caught up in your own accomplishments to the point where you cannot effectively serve your nation.

Heavenly Father, I would be nothing without you. You have given me so many gifts, but I submit to you and ask you to help me avoid participating in or committing any evil acts and to fear you in a holy, reverent manner. Amen.

Do not be wise in your own eyes;
fear the Lord and shun evil.
PROVERBS 3:7

November 24

Call for Assistance

There's no question who the world calls on when they are in trouble—they call +1 (911) USA-HELP. Being fit for duty means we are fit not just physically but also mentally, emotionally, and in every way possible. So that leaves the question, who do we call on when we are in trouble? Like Jeremiah 17:14, calling on God through prayer is our plea for help. We can call on him, and he will hear us. When others call on us for help, they have confidence that we will respond, stand up for what is right, and do our best to make things right.

You can call on God today knowing he will hear you, respond, and solve the matter. My challenge to you today is this: be open to the *way* he solves the matter. Often, we have an idea in our mind of how we believe God should handle a situation, but his plans are better than ours, and as difficult as that is to understand, we must trust his plan. If you call on God for assistance, then he will come, and he will not fail you.

> *Heavenly Father, thank you for being a call, a breath, a whisper away from responding to me. You live in my heart, you are always with me, and you eagerly await my requests for assistance. Thank you for coming to my assistance. Amen.*

Heal me, LORD, and I will be healed;
save me and I will be saved,
for you are the one I praise.
JEREMIAH 17:14

November 25

Give Me the Truth

If you want to grow in your faith, it is necessary to have someone with whom you can walk the journey, thus the need for the body of Christ to function as a healthy unit in this world. You have to be honest with yourself before you can be honest with a brother or sister in Christ. In war, you seldom walk alone. You go to work with a team. You develop strong bonds with warriors with whom you serve, and these bonds last a long time. How much more do we need Christ-like relationships with brothers and sisters of like-faith?

Our confession of sin before God leads to abundant life, but only when we allow his word to change our hearts, minds, and lives. When we reject Jesus, we reject the power of confession, healing, and the effectiveness of prayer. Today, spend a few moments asking God to reveal any suppressed sin in your life and ask him for wisdom regarding this issue. If you have an accountability partner at church or in a small group, talk with him or her about it. You will be glad you did when you experience a new level of power and effectiveness in prayer.

Heavenly Father, thank you for a clean conscience, for power to overcome sin, and for courage to confess when I do sin. Thank you for healing and restoration in my life. Amen.

Confess your sins to each other and pray for each other so that you may be healed. The prayer of a righteous person is powerful and effective.

JAMES 5:16

November 26

Your Fine Has Been Paid

A wealthy man made his way to the municipal court late one afternoon with a pocket full of money. He walked into the magistrate's office and said, "Good afternoon, I needed to see if I could pay a few fines off please." The magistrate looked up his records only to find he had no fines: "Sir," he said, "you do not owe any outstanding fines." The generous man went on to pay off the fines for minor traffic violations for several random people. Can you imagine how those people reacted when they came to pay their citations and found out someone had paid their fines?

We were born into a sinful nature that was doomed from the start. But because God loved us so much, he sent his Son to live and die for each of us, and he paid our price for all our sins forevermore. If we reject the belief and refuse to accept his gift, then we cause double the trouble for ourselves. The peace we have now and for all eternity is because someone else paid our price, and that someone else is Jesus Christ. Your fines have been paid.

Heavenly Father, thank you for loving me so much that you sent your only Son to die for my sins. I love you, I receive and accept the gift of salvation, and I ask you to reign in my life. Amen.

He was pierced for our transgressions,
he was crushed for our iniquities;
the punishment that brought us peace was on him.

ISAIAH 53:5

November 27

Unbroken

A military career can span two decades or more, and with that comes a lot of suppressed memories, some of which are good and some are nightmares. There are certain experiences that will break the heart and soul of any man or woman in uniform, no matter how tough he or she is on the outside. The longer we let these pains go unaddressed, the worse they will be when we finally face them. But there is a better way. Science has shown the power of faith and its integral role in dealing with trauma in our lives.

Psalm 147:3 is one example of how God heals our physical wounds and pains and our emotional and mental pains. When we allow healing through seeking assistance, reading his Word, prayer, and healthy fellowship, God will take those broken memories, those broken emotions, and bring healing to us. As warriors, it would be foolish to assume we never encounter violence or have negative emotions and thoughts along the journey in serving our nation. Today, surrender those vulnerabilities to your Creator. He wants to bind up your wounds and heal your broken heart.

Heavenly Father, thank you for the promise of healing. I surrender the negative painful memories I may be harboring from my past and give them to you. I now ask for total healing and peace and discernment and wisdom on how to move forward. Amen.

He heals the brokenhearted
and binds up their wounds.

PSALM 147:3

November 28

In Good Hands

Some people say God doesn't have favorites, but I tend to disagree. If there are two people in a room with God (figuratively speaking, of course) and one of them uses his or her gifts to serve while the other sits and complains about everything, never contributing with his or her gifts, which one do you think God will honor? When we live in alignment with God's Word, our lives are covered with his favor and blessing. That is not to suggest there will never be times of adversity, but we will experience a level of living like no other can offer.

When we live in "God's hand," when we live according to his ways and principles, we are under his umbrella of protection and blessing. We continue to live in a fallen world, but we are in good hands with God. He will take what used to bring us down and use it to propel us to blessing, victory, and abundant life. Military life is not always easy, but with faith in God, we can be victorious in anything we pursue.

> *Heavenly Father, thank you for holding me in your hands, right where I need to be, safe from the dangers of the enemy. Direct my steps today and every day. Amen.*

I put to death and I bring to life,
I have wounded and I will heal,
and no one can deliver out of my hand.

DEUTERONOMY 32:39

November 29

Help Is on the Way

For a QRF (Quick Response Force), response time is measured in minutes and seconds, which can mean the difference between life and death for fellow service members. Time is how we measure our lives, our progress, and many other things along our journeys. However, God's watch measures it significantly differently. When we are in a place of need, we often expect a response immediately. When we base our faith on the speed of God's response to our needs, we are foolishly using two separate standards of measurement. God's time is not our time and will often not align with our clocks.

When we call on God for help, he will come. He will address our needs according to his Word, and he will not fail us. However, when we place worry and anxiety ahead of our faith in what his Word says he will do for us, and when we allow God's timing to discourage us, we can further delay the victory he has prepared for our lives. Know that, if you are in need, help is on the way the moment you call for it. It will arrive, not a moment too late.

> *Heavenly Father, thank you for confidence in your timing. Thank you for a heart that leans on your clock and your timing and has total faith that you will come to my aid. Amen.*

*LORD my God, I called to you for help,
and you healed me.*

PSALM 30:2

November 30

Keys to the City

There are no magic formulas for eradicating evil from this world. It can come only through good people willing to stand in the face of it and strike it down. If every leader were to seek the will of God, what would our country look like? It wouldn't take long before we experienced a nationwide movement of healing. If we are going to be completely fit for duty as believers in Jesus Christ, we need to have our hearts aligned with the mission of God.

We've received access to the heart of God through Jesus Christ. He desires for this nation and our world to experience healing from ravaged, evil rampages and to be restored to a time of peace and order. Believe it or not, he is using you to accomplish his mission today. Don't take your eyes off the prize and don't be discouraged. Instead, call on God, humble yourself, and pray, and he will come to your aid. Give God the keys to your city.

Heavenly Father, thank you for giving me a right heart to pursue you, to turn from my sin, to humble myself before you, and to call out to you. I know you will hear me, forgive me, and heal my nation and this world. Amen.

If my people, who are called by my name, will humble themselves and pray and seek my face and turn from their wicked ways, then I will hear from heaven, and I will forgive their sin and will heal their land.

2 CHRONICLES 7:14

December 1

Called for Redemption

We often hear of adolescents who grow up without a father. As well, a father may be physically present but not interested in the details of the child's life. Studies have shown that father-less children face a higher risk of alcohol abuse, drug abuse, sexual abuse, and other issues.[8] When children grow up in father-absent homes, other men must step up to the plate. We often view God as a heavy-handed authoritarian waiting for us to mess up so he can destroy us. But he is a loving, kind, and merciful Father.

As the father of the prodigal son welcomed him home with a great feast, so God is prepared and ready to accept anyone who will seek him. Maybe you have saved the life of another during your service. Your day began like any other, and then the opportunity arose. You weren't seeking it, but you were on the lookout and prepared to respond. So God is proactive in his approach. He is searching. When you join the family of God, much like the military family, you come under an umbrella of protection and provision.

Heavenly Father, I ask you to reveal your unfailing love to me in a way I have never experienced. Allow me to radiate that love to others so they may see you through my life. Amen.

Do not fear, for I have redeemed you;
I have summoned you by name; you are mine.
ISAIAH 43:1

---

8 "The Father Absence Crisis in American [Infographic]," National Fatherhood Initiative, December 12, 2013, http://www.fatherhood.org/the-father-absence-crisis-in-america, accessed December 1, 2017.

December 2

Love Exemplified

When we try to determine someone's worthiness of love based on actions, it becomes a game of performance whereby we keep tally of wrongs and rights. Love isn't measured by wrongs and rights. Rather, those who truly love do so regardless of whether love is ever reciprocated. The single greatest example of love demonstrated in history is the birth, life, death, and resurrection of Jesus Christ. While we were undeserving and still sinners and did not love him, he came to give his life for each of us.

Each day we live and serve is a day where we can exude the same love Jesus has for us because, as believers in his Word, we have his love in our hearts. From our daily duties to parenting and everything in between, there are numerous opportunities to show our love today and every day, even to people we may deem undeserving. Through these opportunities, we can demonstrate the true love of Christ to a hurting world through our words, actions, and service, all of which we do in love.

Heavenly Father, thank you for demonstrating how you want me to love and for giving me a heart to love and serve others. Amen.

God demonstrates his own love for us in this: While we were still sinners, Christ died for us.

ROMANS 5:8

December 3

In Spite of Terror

The number one goal of most of America's enemies, both domestic and abroad, is to create fear in the hearts and lives of the American people. These evil monsters not only wish to physically harm and murder innocent human beings, but they also want those who survive to live in fear every day. When you prepare for duty, preparing your heart and mind for the day to come, you prepare to confront the darkest fears of humanity.

Your service is not in vain. Stopping the attacks of mad people, regardless of their method of attack, means you save countless lives. Serving as a warrior *in spite of fear* means you provide your nation with the hope of peace. When the opportunity arises and justice is issued to those who destroy the lives of innocent people, you are part of restoring joy to many righteous and good citizens and ruining the lives of those who seek to harm others.

Heavenly Father, thank you for courage to stand and face the darkest terror, the darkest fear, and the vilest of enemies and for granting me victory over them. Amen.

When justice is done,
it brings joy to the righteous
but terror to evildoers.

PROVERBS 21:15

December 4

Security Clearance Required

Is Jesus the only way to heaven? This is a question that has been debated and argued for thousands of years. In a time when exercising our rights and freedoms is justification for committing every sin under the sun, we should strive to hold true to the roots of our faith and God's Word. There is power in the Word when we read, understand, and apply it to our lives. This doesn't mean our lives will always be easy or everything will always go our way, and it doesn't mean we have to like everything we endure.

What it means is that we submit to the lordship of Jesus Christ, to his leading and promises, and when we do, we abide in his abundant life. As warriors know their chain of command, having access to God the Father through Jesus means accepting his sacrifice, believing in him, and developing a lifelong relationship with him. This is one of the most profound, life-changing, and empowering decisions anyone can ever make.

Heavenly Father, thank you that I have access to you through your Son, Jesus, who lives in my heart as my Lord and my Savior. Reveal to me your nature, as my Father, as God, as my commander and leader. Amen.

Jesus answered, "I am the way and the truth and the life. No one comes to the Father except through me."

JOHN 14:6

December 5

The Empowered Warrior

Day one, you raised your right hand, took an oath to serve, and became part of the world's largest fighting force, the United States armed forces. But that event, albeit a grand one, did not equip you or empower you to serve. It was only through your training that you were equipped for battle and only through great leadership that you were empowered to serve. We can celebrate the moment we receive the authority to join, but it's truly the moment you are empowered as warriors that warrants celebration. For every warrior must be empowered with the proper training, mind-set, and physical skill set before combat ensues.

Without proper authority, no service member would be any different than the average person responding to combat. But because of the training, authority, and lawful power afforded to each of them by the Constitution of the United States, they become empowered warriors. When we have the power, we can overcome any challenge. I challenge you to seek the infilling of the precious Holy Spirit today. You will be better equipped to face the challenges of this world with him.

Heavenly Father, I ask you to fill me with your Holy Spirit. Direct my steps, order my path, and empower me for victorious living. Amen.

You will receive power when the Holy Spirit comes on you; and you will be my witnesses in Jerusalem, and in all Judea and Samaria, and to the ends of the earth.

ACTS 1:8

First Is Last, Last Is First

Most young military warriors are ambitious and have a strong desire to achieve promotions and jump on every school and operation available. Others are perfectly content with just serving and doing their job well. There is nothing wrong with either ambition. However, the person who seeks the seat of leadership is not always the best candidate for the job. In some cases, the best candidate for the job does the everyday, mundane, simple tasks seemingly below his or her pay grade.

The misconception that "we arrive" when we achieve some specific rank or position is misleading at best. To be a true leader, regardless of the division you serve in, you must seek to serve. This is the most accurate and telling sign of a true leader, even if he or she is not yet fully qualified to do so. Be an excellent servant and you will reap the rewards beyond anything you could imagine.

Heavenly Father, please keep my eyes attentive to opportunities to serve your people today and to lead our teams by example through following you. Amen.

Seek first his kingdom and his righteousness, and all these things will be given to you as well.
MATTHEW 6:33

December 7

Seek Godly Counsel

Joint operations between commands, services, and nations are often critical to the success of many missions where a multitude of resources and capabilities are required. For example, in a major combat engagement stretching over a region of the battlefield, you will likely see numerous different entities work together in a coordinated operation to defeat the enemy. What separates the great from the average? Leadership. Unity. Godly counsel.

What foolishness it is to run headfirst into conflict without training or strategy, and it is incredibly dangerous to do so without godly counsel. The war between evil and good is not something individuals can accomplish on their own merit, only as a team. Think back over your life to the times when you faced great conflict and how you often overcame it. Maybe your godly counsel is your chain of command or a chaplain, pastor, friend, or spouse. Create a strategy now, in times of peace, to address conflict when it comes. Because it will come. With good counsel and planning, we can accomplish anything. It is our prayer for you that you would take time to seek good, godly counsel in your next crisis instead of reacting based on emotion.

Heavenly Father, I ask you to give me wisdom and discernment and the common sense to know when to seek good help. Amen.

Plans fail for lack of counsel,
but with many advisers they succeed.
PROVERBS 15:22

December 8

Stolen Valor

We've all seen stories of people who dress in military attire and claim certain achievements and awards when, in fact, they never served or never earned the awards they claim to have received. Who are we to pretend we are the reason for our own successes? Who are we to pretend we are the sole reason for our own salvation, breakthrough, or miracle? We could not save ourselves! It was by grace, through faith, and not from ourselves. God has equipped us to accomplish every mission he has given us.

In this world, if a king lays down his life for others, he is immortalized as a hero and legend. If a service member gives his or her life in the line of duty for others, that officer is a hero forever. We dare not take credit or participate in the victory for which they paid the price. In God's kingdom, we are the beneficiaries of the sacrifice God made in sending his Son, Jesus Christ. It is because of his sacrifice that we can experience freedom and abundant life today.

Heavenly Father, if ever I should forget, remind me that in all my doing, I am not my own hero, but you, my Savior, have always been my shield, my protector, and my rescue. Amen.

It is by grace you have been saved, through faith—
and this is not from yourselves, it is the gift of God—
not by works, so that no one can boast.

EPHESIANS 2:8–9

December 9

Born for This

Paperwork is seldom an exciting task, but if it's not done correctly, thoroughly, and accurately, then it can have serious repercussions. Complacency will lead to poor quality work in your military service, and it can get you or your teammates injured or killed. Be someone who pays attention to detail, even the smallest of details, and leave nothing uncovered. This will help lead you to a prosperous career.

Going the extra mile means putting in extra work, doing your work with excellence, and doing this with a consistent commitment over a long period of time. You are the handiwork, the custom-crafted work of God, created in Christ Jesus to do good work, which he made you to do from the beginning. So when people say, "You must have been born for this!" know that you were born for this. But don't do it halfway. Do it with excellence.

Heavenly Father, thank you for creating me and calling me to serve my country. May all my work glorify and honor you and may it all be done in excellence. Amen.

We are God's handiwork, created in Christ Jesus to do good works, which God prepared in advance for us to do.

EPHESIANS 2:10

December 10

Identify Yourself

Life has a way of causing people to change over time. Whether it is due to success, failure, pain, or great loss, our minds, hearts, and outlooks change as we mature and age. Another part of our life that changes is our outward appearance. Most people do not look the way they did when they graduated high school. If you encounter someone you used to spend a lot of time with and your appearance has changed drastically, one of the first things you will hear is, "I hardly recognized you!"

Seeing someone you have not been around in over twenty years and not being recognized is one thing, but what if you went into your own home and your family did not recognize you? As believers, we find our true identity in Christ, and those who do not know him do not recognize him for who he is. They do not recognize him as Savior or Healer, and sometimes they do not recognize his existence at all. Today, think about the traits you display to others. Will others recognize Christ in you, or will they see the world in your actions?

> *Heavenly Father, thank you for giving me a true identity found in you. May all I do cause others to recognize you and your nature through my actions, my words, and my service. Amen.*

He was in the world,
and though the world was made through him,
the world did not recognize him.

JOHN 1:10

December 11

A Hero's Courage

When the world thinks of a hero, one of the first things many think about is someone just like you. The reason they picture you as a hero is because you are willing to leave home and place yourself in the face of imminent danger, making split-second decisions to save lives, fight evil, and serve our nation and those who can't defend themselves. The courage you possess is not in vain, and you do not use it foolishly.

One of your greatest assets is your relationship with God, especially in difficult times. It is in those times when you can rely on your relationship with God, his Word, and prayer to sustain you. A hero's courage is not blazon and boastful nor is it careless and reckless. A hero's courage perfectly balances faith, training, and confidence in self, God, skills, and your team. It is because of a hero's courage that our world is not in total and utter chaos today. Hold the line, hold the faith, and cling to the promises of God. He will not fail you.

Heavenly Father, thank you for your promises that you will not fail me, that I can cast my fears at your feet, and that you will strengthen me in the time of need. Give me righteous courage in the moment of fear. Amen.

For I, the LORD your God, will hold your right hand,
Saying to you, "Fear not, I will help you."
ISAIAH 41:13 NKJV

December 12

When You Fall

There are going to be bad days, days where you want to curl up in a hole and hide. You're going to make mistakes. That's a part of life. If you aren't making mistakes, then you probably aren't trying, progressing, or taking risks. Anyone can soar through life unscathed. A boxer can get in a ring, throw all the punches, and bounce around like a champion for twelve rounds, but until he gets punched in the mouth, nobody knows what he's made of. We will all fall, but those who keep getting up are the ones who succeed.

During your career, there will be moments you will fall on your face. You can either keep going or just quit—it's your call. But if you want to be excellent, if you want to glorify God in all you do, if you want to leave a legacy of greatness, then you have to get back up *when* you fall. Every single time. Today, wipe the nasty memories of past mistakes from your mind. Just because you did it in the past doesn't mean you are going to do it again. You will succeed, and you will not fail because you will not quit.

Heavenly Father, thank you for giving me the tenacity, resiliency, grit, and courage to keep getting back up after I fall. Amen.

When people fall down, do they not get up?
When someone turns away, do they not return?
JEREMIAH 8:4

December 13

Ticktock

Time never stops. Even when our life ends, time is still continuous. Many of us are guilty of putting off so much good in our lives in the name of finding the "right time." But when we think about it, when will that be? The average life expectancy of a male in America is 76.4 years of age, which is roughly 27,886 days. It's essential to move in the right season and in the right time.

All people have different goals and desires they want to achieve. What is yours? If you can honestly say that you have accomplished everything you want in life, then good for you. If you have a lot of loose ends undone, the good news for you is that the hand on the clock is still moving. As long as time is moving, you are winning. Getting in sync with God's plan for our lives can seem like an impossible task, but it is possible when we seek his plan and direction first. Ask God what time it is in your life, on his watch. As he begins to reveal your season, align yourself with him and watch his promises fulfill in your life.

Heavenly Father, thank you for the gift of life and time here on earth. Help me to get the most out of my time so that I can accomplish my tasks and the purpose for which you created me. Amen.

There is a time for everything,
and a season for every activity under the heavens.

ECCLESIASTES 3:1

December 14

Display of Honor

While many people voice their opinions of dislike, hate, and political agendas against the military, the majority of Americans support you, and we do have a grateful nation. There are still children who want their pictures taken with warriors and dress up like their favorite military superhero. There are still media outlets who give honor to our warriors for their heroic actions and communities that have welcome home events and military parades. If we're honest, the decline in our society began when we devalued honor. Whether it was for parents, elders, teachers, or for some other deserving people or causes, somewhere along the way, we justified the reasoning for it.

We cannot repair our society overnight. Restoring honor will take generations of intentional leadership and a return to people taking responsibility for their actions. Even parents will have to begin instilling the meaning of honor in their children. Today, think of ways you can honor those in leadership. It may seem foolish, and it may seem like a waste of time, but if you will give honor, then in your season, honor will return to you.

Heavenly Father, thank you for revealing to me the true power of honor in our world. Help me to first honor you and to honor the deserving people in my life, all for your glory. Amen.

Whether you eat or drink or whatever you do,
do it all for the glory of God.

1 CORINTHIANS 10:31

December 15

Ties that Bind

There is no greater power for an organization than unity. When a group of people come together with no divisiveness among them, for one mission and one goal, they will achieve what they set out to do. When you talk to other warriors, many will tell you the bonds of our military ranks are in shambles and not as strong as they used to be. Whether that is true or not, let's address it.

With over nearly twenty million veterans in the United States from every walk of life, every faith background, every race, and every sexual orientation, we are bound to have disagreements. When it comes to caring for each other, those disagreements, valid or not, should stay off the table. We are brothers and sisters. We are family. When one suffers, we all suffer, and when one hurts, we all hurt. Let us not allow our differences to weaken the bonds of our unity, but let us come together across every boundary to unify for the common good of our community.

Heavenly Father, thank you for the power of unity. Let me never be a reason for division in my family or the military community, but help me to bring peace and unity. Amen.

I appeal to you, brothers and sisters, in the name of our Lord Jesus Christ, that all of you agree with one another in what you say and that there be no divisions among you, but that you be perfectly united in mind and thought.

1 CORINTHIANS 1:10

December 16

Nerves of Steel

The legacy of so many service members is forged into the core of our nation's history. Your children, grandchildren, and all future generations must know of these bold, courageous moves of bravery by men and women over the years. We won't even try to begin naming the names, there are too many of those who have lain down their lives by falling onto a grenade to save others or those who have given up their own lives by running into the line of fire to save one person's life. It requires a perfected sense of duty, a masterful demonstration of love, and nerves of steel.

Maybe you don't recognize it because it is your nature. The nerves it takes to make those instant decisions are not common in everyday people. It is like your actions bring the words of God to life when you do things like that. Throughout your service, you will do heroic deeds, some of which no one will ever know about. Even so, you are his witnesses through your courageous actions, working through the fear, serving with excellence and honor, and never quitting.

Heavenly Father, thank you for courage, for nerves of steel, and for reminding me that you have told me not to be afraid or not to tremble. I know you are in control and will guide me. Amen.

Do not tremble, do not be afraid.
Did I not proclaim this and foretell it long ago?
You are my witnesses. Is there any God besides me?
No, there is no other Rock; I know not one.

ISAIAH 44:8

December 17

Perfected Judgment

Learning from each other is something we should do on a regular basis. As military service members, we represent the United States of America, the nation we swore to serve. Outside of our oath, our uniforms, gear, and training mean nothing. Think about what Jesus said in John 5:30. The only person to walk this earth in perfection knew that his purpose was to please the Father, not himself.

Throughout our lives, we see a pattern of Christ in our world, even in places where he is rejected. From the order of our society, family, government, law, and even interpersonal decision-making, the patterns and examples of Jesus are evident. We are to please the Father in all we do, to be fair in our judgment, and to honor him, but we are also to be pleasing and honorable to those who are in leadership over us, which is the order God's Word has established. As we seek to please the Father, we will become better subordinates, leaders, spouses, and parents.

> *Heavenly Father, thank you for showing me the pattern of pleasing you through your Son, Jesus. Help me to please you by hearing your Word, obeying your Word, and being fair in all I do. Amen.*

By myself I can do nothing;
I judge only as I hear, and my judgment is just,
for I seek not to please myself but him who sent me.

JOHN 5:30

December 18

A Timeless Gift

Our family has a tradition of playing "Dirty Santa" every year during our Christmas gatherings. It involves everyone bringing cheap gifts and then all drawing numbers and trying to steal the best gift—in an orderly fashion, of course. It's only appropriate at Christmastime. Many of those gifts are stored away for us to reuse the next Christmas, so it's truly a vicious cycle. This often lightens the mood and, to be honest, makes us thankful for what we receive.

Timeless gifts are often things that are not purchased with money but are handmade or required a great deal of thought put into the idea. From before the beginning of time, grace was given to us in Christ Jesus for all we need. His mercy, grace, and perfect sacrifice are the eternal and timeless gifts that no other gifts can compare to. Today, think about the perfect and timeless gift God has given you and how it has empowered you to be victorious in every area of your life.

Heavenly Father, thank you for the perfect and timeless gifts you have given me. May I always live in a way that reflects a thankful heart to you, in my thoughts, words, and actions. Amen.

He has saved us and called us to a holy life—not because of anything we have done but because of his own purpose and grace. This grace was given us in Christ Jesus before the beginning of time.

2 TIMOTHY 1:9

December 19

Evil Intentions

There are always people who are doing good deeds, but recently I heard about someone who was upset because there was no local media covering his efforts of "good deeds." The purpose of doing good should not be to receive something in return, even if those good deeds are done for media attention or exposure for a business or product. At the end of the day, if our heart is out of alignment with God's intentions, then our actions will be out of alignment also. Everyone will eventually see through our actions. One of the secrets of blessing comes as we serve or give in secret and do so anonymously.

When we read the phrase "your heart" in Matthew 6:21, it is referring to our mind, emotions, and will. Knowing that, if our heart is out of sorts before we speak or act, no matter how good the deed or word is going to be, the seed we were going to plant is poisoned from the beginning. Ask God to check your heart, your mind, your emotions, and your will to ensure they are aligned with his nature, will, and Word.

Heavenly Father, thank you for giving me a heart that treasures your ways, your Word, and seeks to honor you. Amen.

Where your treasure is, there your heart will be also.

MATTHEW 6:21

December 20

Trained for Greatness

It is not by accident that you are in a position of authority. You have tremendous power to have a good influence on society, and with that power comes tremendous responsibility. Throughout the Old Testament, there are times when God raised up and rewarded leaders who honored him, and there were times when leaders dishonored God and faced harsh consequences. What a joy it would be for you to be a light for your community through the position you hold and for the name of God to be proclaimed through your love and service.

From the moment you raised your right hand to swear in making an oath to serve this nation, to being promoted and climbing the ranks, the authority and position you are entrusted with is to be honorable to the people you serve. Through all you do today, let those you encounter and interact with see the hand of almighty God in your life, guiding you, leading you, and changing you for his good. He has not placed any leader in authority for his or her own benefit but for his own glory so that others may come to salvation through Christ.

Heavenly Father, thank you for the responsibility and authority I am entrusted with. Today, I ask you to bless my decisions, and may all I do honor your name. Amen.

Scripture says to Pharaoh: "I raised you up for this very purpose, that I might display my power in you and that my name might be proclaimed in all the earth."

ROMANS 9:17

December 21

The Power of Articulation

A poorly written AAR (After Action Report) can mean the difference between the success and failure of future missions to protect the life and safety of others. Failure to articulate the details of the operation, especially if it is enemy activity and tactics, can lead to severe consequences against you, teammates, other service members, and civilians. There is tremendous power in articulation in all your reports. There will be many people who read them over the years.

Our plans in life may seem good in our own eyes, like our own reports may seem good at times, but without the divine blessing of God, his direction and leading, and his power articulating those plans, we will never reach the fullness he desires for us. Take time today to listen for his voice through his Word for the proper answer for your life. There are many answers, but only he has the *proper* answer for what you need.

> *Heavenly Father, when I pray, help me to speak clearly and to remember you desire relationship above performance. Open my ears to understand, my eyes to see, and my heart to move when you speak. Amen.*

To humans belong the plans of the heart,
but from the LORD comes the proper answer of the tongue.

PROVERBS 16:1

December 22

Thorough Investigations

After an act of terrorism there are many details to investigating a crime scene, such as gathering evidence, interviewing witnesses, taking photographs, and documenting important notes, not to mention preparing to run down leads to locate those responsible and hold them accountable. A thorough investigation means that from the time the person arrives on scene to the time justice has been served, everything is done with excellence. The victims deserve thoroughness, and thoroughness is essential to prevent such tragedies from happening again.

When we overlook details and do not thoroughly conduct investigations, the enemy could get away with it and strike again. Think of the work God has begun in your life and how you would be if he overlooked the details of your life. He promises to finish what he started in us until Christ returns. As such, we should strive to mirror his nature of excellence and thoroughness in all we do. We received the promise that God began a good work in us, and he will not stop until it is finished. Don't become stubborn and refuse to allow him to do what he said he would do.

> *Heavenly Father, I invite you to complete the good work you began in me. May my service to my nation reflect your nature of excellence, both today and forever. Amen.*

Being confident of this, that he who began a good work in you will carry it on to completion until the day of Christ Jesus.

PHILIPPIANS 1:6

December 23

Abundance Mindset

Rarely do we achieve our full potential in life. Supposedly, the average person uses only a small portion of his or her brain. What would this world look like if the opposite were true? Fear, doubt, anxiety, worry, and hate were never supposed to be part of our lives. It's *not* natural to have these emotions, which is why they are called negative emotions. When we buy into the lie of negative emotions, we cannot access the power of the mind of Christ.

Yes, God is good and his power is greater than anything, but we must allow him to work in and through us. When we surrender our negative emotions and thoughts, we surrender what has been serving as barriers between where we are and the fullness of where God has called us to be. This is the abundance mindset. Cut the ties with what has been holding you back from reaching your full potential in Christ and watch how much more fruitful your life becomes in Christ.

Heavenly Father, I submit to you all my thoughts and emotions. If there are any that hinder you from moving and having control in my life, I surrender them. I ask you to do immeasurably more than I could ask or think in my life, according to your power. Amen.

Now to him who is able to do immeasurably more than all we ask or imagine, according to his power that is at work within us.

EPHESIANS 3:20

December 24

Blinded by the Light

While many have protection, numerous people around the world still live under oppression because of hate, tyranny, and evil ideologies. These people are scared to speak out, to ask for help, or to say something about the issues. There is only one solution to their problem, and that is people like you. Fear may have these oppressed people thinking no one can help them, that you cannot come to their rescue. But darkness must go when light enters in and dwells.

Have you witnessed innocent people living under such oppression and justifiable fear for their life? You are placed here on this earth, not only as a believer in Jesus Christ but also as a warrior, to be the salt and light to this world. Today, provide hope to those who are hurting, afraid, and oppressed so they regain their lives of peace. How can you help flush out those who torment the innocent and helpless?

Heavenly Father, thank you for using me to be the salt and light of this world and to free those who are oppressed and afraid because of the evil of others. May my work shine your light in the dark places of this world to flush out the evil that lurks. Amen.

The people living in darkness have seen a great light; on those living in the land of the shadow of death a light has dawned.

MATTHEW 4:16

December 25

The Depths of Your Heart

The structure of American military branches is uniform, but it is not wise to assume the culture of any one branch to be the same as the next. But there's one thing for certain, and that is that interview and interrogation skills apply across the board. These skills are like our firearms skills though. If we don't stay current with them, then when we need them the most, we will have nothing to pull from. As troops interview locals in foreign lands, they learn the value of effective communications skills and the fruit they can produce.

Learning to communicate with other people is a powerful and often underutilized skill in our society, especially considering the abundant use of smartphones today. If we take time to actively listen to what other people are saying, we can gain valuable insights without them telling us specifically what we want to know. If you want to determine someone's motive, then draw it out. Insight is a powerful tool, according to King Solomon. Think outside the box today. Think about Proverbs 20:5 and how it applies to you. It may just take you down the road to some big leads you need.

Heavenly Father, thank you for giving me insight, teaching me the value of insight, and helping me to hear beyond the words a person speaks. Amen.

The purposes of a person's heart are deep waters, but one who has insight draws them out.

PROVERBS 20:5

December 26

The New You

Everyone around us has something in common: we all have a past. If we are honest, does it matter how bad that past is? Maybe your past has things you don't want to ever think about again. But the joy of God's mercy and grace is that he washes that guilt and condemnation away forever. This world may want to bring it up again, but we know what God's Word says about our sins. Once God forgives them, they have been separated from us as far as the east is from the west. You are a *new* creation, and the old is no more.

Getting accustomed to the new you may take some time. The old desires may want to creep up every once in a while, but you have power over those things in Christ. As a warrior in the United States Armed Forces, you know the power of a clean slate and what it can do for a person. Maybe you need a fresh start, a clean slate, a new you. Maybe you just need a spiritual upgrade. Today, you can be made new in Christ, and the old will never be known again.

Heavenly Father, thank you for making me new in you, for new mercy every day, for grace, for forgiveness, and for removing my old ways. May my life glorify you, both now and forevermore. Amen.

If anyone is in Christ, the new creation has come:
The old has gone, the new is here!

2 CORINTHIANS 5:17

December 27

Firmly Established

Your plans in life will change. You will have a need to plan for contingencies, but being flexible is just one element to consider. It is more valuable and prudent to adhere to the leading of God, which you can discover through relationship with him in Bible study, prayer, and worship. Think about it like this: when a superior ranking officer orders you to follow a plan, you do it. If you abandon it, there are consequences. Now you are equipped with the plans and ways of God, and this firmly establishes you in the mission of life he has called you to.

Never allow the plans you have for your life or your ideas of what the future should be like serve as an inhibitor to the growth and direction God has for you. Our hearts can lead us astray if we do not fully focus on the Father. As we pursue him, however, our feet will move swiftly with established steps. Let us pursue the Master today. May the plans in our hearts become his plans, and may our steps be established firmly in his order.

Heavenly Father, thank you for giving my steps firm establishment with each landing, for keeping me from any hazard or trap. May my plans be yours and yours become mine. Amen.

In their hearts humans plan their course,
but the LORD establishes their steps.

PROVERBS 16:9

December 28

Remember the Reason

Life has a way of causing us to forget *who* we are in Christ, a way of trying to keep us depressed and frustrated if we stay focused on the pain, evil, and sadness surrounding us. Jesus Christ does not call us out of our old life of darkness to go into the shadows. He calls us, as believers in him, to be his light to this world. But too often we allow our selfish desires to get in the way of that.

As a child of the King, commit to studying his Word and knowing it like you know military code of conduct. Study and be prepared so that you can give an answer. At the end of the day, whether you are wearing the uniform in service to our nation or if you are off with your family or friends, you are called to serve. Above all, remember that you are special to God and unique. You may be the cream of the crop, but you are the apple of his eye.

> *Heavenly Father, thank you for loving me the way I need to be loved, for using me to be your light in a dark world. May I always remember why you saved me, not only for my own sake but also to tell others. Amen.*

You are a chosen people, a royal priesthood, a holy nation, God's special possession, that you may declare the praises of him who called you out of darkness into his wonderful light.

1 PETER 2:9

December 29

Time to Unite

America has experienced its share of horrific, violent tragedies over the years. One thing about all of these horrible incidents is what happens to us as Americans. For a brief moment, most of us lay down our differences, unite, and come together. Have you ever noticed this? It's almost like the plans of the enemy backfire. Of course, we cannot undo lost lives, and we cannot permanently heal scars and horrible memories, but when we unite as one people, we become the most powerful force on the planet.

There will be more violence in America; that is a given. But in those times, as men and women like you rise up to the challenge, as you set the example for the citizens of this nation in service, they will begin to see how God can and does cause good to come out of horrible situations. He will work for the good of those who love him. There has never been a better time than now to unite as Americans. What a legacy it would be for generations to come.

Heavenly Father, thank you for working for the good in my life, even through the terrible and devastating times. I know you have called me according to your purpose, and I trust you. Amen.

We know that in all things God works for the good of those who love him, who have been called according to his purpose.

ROMANS 8:28

December 30

Plans to Prosper

O ver the span of your career, you will meet a lot of people who tell you how much they appreciate you. But you will also encounter those who hate you, despise you, and want to bring you harm. When you took your oath to serve, you knew the risks, the dangers, and what the world that you would be entering was like. But to know that the God you serve has a plan for your life means that his power, his plan, and his destiny will always outweigh that of this world and the enemy.

If the day comes and the burdens of your calling seem like they have become too heavy to bear and you cannot continue, then remember: "I know the plans I have for you." If you ever feel worthless, useless, and forgotten in this world, then remember that God "plans to prosper you and not to harm you." You serve a loving, heavenly Father who knows all your needs. He will not abandon you in the middle of battle, and he will never turn his back on you. God has a plan for your life.

Heavenly Father, thank you for giving me a plan for my life, plans to prosper me, to protect me, and to give me a hope and future. Amen.

"I know the plans I have for you," declares the LORD,
"plans to prosper you and not to harm you,
plans to give you hope and a future."

JEREMIAH 29:11

Deecember 31

Rewarded as Royalty

If your superiors thoroughly rewarded you based on your performance on the job, you would likely receive numerous commendations and medals, maybe even a meritorious promotion. But you did not take your oath of service because of the money and accolades. You did it out of a heart of service to something bigger than yourself. But let's be real for a moment: It would be nice to see the treasures you have laid up because of the good you do on a daily basis, wouldn't it?

Only the perfect sacrifice of Jesus makes us clean. Because of him, we have access to the Father and are empowered by the Holy Spirit. Therefore, when God deals with us according to our righteousness, the Father sees his Son's payment for our sins and not our filthy past. Therefore, if we hold true to Psalm 18:20, when the Lord deals with us according to *our* righteousness, he sees Jesus, and we are rewarded as royalty. This is only possible through a relationship with Jesus Christ. Now that's a commendation I'd like to receive.

> *Heavenly Father, thank you for the gift of salvation made possible only through the sacrifice of your Son, Jesus. Let my life be seen through the lens of what Jesus did for me and not my own filthy rags. Accept me as your own, Father God. Amen.*

The LORD has dealt with me according to my righteousness; according to the cleanness of my hands he has rewarded me.

PSALM 18:20

Acknowledgments

We would like to express our gratitude to the team at BroadStreet Publishing for their efforts and assistance in making this book possible. Thank you to Lt. Col. Dave Grossman for taking time to review this book and provide a foreword. We also thank our families, the team at Mighty Oaks Programs, and all our friends who stood by us during the writing process.

About the Authors

Adam Davis is an unrelenting force of inspiration. He believes we all have a unique purpose and that we must be good stewards of the time we are given in this life. Described as "a dynamic and powerful writer and speaker," Adam has devoted his life to inspire others to take positive action in their professional and personal lives. His writing and speaking are not only inspirational but also thought-provoking and challenging.

He inspires, challenges, and motivates others through his books. The most popular books by Adam include: *Behind the Badge: 365 Daily Devotions for Law Enforcement* (recommended and read by law enforcement leaders nationally and a perennial bestseller); *Bulletproof Marriage: a 90-Day Devotional* (2020 Christian Book Awards Finalist and a perennial bestseller with Lt. Col. Dave Grossman); and *On Spiritual Combat: 30 Missions for Victorious Warfare* (with Lt. Col. Dave Grossman).

A former law enforcement officer and FBI trained hostage negotiator, Adam knows the challenges faced by law enforcement officers and their relationships. Since leaving his career in law enforcement in 2015, he has devoted his time to delivering proven tools and resources for the mind and soul. He has devoted his life to serving others and sharing his words, in writing and speaking, to inspire others to make positive changes in their lives.

Adam has an uncanny ability to speak "grunt" and to the heart of warriors. His raw, unfiltered story of overcoming the trauma of childhood sexual abuse, experiences from law enforcement, and battle with suicidal thoughts and substance abuse position him as a powerful force of hope for millions of people today. His work has attracted the attention of many influencers, and he is best known for his work to deliver faith, hope, and love to those who serve.

From major universities to government entities, Adam has presented his story of conquering some of life's most smothering battles and how these principles can be applied in every life to achieve optimal performance and fulfillment. His work has been featured in *Entrepreneur Magazine*, Fox News, The Huffington Post, PoliceOne.com, and *Law Enforcement Today*. As a speaker, he has presented for the University of Alabama, Auburn University Department of Economic Development, TEDx Troy University, law enforcement agencies, military bases, and many seminars with Lt. Col. Dave Grossman, Taya Kyle, and other American patriots. His media appearances have included *The Rick & Bubba Show*, The Blaze Radio Network, Family Life Today, *The 700 Club*, *The Glenn Beck Program*, Team Never Quit Podcast with Marcus Luttrell, and many others.

Adam is the spokesperson for REBOOT Recovery First Responders, a nonprofit organization which focuses on providing faith-based trauma healing for first responders and service members. He is supported by his wife, Amber, of twenty years and three children. You can learn more about Adam by visiting his website at www.theadamdavis.com.

About the Authors

Chad Robichaux is a former Force Recon marine and Department of Defense contractor with eight deployments to Afghanistan as part of a Joint Special Operations Command (JSOC) Task Force. After overcoming his personal battles with PTSD and nearly becoming a veteran suicide statistic, Chad founded the Mighty Oaks Foundation, a leading nonprofit serving the active duty and military veteran communities with highly successful faith-based combat trauma and resiliency programs.

Having spoken to over 150,000 active-duty troops and led life-saving programs for over 3,800 active military and veterans at four Mighty Oaks Ranches around the nation, Chad has become a go-to resource and is considered a subject matter expert on faith-based solutions to PTSD, having advised the Trump administration, Congress, the VA, and the highest levels of the DoD. Currently, Chad serves as the chairman for the Faith Based Veterans Service Alliance (FBVSA), collaborating with the White House on behalf of a coalition of faith-based Veteran Service Organizations, and is a surrogate speaker and national board member for Veterans Coalition for Trump.

Chad has written five books related to veteran care, donating over 100,000 copies to the troops during his resiliency speaking tours. He is regularly featured on national media, such as Fox News, OANN, *The O'Reilly Factor*, The Blaze, *TBN*, *The 700 Club*, and *USA Today* and has appeared in a short film by I Am Second. Currently, a life-story motion picture is being produced based on the stories in his book, *An Unfair Advantage*.

In addition to Chad's military service, he is a former federal agent and law enforcement officer who was awarded the Medal of Valor for bravery. Chad is married to his wife, Kathy, and they have a daughter and two sons. Hunter is a third-generation Marine Combat veteran in the Robichaux family. Chad and his two sons are lifelong martial artists. Chad is a third degree Brazilian jiu-jitsu black belt under Carlson Gracie Jr. and is a former Professional Mixed Martial Arts Champion, having competed at the highest levels of the sport.